FOURTH EDITION

Decision-Making Group Interaction

Achieving Quality

Bobby R. Patton

Central Missouri State University

Timothy M. Downs

Gannon University

Boston   New York   San Francisco
Mexico City   Montreal   Toronto   London   Madrid   Munich
Hong Kong   Singapore   Tokyo   Cape Town   Sydney

Executive Editor: *Karon Bowers*
Editorial Assistant: *Jennifer Trebby*
Marketing Manager: *Mandee Eckersley*
Production Editor: *Paul Mihailidis*
Composition and Prepress Buyer: *Linda Cox*
Manufacturing Buyer: *JoAnne Sweeney*
Cover Administrator: *Kristina Mose-Libon*
Compositor: *Galley Graphics, Ltd.*

For related support materials, visit our online catalog at www.ablongman.com.

Library of Congress Cataloging-in-Publication Data

CIP data not available at time of publication.

ISBN: 0-321-04919-5

Printed in the United States of America

10 9 8 7 6 5 4 3 2   06 05 04 03

CONTENTS

PREFACE

As we begin the first decade of the twenty-first century, we are prompted to question those learning and research findings from the past to determine what will prove enduring. The significance of groups in our society becomes more and more pronounced with each passing year. Effective group decision-making is vital to the maintenance of participative democracy, both in politics and in the workplace. The past few decades have witnessed people having a greater voice in decisions affecting many different aspects of their lives.

We live in an information age; data are readily available at our fingertips through electronic terminals. Decisions, however, depend upon more than just data. Analysis and critical judgments are necessary to determine the validity of data, and effective communication is required to determine the focus, relevancy and application of information used to make decisions. The human ability and necessity to work together is greater than ever before.

In earlier editions of this book we attempted to sort, select, and focus on multidisciplinary research that enhance our understanding of group process. In this edition we go a step further to attempt to delineate the factors that promote *quality* in the group activities. We have incorporated examples from various organizations that have proven successful in promoting positive decision-making results.

The capacity to make sound, complex decisions are the hallmark of both the educated person and the functional organization. The skills required to make such decisions demand higher levels of training and education in communication. This book attempts to establish both a theoretical framework and a design for applied learning that will promote quality. Our combined experience in teaching about groups and in watching them in action has given us a perspective that is both analytical and prescriptive.

The writing and development of this book was aided by the help and encouragement of several individuals. Specifically, we would like to thank Karla Hutcherson (Wichita State University), Peggy Anderson (Emporia State University), Brad Goebel (Emporia State University), Vanessa Volpe (Emporia State University), Tatiana Pachkova (Emporia State University), and our editor, Karon Bowers. John Inglish gave valuable and insightful editorial assistance. We would also like to thank our respective spouses, Elle Patton and Mary Downs, for their constant support of this endeavor, as well as colleagues and friends for their encouragement and insights. Lastly, we would like to thank the following reviewers for their input and opinions: Patricia Amason (University of Arkansas), Mary Helen Brown (Auburn University), Betsy Gordon (McKendree College), Laurie Haleta (South Dakota State University), Cary Horvath (Westminster College), Lawrence Hosman (University of Southern Mississippi), Robert Martin (Ithaca College), Beatriz Duran McWilliams (MiraCosta College), Robert E. Mild (Fairmont State College), Jerry Pepper (University of Minnesota, Duluth), Mary-Jo Popovici

(Monroe Community College), and Glen Stamp (Ball State University). We sincerely hope that this book provides information to assist readers in improving group decision-making processes and enhance the quality of group interactions.

Bobby R. Patton
Professor of Communication and President
Central Missouri State University

Timothy M. Downs
Professor of Communication
Dean of the College of Humanities, Business and Education
Gannon University
Erie, PA

1

Communication in Decision-Making Groups: An Introduction

Scenario

You receive a letter from your dean requesting that you serve as a student representative on a committee charged with improving campus climate. While you feel honored to have been selected, you're concerned about the expectations and the amount of work. The first meeting is called for Thursday afternoon at 3:30 in the conference room in the library. Even though not fully committed to participation, you attend the first meeting to see how much time is going to be expected, the makeup of the group, and what outcomes are anticipated. You find that you are one of eight undergraduates along with an associate dean, three faculty members, a staff member from the student union, a staff member from the student affairs office, and a graduate student. The associate dean leads the meeting and distributes a brief outline. She explains that the formation of the group is in response to a presidential concern about the quality of student life, including campus safety, the number of events taking place on campus, and the adequacy of facilities. The makeup of the committee is intended to be a cross section of people affected by the topic. The group is asked to meet every other week for the remainder of the semester, or until such time a list of recommendations can be made. The president has guaranteed that the recommendations will be taken seriously.

Would you accept appointment to such a group? Have you participated in groups that had such a focused problem?

The number of groups an individual can belong to (personal and professional) and their importance in our culture continues to grow. There are literally more groups than people in the United States, for each of us is a member of a number of groups, often diverse in their nature. These groups have immense impact on our lives as we invest our time, livelihood, and well-being in them. Further, groups to which we do not belong can significantly influence our lives: an educational policies committee, the U.S. president's economic advisors, or an employment team.

Within the modern organization a considerable percentage of time is spent in group meetings. One major company recently stated that over ten percent of its total operating costs go to fund such meetings. Decision making in a group involves people talking together in order to cooperatively resolve a mutual concern. This process is the essence of democratic action. It is cooperative in that all viewpoints are encouraged to be voiced (although a view held by several persons actually may be voiced by only one). It is purposive in that an attempt is made to identify and resolve a need felt by a number of people. In many cases the membership of the group—who is in the group and who is not—is determined by the degree of mutual concern shared by group members. For example, a mutual concern may be the need for agreement on a policy committing group members to a selected way of behaving, a mutual concern that requires group action as one that each individual working alone probably could not resolve. Even if the concern is simply to be with other people, to share thoughts and feelings, certain ways of interacting are facilitative and desirable.

The decisions sought by people cover a wide range of goals and conditions. Examples include:

- A group of students and teachers attempt to develop a new set of required courses for an academic program.
- A group of students living in a dormitory reaches an agreement on a revised set of rules for behavior in their living area.
- Two families share their resources and build a beach cabin.
- A small unit of an industrial organization prepares a report defining a company problem, evaluating a proposed change in policy, or outlining a specific plan of action.
- Six commuters arrange a route and set a time for departure for a car pool.
- An industrial task force prepares a plan for reducing air pollution in a chemical fertilizer plant.
- People living on the same city block develop plans for a neighborhood youth recreation center.

In each of these examples, there are certain common factors: identifying a mutual concern, an analysis of the situation, and producing the desired change in the form of a contract, product, event, or procedure.

The most common definition of a group involves two elements. It is a small number of individuals in interdependent role relations, and it has a set of values or norms that regulate the behavior of members in matters of concern to the group. This definition reflects both the size of the group and the individual's behavior as it affects other individuals in the group.

This book focuses on communication within the group attempting to make decisions. We believe that communication is the essence of the small group experience and the key to the success of the group. By focusing on decision-making groups, we limit our concerns to situations in which members recognize that they form a unit and are acting intentionally together. We see five conditions necessary for such a group to exist.

1. *People joined together by common issue or concern:* We are primarily concerned with groups small enough that the presence of each person is significant to the decision-making process. When a group exceeds 20 people, some loss of individual contributions can be expected. We shall rely upon studies that examine the importance of group size to the optimal accomplishments of task. Typically, the small group consists of three to eight members.

2. *Interdependence:* We all know what it means to depend on another person, but if people depend on each other in equal degrees, so that they unavoidably influence each other, they are interdependent. The behavior of each member of the group determines and is determined by that of the others. This interaction can be viewed as circular, with cause producing effect, and effect turning into cause as it feeds back to the original cause. Face-to-face interaction may vary from mediated interaction in results. We shall discuss these differences.

3. *A common goal:* Individuals may board an elevator. From our perspective, this collection of people is not a group. However, should the elevator fail to function properly and become stuck between floors, a group will be quickly formed, as all of the individuals become concerned with dealing with their mutual problem. People may join together to engage in an issue of personal growth, which becomes the unifying goal. Even if the goal is not perceived as a problem to be solved, decisions will likely need to be made.

4. *Norms:* A common set of values is necessary to regulate the behavior of members if a group is to continue to exist. Group members articulate their values and in the process establish a consensus regarding judgments to be made. Unless people ascribe to the values of the given group, they will not choose to join or continue to be a member. Such norms allow members to think of themselves as a group and to have a collective perception of unity, a conscious group identity.

5. *Communication:* Individuals working together collectively on an assembly line do not constitute a group unless they are interacting. This is because communication is required for individuals to coordinate and act as a single unit. How well group members understand one another, how clearly they are sharing their ideas, values, and feelings, are important determinants of the effectiveness of the group. Communication includes all verbal and non-verbal behaviors to which meaning can be attributed. We believe that communication is the essence of the small group experience and the key to the success of the group.

Why Groups?

During the last decade, the use of groups and teams of individuals in organizations has increased dramatically. Our society has recognized that groups provide an appropriate structure for the implementation of strategies formulated to deal with performance demands and to address changes needed in the workplace. Americans have had to completely rethink the notion of quality and how to focus on it.

Without effective group communication, quality programs cannot happen and organizational execution will be limited. Groups are used for planning, problem solving, assessment and training, as well as for routine business meetings.

Consider a couple of examples of successful outcomes of groups. Texas Instruments in Houston was spending an exorbitant amount on waste disposal. A project group reduced the cost of hazardous waste disposal by $87,000, a savings that represented seventy percent of the total yearly costs for disposing of wastes.[1] The General Electric plant in Salisbury, NC, reduced operating costs by more than thirty percent and eliminated a number of supervisors, shortened the delivery cycles from three weeks to three days, and reduced customer complaints by 90 percent.[2]

With the proliferation of groups has come challenges and opportunities including an increasing emphasis among people in the process of creating teams in building relationships, rather than building a strong structure to support the team's development. Without clarity of roles, goals, and procedures, the teams falter. Unclear, vague, excessively broad purpose statements cause members to become frustrated and confused. For example, the group meeting on campus climate would need to know what is expected, and would need to define what is meant by "campus climate."

Various time and dollar estimates have been prepared to determine the cost of time spent in groups. It has been estimated that managers and technical professionals spend the equivalent of one day a week in meetings, while middle and executive managers spend two days per week, and senior executives spend three or four days per week. In fact, group attendance and participation is often the main focus of a senior manager's responsibilities.

Time spent in meetings can either be productive or wasted. One Fortune 500 company estimates that it wastes over $50 million annually on ineffectively managed meetings. Another estimate says that fifty percent of the time spent in group sessions is wasted. Such time waste is caused by poor planning, too many participants, communication overload, an unclear reason for the meeting, poor participation, and/or poor communication.[3]

Other problems concern the amount of training and the knowledge of skills required. People must be able to communicate openly without fear, suspicion, or reasons to withdraw. If a student member is intimidated by the presence of faculty members, free and open communication will be inhibited. Such a problem is clearly related to ineffective communication and a limited knowledge of group dynamics.[4]

Groups as Systems

In the dictionary, a group is defined by such words as interaction, interdependency, harmony, and networks. In this book the small group is considered the primary system of people working together for making decisions that impact the well-being of the members of the group. Thinking in terms of systems is important for understanding the processes and potential of any group. Systems thinking means anticipating the diverse effects of contemplated action. A single group is but one component in a vast, multi-level organization.

Every group meeting can be measured in terms of what the time spent together adds to the participants and the larger society. In today's complex world, resources such as time, money, people, space, and technology cannot afford to be wasted on matters such as internal competition or limited thinking.

Systems theory suggests that group decision making can be thought of as interdependent forces able to be analyzed and set in the perspective of other forces. The behaviors of individuals in groups result from many causes, and the systems method emphasizes multiple causation and a complex interrelation of forces. We shall examine the personal factors that make a difference as people come together, the internal influences that take place within the decision-making process, and the consequences of the actions of the group.

In the committee studying campus climate in the scenario, an absence of ethnic diversity on campus is likely a result of many factors. For example, every student chooses a college for different reasons. Entrance requirements may impact some groups of students more than others. The presence of cultural sub-groups and social activities may also be factors. The committee must avoid thinking in terms that do not reflect the multiple causations. The dynamics in each sub-group must be considered in the context of the total university.

A fundamental principle of a systems approach is that the whole should be greater than the sum of its parts. From a group perspective, interdependence is promoted through effective communication. We agree with systems writers who have advanced the argument that groups can best be understood from a communication perspective.[5]

Quality and Accountability

It is difficult to read business publications today without encountering Total Quality Management (TQM). In an attempt to focus on the quality of goods produced, rather than the quantity, the economic success of Japan caught America's attention. The first wave of TQM came to the United States in the mid-70s in the form of "quality circles," based on a Japanese practice in which workers would meet once a week for an hour or so to discuss work problems. The early results of quality circles in America were not successful. Basically, they were introduced with very little group training or emphasis on communication skills, and appeared to be more of an appendage, rather than an integral part of the organization, as had been the case in Japan. Actually, the technique was not of Japanese origin, but had been developed in the United States in the 1940s. The person considered by most people to be the father of production quality and quality control is W. Edwards Deming, an industrial engineer. Ignored in the 1940s by American industrial leaders, Deming lectured in Japan, where his ideas were widely accepted. Deming developed what is known as the Deming Cycle: Plan, Do, Check, and Act (PDCA).

The "total quality" philosophy has evolved over the years and has now taken a place in American culture that transcends thinking of it as a fad. In July 1994, the *Academy of Management Review* published a special "Total Quality" issue. In it, Barbara Spencer summarized its major components as follows:

Goal: TQM establishes quality enhancement as a dominant priority and one that is vital for long-term effectiveness and survival. It claims that improving quality can decrease rather than increase costs and facilitate attainment of other demands and objectives.

Definition of Quality: Quality is satisfying or delighting the customer. All quality-improvement initiatives must begin with an understanding of customer perceptions and needs.

Role/Nature of Environment: TQM blurs the boundaries between the organization and the environment. Entities previously regarded as outsiders (e.g., suppliers, customers) are now considered part of organizational processes.

Role of Management: Management's role is to create constancy of purpose for improvement of product and service and to create a system that can produce quality outcomes. Managers and the system, not the workers, are held responsible for poor quality.

Role of Employees: Employees are empowered to make decisions, build relationships, and take steps needed to improve quality within the system designed by management. Additional training and educational opportunities provide necessary skills for this broader role.

Structural Rationality: The organization is analyzed as a set of processes that begin with the supplier and end with the customer. Each step in each process relies upon teams organized to facilitate task accomplishments.

Philosophy Toward Change: Change, continuous improvement, and learning are encouraged. Ideally, all organizational members are motivated to improve the status quo.[6]

The Deming model extends beyond management theory to a way of looking at group performance and accomplishment. According to Deming, groups, like every other aspect of our society, must be subject to strict principles of accountability. We should know how well a group has performed through such devices as benchmarking, a concept we shall discuss in Chapter 10.

The extensive literature on quality performance suggests principles that relate directly to the quality of performance in groups.

The groups are vision, mission and outcomes driven. The quality group has a clearly defined purpose and desired results. Such focus allows it to have considerably more impact and abilities to determine successful outcomes.

A systems approach to collaboration is required. If people are to work together effectively, the information, ideas, and sense of common purpose must be shared. The greater the collaborative teamwork within the group, the more effective the interaction. Systems must be interrelated within the larger organization. Understanding the linkage to other parts of the system can greatly improve decision-making.

Supportive leadership is integral. Organizational leadership must create a quality culture to which all members of the group subscribe. Further, leadership is necessary to secure the resources and support necessary to implement decisions of the group.

Decisions should be based on factual data. Problems occur when groups do not take the time to define the problem clearly, collect data to identify the reasonable causes of the problem, and then work to implement solutions until the most effective one is found. To the extent that problem solving is based on fact-finding and critical evaluation, the greater the likelihood of quality decision-making.

The group values each individual's participation. If people contribute based on their knowledge and experience, and everyone carefully values the contributions of others, better decisions will result. Interpersonal skills are necessary within the group to assure maximum interaction.

The group must anticipate and plan for change. Such planning is the foundation for continuous quality improvement, and involves the reengineering and reassessment of assumptions. The group needs to embrace change as a cultural value and perceive it as a positive factor. Figure 1.1 presents a flowchart citing the steps in the quality process as they relate to the decision-making process. These steps and various options will be discussed in subsequent chapters.

In this book, we shall elaborate upon these principles and provide illustrations and examples that are intended to assist in implementation.

Groups as Interdisciplinary Study: A Brief History

Although the study of groups was largely a twentieth century phenomenon, research began in the nineteenth century. This research focused on "the pathological crowd," the nature of social-interaction processes, two person dyads as the basic social unit, and the family as the primary group. Researchers were philosophically oriented in their investigations, and they argued about the fundamental origins of people's social behavior. The argument was between the environmentalist-behaviorists and the innate-environmentalists; the latter eventually won the debate. The controversy ended in the 1920s, when attention no longer centered on philosophy, but focused on the development of a more rigorous scientific methodology.

In the late 1930s, Kurt Lewin was instrumental in applying experimental methodologies to the study of small groups. One of his techniques was to create different groups with known characteristics and observe their operation. For example, he might set up groups under different types of leaders, observe how the leaders acted and the members responded, compare the various interactions, and draw empirically based conclusions about the dynamic effects of leadership. Through such simple yet sound procedures, theoretically relevant hypotheses were tested

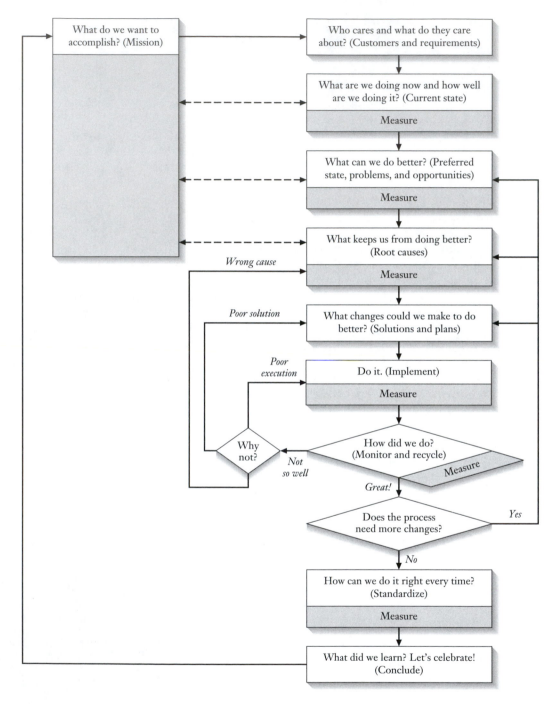

FIGURE 1.1   A Flowchart of the Quality Group

Source: Nancy R. Tague, *The Quality Toolbox* (Milwaukee: ASQS Quality Press, 1995), p. 13.

under experimental conditions. Lewin was thus successful in linking group theory, real-world problems, and experimentation.

Research in the 1940s expanded in two directions: extensive methodological improvements were made and quantities of empirical knowledge were accumulated. Valid and reliable theory, however, remained sparse.

The field of small groups was accepted as a respectable area of study. Following Lewin's leadership, Morton Deutsch tested the differential effects of cooperation and competition on groups.[7] In other studies, Alex Bavelas controlled experimentally who in the group could send information to whom and tested the effects of communication networks on group satisfaction and efficiency.[8] A major theme in post-Lewinian research on the nature of groups was the instruction in group process and discussion developing in college social psychology and speech communication departments. Teachers were challenged to translate the findings of the researchers into methods of improving communication within the groups. Business and industry joined this move as size and organizational complexity provoked problems of decision making at all levels.

Another approach to the study of groups is the "laboratory method" in which a group studies itself. In 1947 the National Training Laboratories were founded in Bethel, Maine. They were "designed to try out new methods for re-educating human behavior and social relationships." In these laboratory groups, called t-groups (for "training"), the members diagnosed and experimented with their own behaviors and relationships.[9] An enduring feature of the t-group throughout its development has been its emphasis on feedback, a built-in mechanism for personal change. Research in this area has tended to emphasize the possibilities for human growth when individual members expand their awareness of their own feelings and those of others.[10]

The 1950s and 1960s saw a research boom. Of special significance was the contribution of Robert Bales.[11] Bales developed an empirical technique for observing groups in action. He applied a standard method of classifying interaction to determine how decision-making groups function in different phases of meetings and how the members assumed duties that contribute to the well-being of the group. How do variables such as leadership styles, member personalities, and group size affect the interaction process? Bales's observational technique has been used widely in studying groups and in the development of theory.

In the 1970s, group researchers made several significant contributions. First, the gap between the study of the individual and that of the group diminished; instead of viewing the individual as being apart from the group, often pitted against it and contending with it, researchers typically saw the individual as being *within* the group. Second, there was a shift from focusing on the external effects of the group to a genuine concern with group process; instead of measuring opinions before and after a meeting, researchers now tended to concern themselves with what went on within the meeting. Third, the laboratory groups provided self-analytical data, giving researchers new insights into emotions and feelings as they affect behaviors in a group.

In the 1980s, investigations of small-group behavior once again affirmed that any major research effort faces a dual problem. Researchers from varying disciplines (e.g., communication) identified certain parts of their discipline to understand relationships among those parts—a process called *conceptualization*. They also developed ways of measuring those parts of their discipline—a process called *operationalization*. Inquiries into the behavior of small groups have been plagued by the fact that the parts of reality to be studied and the ways in which they should be measured are neither obvious nor static. Efforts have been made and are being made to find the most useful concept and measurement combinations readily, as they are discovered.[12]

In the 1990s, the study of groups became a truly interdisciplinary activity. A behavioral model was used primarily in the disciplines of political science and philosophy. In this model emphasis was placed on the possibilities of manipulation, power, and dominance. Compromise as a strategy was introduced as incremental decisions are made through adjustments, and the views of participants become known. This political model was founded on the concept of "incrementalism," and was characterized by a limited number of alternatives considered and evaluated. The problem is not viewed in terms of making the "right choice," but rather as making a manageable decision acceptable by the people involved.[13]

Sociology tended to work from a theory-driven model. The work emphasized formulating knowledge claims, stating them in abstract terms, and deriving hypotheses from them. This tradition is based on the idea that theories must be put to an empirical test for validation. Sociologists emphasize social structures—how they merge and change, how they affect and are affected by individuals. The unit of analysis is characteristically the person in a context.[14]

Business and industry were interested in groups from a pragmatic perspective. In the competitive struggle for survival, groups were looked at as a means to survival, whether engaging in strategic planning, determining market strategies, or discussing delivery of services. Management teams became a focus of business and management studies.

Other academic fields used groups in their own contexts. These include studies of classrooms by professional educators, health care delivery by health professionals, research teams of engineers, and art management teams. The overriding and most interdisciplinary research was done within Communication Studies. The common core or research in all fields has been concern for communication and effectiveness.

The spring 1994 issue of *Communication Studies* focused on the topic "Revitalizing the Study of Small Group Communication." The lead article by Lawrence R. Frey stated:

> I sincerely believe that the small group is *the* most important social formation. Every segment of our society—from the largest multinational organization to the political workings of federal, state, city, and local governments to the smallest community action group to friendship groups to the nuclear and extended family—relies on groups to make important decisions, socialize members, satisfy emotional needs, and the like. From birth to death, small groups help define who we are and want to be, how we live and relate to others, whether we will be successful professionally,

and even how we are put to rest after we die. Our life in groups starts with the "birthing" group that brings us into this world, continues in the family that raised us, the school systems that educate us in small classrooms, the peer groups that influence us, the group sports in which we participate, the small office groups or teams in the organizations where we work, the family we start, the time we spend socializing with friends and neighbors, the support groups 75 million of us (40 percent of the U.S. adult population) belong to currently, and ends with the gathering of significant others to pay their respect at our funeral.[15]

Now in the twenty-first century, researchers approach decision making in groups as a process model. The process model draws from the quantitative models of mathematics, statistics, and economics, as well as the behavioral models of political science, psychology, philosophy, and sociology. This process model is governed by highly dynamic objectives that recognize that choices are determined within identifiable constraints, such as time and knowledge of the participants. The process model looks toward the future and the long-term implications of decisions. Electronic technologies, especially computers, are widely regarded as essential to efficient performance at all levels of organizations. Beyond the obvious impact on an individual's work, computers also play a large part in the work of groups.

Even with the strong utilization of computers and other electronic technology in the area of group support systems, the emphasis has been on specific techniques to improve group functioning at the expense of group theory. The efforts to provide groups with technological support have been driven by three basic ideas: (1) improving group task performance, (2) overcoming time and space constraints on collaborative efforts, and (3) increasing the range and speed of access to information. We shall look at these ideas in greater detail.

In earlier writings we have limited our definition of groups to individuals who meet face to face; that is, requiring that all members be present at the same place at the same time. The advent of enhanced communication systems now makes this definition obsolete. There has been considerable research testing the effects of physical separation on group interaction and task performance. We are now open to all possibilities for individuals working together, whether in the same room or at different places around the world.

Computers can increase the range and depth of information beyond what a single individual can reasonably accomplish. In this book we shall attempt to address the problems regarding groups, theory, and time as related to the information technology available. In Chapter 9 we will focus on the use of technology and the development of functioning groups, both in terms of information acquisition and processing as well as the issues in individual and group behavior.[16]

Case Study

Most people don't know what happens to their mail after they drop it in the mailbox or the out basket at work. Obviously, it winds up in U.S. Postal Service distribution centers where four million pieces of mail from 160 post offices are sorted and sent on in the state of Michigan alone. Each distribution center's goal is next day delivery of letters addressed to its own territory. Each day around 4 p.m., sacks and cartons of mail start arriving to be sorted by a large machine. The machine separates the mail by zip code, size, and postal class, affixes a bar code, and cancels the stamp. The goal is for that day's mail to leave the distribution center by 12:30 a.m. without excuse.

The task is easiest when a letter is standard size with the address clearly typed or written, the bar code prestamped, and the zip code correct. It is harder, but not impossible, to automatically sort oddly shaped letters, thick or colored envelopes, and letters addressed in unusual type; such mail can go through the machine, but in recent years much of it has ended up in the hands of manual sorters. This makes the process more expensive, as manually sorted mail costs $44 per thousand letters versus $3 for automated sorting. In response, the postal workers were challenged to find a way to improve the process and allow themselves to continue to reach their goal of next day delivery. What do you think should be done?

Response

A team of manufacturing, marketing, delivery, and collections employees from within the U.S. Postal Service attacked the problem. They discovered that 32 percent of the mail sent to be manually sorted could have been processed by the machine. They determined that they would attempt to cut this by 15 percent, a goal that would save the center about $380,000 a year.

The team discovered two big problems: first, some of the mail that could have been automated was being routed to bins for manual sorting because no one was stopping it; second, some frustrated manual sorters were sending mail they thought could be automated back to the machine, which then kicked it right back to them, creating a loop that delayed letters up to six days.

The group determined that clerks should check to see whether mail that is rejected by the cancellation machine can be automated. If so, it is fed back through the sorter. Meanwhile, manual sorting employees have been trained to decide whether to send the rejected mail back or to process it themselves.

As a result, rejected mail is down to less then six percent, and savings are running at a annual rate of $700,000, even more than anticipated by the team.

Chapter Summary

Groups today are challenged to work together on a variety of problems and to make effective decisions. The advent of the climate in which quality is demanded requires knowledge and skills of effective communication. We believe that the theories of decision-making groups can be subject to observation, application, and verification.

As we examine various research reports, we shall note what seem to be tendencies of most similar groups. Since each group is unique, all-inclusive generalizations cannot be made; on the other hand, to include all relevant qualifiers would make valid generalizations about most groups impossible. Therefore, we have attempted to walk the thin line between overstated generalizations and overly cautious reservations.

Decision making is a province claimed by many disciplines, such as sociology, economics, psychology, management studies, statistics, operations research, education, social work, political science, philosophy, and, of course, communication. As a result, scholars of decision-making differ widely in their models, approaches, methods, and applications. Still, a common core in the research is the concern for communication and quality.

In examining group communication as a process, we wish to equally avoid explaining the behavior of the parts as being simply a function of the group as a whole, and explaining the nature of the whole as a total of all individual members' actions. Our goal will be to consider both the individuals involved and the group as a unit, noting the interaction within and the relationship between process and outcome.

"If we can just talk it over, we can find the right answer." This is one of the number of popular myths concerning groups. We shall try to point out the error of such myths and show how they can seriously undermine the quality of decision-making groups. Good communication does not assure quality decisions, but a group with communication problems will always have difficulty arriving at desirable outcomes.

The utilization of both total quality management and total quality performance principles should be known and utilized when appropriate in our study of groups. In the post office case for example, by using effective decision-making a team found ways to reroute mail that had been sorted by hand so it could be processed by automatic sorting machines. This team's work helped the U.S. Postal Service reach its goal of next day delivery for all letters mailed within the region and saved that post office $700,000 a year.

APPLICATIONS

1.1 Meet in a small group of four to six of your classmates. Compile a list of all the groups to which the members of your group belong. Classify the groups and discuss differences in the communication processes.

1.2 A number of groups are formed to deal with personal problems. Discuss any experiences you have in such groups, for example, support groups and church groups.

How do the experiences in these groups differ from those of decision-making groups?

1.3 Attend a meeting of a campus decision-making group, such as a planning group for a dormitory or house party. Form impressions about the goals of the group and the ways in which the communication either helped or hindered achievement of the goals.

REFERENCES

1. J. Gordon, "The Team Troubles That Won't Go Away," *Training,* August, 1994.

2. J.R. Katzenbach and D.K. Smith, *The Wisdom of Teams: Creating the High Performance Organization* (Boston: Harvard Business School, 1993), p. 198.

3. R.S. Johnson and L.E. Kazense, *The Mechanics of Quality Processes* (Milwaukee: ASQC Quality Press, 1993), p. 1.

4. D. Harrington-Macklin, *Keeping the Team Going: A Tool Kit to Renew and Refuel Your Workplace Teams* (New York: AMACOM, 1996), p. 44.

5. P.H. Andrews and R.T. Herschel, *Organizational Communications* (Boston: Houghton Mifflin Company, 1996), p. 44.

6. B. Spencer, "Models of Organization and Total Quality Management: A Comparison and Critical Evaluation," *Academy of Management Review,* 19 (1994), p. 447.

7. M. Deutsch, "An Experimental Study of the Effects of Cooperation and Conflict upon Group Process," *Human Relations,* 2 (1949), pp. 129–152 and 199–231. Discussed in Chapter 6.

8. A. Bavelas, "Communication Patterns in Task-oriented Groups." *J. Acoust. Soc. A.,* 20 (1950), pp. 725–730. Discussed in Chapter 2.

9. L. Bradford, J.R. Gibb, and K.D. Benne, *T-Group Theory and the Laboratory Method* (New York: Wiley, 1964), p. viii.

10. J.R. Ogilvie and B. Haslett, "Communicating Peer Feedback in a Task Group," *Human Communication Research,* 12 (1985), pp. 79–98.

11. Bales' work is discussed in detail in Chapter 10.

12. D.E. Warnemunde, "The Status of the Introductory Small Group Communication Courses," *Communication Education,* 35 (1986), pp. 389–396.

13. E.F. Harrison, *The Managerial Decision-Making Process* (Boston: Houghton Mifflin Company, 1987), pp. 83–84.

14. M. Foschi and E.J. Lawler, *Group Processes* (Chicago: Nelson-Hill Publishers, 1994), p. vii.

15. L.R. Frey, "Introduction: Revitalizing the Study of Small Group Communications," *Communications Studies,* 45 (1994), pp. 1–2.

16. J.E. McGrath and A.B. Hollingshead, *Groups Interacting with Technology* (Thousand Oaks, CA.: Sage Publications, Inc., 1994), pp. 1–10.

2 Quality Communication in the Group

Scenario

Fred and Roger had just attended the monthly meeting of the marketing department with the opportunity to meet the new director.

"Well, what did you think of that meeting?" asked Roger.

"Okay," Fred responded guardedly, waiting to see Roger's reaction.

Roger had made such an attempt to impress the new director that Fred thought he had been obvious and amusing.

"I really thought the new director hit the nail on the head," said Roger. "He zeroed in on the problems and saw that some of the people aren't doing their jobs. I think he's really going to change things around."

Fred wondered if he had been at the same meeting; he felt only generalities and polite comments had been made. He thought that the time spent had been wasted.

The point here is obvious in that different people interpret situations in different ways. While we have many things in common including a shared language, shared beliefs and shared norms, many of the differences of reactions remain under the surface until brought forward in discussion. Quality communication is necessary to provide the bridges between the differences.

A popular adage in communication studies has been, "You cannot not communicate." Whenever we are in the presence of another person, everything that we say or do has some communication potential, including silence. Communication involves the attachment of meaning to phenomena and behaviors, both intentional and unintentional. As both senders and receivers of messages, group members must strive for effectiveness and high-quality communication. In this chapter we will be concerned with the variables that determine quality communication.

Communication Networks

Early research in communication focused upon the structure of the network through which information is exchanged.[1] Such networks are influenced by power factors within groups such as meetings called by the president of an organization, the informality that allows for unstructured relationships, and the ways in which information is transmitted, including the use of technology. The key question is: Who speaks to whom? The most centralized pattern is the wheel network in which one member is at the center and other members are spokes. In this network the person at the center has all of the power and is the only one who communicates with the other members directly. The other members have to go to the center to communicate with each other. Characteristically, this wheel network is unsatisfying to all members except the individual at the center, and although producing low levels of satisfaction among the members, such a pattern is efficient for routine and recurring decisions in which no need exists for group interaction.[2]

The chain network is another communication network close to the wheel in its power structure. In this network, two members serve as in-persons, each of whom communicate directly with only one other person. The middle persons serve

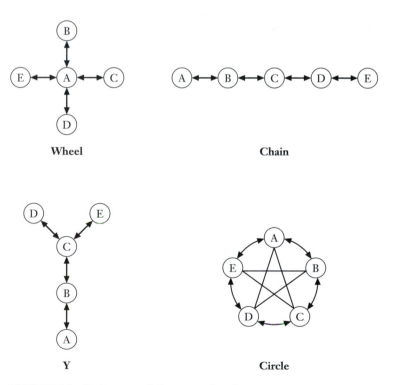

Wheel

Chain

Y

Circle

FIGURE 2.1   Patterns of Communication

as relays, sending messages toward the center. The person at the center of the chain receives information from both ends, decides on the best course of action, and sends it back to the relay persons toward the end of the chain. Thus, the people at the end of the chain communicate directly with only one person, while the relay persons communicate with two, as does the center person. However, the center position is in closest contact with all members of the chain, and that person's position is similar to the wheel. Such a network is satisfying to the center person, somewhat satisfying to the relay persons, and unsatisfying to the people at the end. Like the wheel network, the chain network is most useful in routine, recurring decisions that have a high certainty of outcome.

A third network, the circle network, contrasts with the wheel and chain, allowing each member equal opportunities for communication. In the circle network, information is passed around to all members, and each person acts as a decision-making center. While such a network offers a high level of satisfaction for each of its members, it does take more time to transmit information through the circle network because of the extra links.[3]

Finally, in the completely connected network, there are no restrictions on communication. Individuals in this group make decisions by having members communicate information to everyone directly, each member forming his or her own ideas and tentative alternatives. This group affords the most personal satisfaction because it has many links, but it does take longer to convey information with greater possibility of distortion of the original transmittal. This network is best for decisions that are nonrecurring and uncertain of outcome.

Communication that flows in many directions is slower than a one-way flow of communication, but it is usually more accurate. The senders in the flow of two or more directions feel less anxious and less threatened because receivers respond to the original transmission. However, receivers will feel more sure of themselves and confident in the correctness of the judgments.

Consider the implications of the patterns of communication on two basketball squads. During a timeout, the head coach may provide all of the information in a wheel pattern because of the time constraints. During the halftime, however, the coach may have more of a circle of communication as different players share their opinions as to options available to them in the next half.

Brant Burleson and his colleagues have hypothesized that an open exchange of information, opinions, and criticism is necessary for optimum decision making in complex tasks. They devised a study to determine whether groups employing such interaction procedures produce better decisions than groups employing either averaging or nominal decision procedures. Their work confirmed their hypothesis, even though two groups produced consensual decisions lower in quality than the decisions that would be reached simply by averaging individual preferences. The researchers conclude: "Thus, while social interaction may not result in better decisions for all tasks, it's likely that social interaction will result in high-quality decisions on 'everyday' group decision-making tasks."[4] Effective interaction will likely result in better decisions, while ineffective or inadequate interaction will likely result in relatively poor decisions.

Communication Intentions

Most human communication is designed to achieve a desired effect and elicit a desired response from the other people. We believe that there are three major intentions likely to be served in the quality group environment.

1. *To gain information.* This intention grows from a genuine need to know. Such information opens the doors for the necessary sharing of perceptions and judgments and the establishment of procedures and focus. Information comes from three different levels:
   - *The perceptual level.* This level refers to a report from the sense data a person receives. From touching, seeing, hearing, smelling, and tasting a person can report phenomenal data to others in the group. This level constitutes the first-hand facts that can be verified for accuracy. Like a witness at a trial who is restricted to personal knowledge, permitted neither to draw conclusions nor to give hearsay evidence, data at this level can approximate certainty. If members of the group are not in a position to "see for themselves," they can accept the perceptions of others.
   - *The cognitive level.* With clusters of perceptions and personal orientations, one can communicate a view of reality. This personal cognition is based upon inferences and includes conclusions drawn from facts. The facts of the perceptual level can be verified more easily than those of this level where conflicting viewpoints are likely.
   - *The judgment level.* A person can also communicate values about the world. Such judgments vary greatly from person to person since our ideals, morals, and bases for judgment vary greatly. For example, in the scenario at the beginning of the chapter, Roger reached conclusions quite the opposite of Fred due to his personal impressions that the new director was insightful and impressive. Fred saw the director as shallow and ingratiating.

   While the perceptual level can approach certainty using a scientific mode of validation, the cognitive and judgment levels lack conclusive validation and can only approach varying degrees of probability.

2. *To promote relationships.* Much of our communication within the group is designed to gain social validation from the others. The intent here is to be liked and affirmed. Initially, people will try to establish commonalities and engage in small talk until a clear task has been presented to the group. Even while working on the task, however, much communication is designed to promote particular types of relationships. Smiling and nodding signal an intent to be affirmed. Dominant behavior signals attempts at leadership and may force others into submissive roles. Unless people feel comfortable in the group situation, energy is likely to be lost on the project at hand.
3. *To change the environment and others.* Much of the work of the group is geared toward problems and tasks that require changes. We may choose to participate

in a group because of this option. Issues of power and control reflect this intention.

In studies that differentiate successful groups from unsuccessful groups, Randy Hirokawa has determined three factors that relate to these intentions.[5] The first is the *amount and accuracy of information available to the group*. The better informed a group is about the problem at hand, as well as the positive and negative qualities of optional choices, the better it will be able to reach quality decisions.

The second factor, according to Hirokawa, that makes differences in group decision-making quality is the *amount of effort* group members are willing to put forth in trying to reach a decision. Groups are more likely to reach a high-quality decision when they carefully and painstakingly examine and reexamine the information upon which their decision is based.

The third factor that influences group performance is *the quality of thinking that occurs among the group members* as they attempt to reach a collective decision. A number of studies have discovered the ability of a group to reach a high-quality decision is dependent upon the members' ability to draw correct inferences from the information brought to the group. The group is more likely to reach a high-quality decision when appropriate conclusions are drawn from the relevant data available to them. Such performance is the topic of Chapter 5.

Characteristics of Quality Group Communication

Research has confirmed that a number of characteristics emerge in the communication of groups that are likely to reach quality decisions.

- The members *listen* to one another. Each idea is given a hearing and people are not afraid of being considered foolish by suggesting even extreme ideas. Disagreements are examined with attempts made to resolve them, rather than suppress them.
- The *atmosphere* tends to be informal, comfortable, and relaxed. There is a great deal of discussion in which everyone participates and the discussion remains relevant to the subject at hand.
- The *objectives of the group are well understood and accepted* by all members of the group and assignments to the members are clear and accepted. Members feel free to express their feelings, as well as their ideas, not only on the decision to be made, but also on the group's operations. The group is likely to be self-conscious about its own operations.
- Most decisions are reached through *consensus* in which there is a general willingness to accept the decision. Formal voting with a simple majority is unlikely to be the basis for action.
- The *group leader* does not dominate, and there is no evidence of a power struggle as the group attempts to achieve its tasks.

Let us now consider these five characteristics in greater detail.

Listening

Listening has a number of purposes: we listen to obtain and retain information; we evaluate credibility of the information; we attempt to understand the feelings and point of view of the source of information. Not only must we listen for the content of the message, but we must also seek to evaluate its credibility: should we believe what is said? To what extent does it agree with our experience, the reported experience of other persons with whom we have confidence, and the general wisdom accepted by most people?

Listening for an accurate understanding of the message as well as seeking its credibility are two important functions to use whenever you are a member of a group. However, although you are critically seeking to assess the credibility of a message, you must do so in a way that does not limit (1) your ability to receive it or (2) the speaker's ability to present it. If you are judgmental or hypercritical while trying to listen to a speaker, you may not be able to listen with an open mind. In addition, if your nonverbal behavior is negative the speaker may become inhibited or falter in their presentation. It is not easy to be both open-minded and sensitive to credibility at the same time. However, this is exactly your responsibility as a member of a group.

Critical evaluation of ideas is essential to all of us in the decision-making process. However, to achieve this, we must hear fully what the other members of the group have to say—to hear them and to avoid giving them negative feedback that will impede the full and free expression of their thoughts and feelings. Usually this means suspending critical judgment until we understand their message. Too frequently, we let our predispositions block new ideas or ideas contrary to our beliefs from entering our minds and thus fail to give them consideration. We have perfected the debater's technique of refuting, point-by-point, controversial ideas as they are presented to us.

Let's assume that a person is authentically trying to communicate with us. What critical assessments do we make after we have given a fair hearing to his or her comments? Begin by asking yourself four questions: (1) What is the speaker really saying? (2) Does the speaker make sense? (3) Why should I believe this? (4) Why is this so important?

1. *What is the speaker really saying?* In this first question our search is for the true meaning of the speaker's ideas. Are there hidden meanings? Are there double meanings? If the speaker's meaning appears to be obscure, we may search for probable reasons for their not being more explicit. Deliberate ambiguity is a common tactic of people who feign good intentions in order to deceive listeners. Irresponsible speakers are frequently vague; they fail to use names, numbers, dates, and places, but rely on generalities of all sorts. Terms that mean vastly different things to different people such as *truth, freedom, progress,* and *the people's will,* may be used. If the speaker's meaning is not clear, ask clarifying questions.

2. *Does the speaker make sense?* There are four common flaws in reasoning that you should watch for when you evaluate ideas: non sequitur, false cause,

hasty generalizations, and the bandwagon appeal. Let's look at each of these flaws more closely.

- A *non sequitur* is an instance in which one statement does not follow from another. If someone were to say, "Enrollment in American colleges is declining; I guess I don't need to go to college," that person would be guilty of using a non sequitur. The mere fact that enrollments are declining says nothing about the value of a college education. This particular non sequitur is obvious to most of us, but some of them are much more subtle and much more difficult to detect. Unless a listener carefully reflects upon the sequencing of speaker's statements, such errors in reasoning often go unnoticed.

- A speaker commits a *false cause* fallacy when he or she ascribes something as the cause of an effect when in reality it is not the cause at all. When someone tells the group that we have to curb labor unions because the growth of labor unions has brought with it considerable unemployment, we can quite legitimately ask whether a causal relationship actually exists between labor unions and unemployment. Doesn't a general business recession often cause rising unemployment? We should always test assumptions of causal relationships. The following three questions are especially pertinent: (1) Is the ascribed cause the real cause? (2) Is it the only cause? (3) Is it an important cause?

- We are all given to *hasty generalization*. "I once had a German shepherd dog that was lazy. I just couldn't get it to do anything. I guess German shepherds just can't be counted on for much." Frequently we hear such statements in conversation. Similar statements find their way into group meetings. A hasty generalization occurs every time we generalize about something from too few instances. In the above statement, the "expert" on dogs generalized from a sample of one. It is important that a critical listener ask whether the speaker's conclusions are drawn from sufficient examples. In other words, does it make sense to generalize from the database the speaker is using?

- The *bandwagon appeal* suggests that we should believe something because "everybody believes it," or suggests that we do something because "everybody is doing it." Some people may be convinced by this "follow the crowd" form of reasoning. In such cases they surrender individuality and bow to conformity. Whenever a speaker is trying to ground an argument in the thought that "it is commonly held" or "everybody seems to be doing it," the listener should be wary. Does it make sense to do something merely because there are others doing it? A number of college students each year commit suicide. Does it follow, therefore, that you should commit suicide?

3. *Why should I believe this*? Before making a decision on an issue we should become thoroughly acquainted with the available supporting data. If the primary reason for listening is to find important information about a topic and its corroborating evidence, you should raise the question, "Why should I believe this?" If the speaker fails to answer the question, it is highly appropriate to ask questions about supporting evidence. We suggest that you ask: (1) What is the source of the speaker's claims? Do they stem from the speaker's personal experience? Statistical data? The testimony of authorities? Specific

examples? Direct observation? (2) Is the source of the speaker's evidence reliable? Is the source competent? Is the source prejudiced or biased?

4. *Why is this so important?* Debaters have for years used a device known as the "so what" technique. It consists of questioning the importance of the opponent's arguments. The "so what" technique is equally useful in evaluating the ideas of a group member. A speaker may develop a point with meticulous care but fail to demonstrate that it has significance. If so, you should rightly ask, "So what? Why is this important?" Certainly most commercial testimonials should receive the "so what" treatment. A prominent Hollywood star drinks a certain wine cooler. So what? A baseball superstar eats a particular breakfast cereal. So what? If a member of the group were to argue that you should oppose capital punishment because it was opposed by the greatest criminal lawyer of all time, Clarence Darrow, you should say, "So what?" What you should be interested in is Darrow's *arguments* against capital punishment.

For a group to be successful, it is critical to support the group leaders and other members of the group in learning active listening skills. The following are some active listening techniques that you might want to share with your group.

1. *Pay attention to nonverbal language.* Body language gives important clues to attitudes and feelings. Notice posture, gestures, facial expressions, and eye contact. A shrug, a smile, a nervous laugh, and body positions speak volumes. Start to "read" them. Remember, the vast majority of what we hear comes not from the message, but from the nonverbal signals, including the tone of voice. Gestures, especially hand movements, may reveal feelings and emotional states persons don't intend to reveal. Many of these feelings or attitudes are directed toward oneself. Self-directed gestures may include covering the eyes or touching or covering parts of the face. Other hand movements are designed to groom or hide parts of one's body. Such movements are frequently indicative of shame or embarrassment. One research team asked subjects to view a film and then describe their feelings honestly in one interview and dishonestly in another. Observers were able to identify twice as many self-directed motions when the subjects gave dishonest reports; further, they rated the dishonest reports significantly lower in credibility.

2. *Concentrate and work at listening.* Listening is hard work and is more than just hearing. If your mind wanders and you lose your attention, the speaker will notice that you aren't truly interested in what he or she is saying.

3. *"Attempt to be accepting of what is said" without judging and evaluating until you fully understand the position of the speaker.*

4. *Don't interrupt.* Avoid the temptation to jump into the message of the speaker with stories and examples of your own. Attempts at commonalities are helpful, but interruptions distract from the speaker's thoughts.

5. *Be empathetic.* Put yourself in the place of the speaker, imagining how he or she is thinking and feeling. Listening with empathy requires that we temporarily suspend our own frame of reference and try to get into the speaker's

inner world as he or she experiences it. This does not mean, however, that we necessarily agree with what the speaker has said, only that we continually understand the point of view and the feelings about it. Such an attempt is in itself an expression of respect for the speaker's views, a statement of caring in this situation, and, most important, a desire for understanding.

6. *Listen for the "paralanguage."* Tone of voice is a good indicator of a person's emotional state. Listen for tone, pitch, hesitation or stuttering, loudness, rate, fluency, and inflection to give you clues about how the person is reacting to questions being asked and the memories being recalled.

7. *Guard against asking questions that may get the speaker off the track.* The following are several skills that will help.

   - Gathering information: "Tell me more about that;" "How do you feel about that;" "Let's see if I heard it correctly;" "Is there anything else you remember about that?"
   - Asking questions: Ask questions to get more information to clarify. Thoughtful questions show genuine interest.
   - Clarifying/paraphrasing: Practice reflective listening by paraphrasing and/or summarizing. "In other words you are saying;" "It sounds like you are;" "Is this what you mean?"
   - Summarizing: By summarizing what has been said you give the other members of the group feedback that helps both you and them to better understand and shows the speaker that he or she has been heard.
   - Perception checking: Check to confirm the speaker's emotional state; "It seems to me that you are feeling anxious about that. Am I correct?"

8. *Be comfortable with the expression of emotions.* Allow members of the group to be comfortable if they have strong feelings and are willing to express these feelings. The group should have a norm of permission to express strong feelings when they are called for.

9. *Respond to all group members' concerns.* If someone makes a statement that is not acknowledged or addressed by group members, come back to the issue, feeling, or statement to make sure that the group deals with it. The speaker should feel that what he or she is saying has worth and value. For example, "Let's get back to what Frank said," or "Does anyone have any suggestions on Mary's situation?"

Atmosphere of the Group

As we have indicated, in quality groups the atmosphere tends to be informal, comfortable, and relaxed. Types of behavior relevant to the group's remaining in good working order, having a good climate for working on the task at hand, and having good relationships to permit maximum use of member resources include:

- *Harmonizing.* Attempts to reconcile disagreements; reduces tension; gets people to explore differences.

- *Gate keeping.* Helps to keep communication channels open by suggesting procedures that permit sharing remarks; facilitates the participation of everyone in the decisions.
- *Encouraging.* Is warm, friendly, and responsive to others; indicates by a remark or by nonverbal communication (nodding, smiling) the acceptance of others' contributions.
- *Compromising.* Offers compromises that may yield status when one's own idea is involved in a conflict; admits errors and is willing to modify beliefs in the interest of group cohesion or growth.
- *Standard setting and testing.* Tests whether a group is satisfied with its procedures; points out the norms that have been set for evaluating the quality of the group process.
- *Relieving tension.* Introduces humor or other relief in a tense situation; helps relax the group.

Such behaviors promote a supportive atmosphere in which participants feel comfortable, enjoy the experience, and are willing to take risks, knowing they will be supported. Flexibility and creativity are encouraged, as people listen to one another and attempt to understand feelings as well as ideas.

Clear Objectives and Acceptance of Roles

Every meeting has a purpose (or else it shouldn't be scheduled). The situation or problem at hand must be presented to all participants in an agenda. The purpose should be mentioned again at the beginning of the meeting, as the group orients itself to the problem. All known constraints should be outlined before a meeting begins. Economic, political, legal, time-related, technical, ethical, or organizational restrictions or concerns should be made clear at the onset. Unless there is "buy-in" by the participants to the objectives of the group and the problem being discussed, the group will be unable to arrive at quality conclusions. In a quality group the following factors cannot be disregarded:

1. The motivations of the people to engage in interaction: What are the needs, drives, and modes of fulfillment of each individual member?
2. The individuals' attitudes and value orientations that exist prior to the meeting and that characteristically influence their behavior: Is there dissonance influencing potential action?
3. The individual and collective prejudices and biases brought to the group: Do they limit the decision-making potential?
4. The self-conceptions of individuals within the group: Is self-determination present? What levels of consciousness are present in the group?
5. The degree of individual openness and willingness to communicate honestly with the group: Are the individuals able to disclose honest feelings rather than merely fulfill role expectations?

Reaching Consensus

Two aspects of consensus—cohesion and conformity—are closely linked. Cohesion refers to a group quality that "includes individual pride, commitment, meaning, as well as the group's stick-togetherness, ability to weather crisis, and ability to maintain itself over time."[6] Members have a sense of belonging and are dedicated to the well-being of the group. Indirectly, cohesiveness refers to morale, teamwork, and the so-called group spirit.

While cohesion is essential to the well-being of the group, an extreme conformity can greatly limit a group's effectiveness. If group members conform too readily to the group's norms and reinforce one another indiscriminately, the result is likely to be what Irving Janis has labeled "groupthink."[7] We shall discuss this problem in greater depth in subsequent chapters.

Janis does not suggest that cohesion must necessarily give rise to "group-think." He proposes that individuals be assigned the role of critical evaluator and that a high priority be placed on airing any doubts or uncertainties. An agenda can be altered to pay greater attention to competing alternatives before consensus is reached. The process of group decision-making should include a review of the assets and liabilities associated with the efforts to reach a consensual choice. The assets of group decision making include:

1. *Greater sum total of knowledge or information.* There is more information in a group than within any of its members. Therefore, decisions that require the use of knowledge should give groups an advantage over individuals.
2. *Greater number of approaches to a problem.* Individuals often fall into ruts in their thinking. Interaction with other members of the group who have different viewpoints should stimulate new thought and open up intellectual horizons.
3. *Participation and decision making increases general acceptance of the final choice.* When groups make decisions, more people accept and feel responsible for the decision work. A low-quality decision that has acceptance can be more effective than a higher-quality choice that lacks general acceptance.
4. *Better comprehension of the decision.* There are fewer chances for failures in communication when the people who work together to implement the decision have participated in making it.

The liabilities in the quest for consensual choice include:

1. *Social pressure.* The desire to be a good group member and to be accepted may force consensus and silence disagreement.
2. *Acceptance of solutions.* The first solution that appears to receive strong support from the majority of the group members or a vocal minority is likely to be accepted. Higher quality solutions introduced after the first solution has been accepted have little chance of receiving honest consideration.

3. *Individual domination.* In leaderless groups a dominant individual may emerge and exert more than his or her share of influence on the decision. Even appointed leaders may exert a major influence in selection of preferred alternatives.

4. *Winning the decision.* The appearance of several alternatives often causes the members to support a particular position. These preferences may take precedence over finding the best solution and the result is a compromise decision of lower quality.

The most effective groups attain the objectives that give rise to the formation of the group and at the same time satisfy the needs of the members. A high level of cohesiveness helps satisfy the individual needs of the members and group norms may encourage the attainment of the established goals.

Balanced Power

The effective leader in the quality group allows the group to communicate openly and does not attempt to control and dominate the interactions of the group. Power may be defined as the ability to influence the behavior of others in accordance with one's intentions. Power may be applied by force, domination, or manipulation. Two principle criteria used to measure power include: (1) the number of actions on the part of any person in each of any number of selected types of behavior in which power is exercised successfully, and (2) the number of persons over whom such power is exerted. By these criteria it is apparent that group leaders have ample opportunities to exercise power. The usual bases of decision-making power are legitimacy, reward, and coercion. Legitimacy may come from the rank of the individual, such as a manager of a division or business. Expert power comes from special knowledge and expertise, and referent power is often acquired by being likable, admirable, honorable, or charismatic. These types of power, unlike the others, are available to all group members. Power is not something a person can demand from a group; it is given by the group. Even the legitimate leader who has been assigned the role of leader may find exercising controlling prerogatives to be challenging if the group resists. The way that a person chooses to use power should depend upon the situation and the individual's style. We shall discuss this concept in greater detail in our discussion of leadership in Chapter 8.

Case Study

In Sellersburg, Indiana, a small company named SERVEND builds large beverage dispensers for restaurants and convenience stores. With low salaries and inflexible hours, the employee turnover rate was extraordinary, reaching 70 percent a year. Each defection cut into productivity and cost the company approximately $5,000. The rapid turnover of employees also alienated customers who received the machines built by inexperienced workers. What could the company and employees do to improve working conditions and reduce turnover?

Response

In 1996, Elaine Monson, SERVEND'S director of marketing, and 11 of her colleagues formed the Workplace Excellence Team with the mission to make the company a better and more appealing employer. Executives began studying the management principles of total quality management.

"The real key was learning how to listen carefully to our people," Monson stated. "They told us what they needed to be satisfied at work and in life."

The sharing of information has played an important role in the company's comeback. SERVEND began quantifying performance in minute detail, and lining the halls of the headquarters with charts showing everything from employee satisfaction to plant safety records. The results are impressive: the average annual wage for factory workers, including profit sharing, has nearly doubled since 1994. Individual productivity has jumped more then 66 percent since 1995, and customer's concerns have dropped from a total of 313 in 1995, to just 17 during the first quarter of 1999.

These improvements have made major changes in the workforce as turnover has been reduced to 12 percent and the company now receives some 500 applications annually for 30 new positions. The work of the team received the 1999 RIT/USA Quality Cup for Small Business.[8]

Chapter Summary

Effective communication is the essence of group decision-making. The ability of group members to speak and listen in such a manner as to share meanings permits the group to function as a unit. We have suggested skills that we feel are important to the speaker and the listener.

The effects of communication within a group have been studied in two ways: by careful observation by an outside researcher and by imposing some communication pattern on a group. Observation studies have shown that over time group members vary in the quantity and quality of their contributions. In this chapter we have examined the importance of both verbal and nonverbal messages within the group. Either as participants in a group or as observers of a group process, we should be aware of the range of messages and the outcomes of the options taken. The experimental study of patterns indicates that the more centralized the group structure (that is, the greater the extent to which one member can exchange messages with others), the greater the speed and accuracy in solving simple problems, and the lower the morale and satisfaction of the members.

Improved communication in the case study at the SERVEND Company was able to raise wages and reduce employee turnover from 70 percent to 12 percent.

As one of the judges for the national competition stated, "SERVEND implemented a truly comprehensive quality initiative that's pervasive throughout the organization."[9]

Now that we have considered communication as the focal process in the group, let us consider how people's participation impacts upon the quality of decisions.

APPLICATIONS

2.1 Convene four groups of individuals. Form each group into the "patterns of communication" (see Figure 2.1) and ask each group to simultaneously solve the same problem. Afterward, discuss the differences in the patterns of communication within all four groups.

2.2 Have groups of five to seven individuals meet to discuss a topic. Assign one person per group to become agitated with the group's discussion. Assign a second person to maintain a supportive climate, using techniques outlined in this chapter. Discuss the outcome of these interactions.

REFERENCES

1. A. Bavelas, "Communication Patterns in Task-Oriented Groups," *Journal of the Acoustical Society of America,* 22 (1950), pp. 725–730.
2. J.C. Gilchrist, M.E. Shaw, and L.C. Walker, "Some Effects of Unequal Distribution of Information in a Wheel Group Structure," *Journal of Abnormal Social Psychology,* 49 (1954), pp. 554–556.
3. M.E. Shaw, "Group Structure and the Behavior of Individuals in Small Groups," *Journal of Psychology,* 38 (1954), pp. 139–149.
4. B.B. Burleson, B.J. Levine, and W. Samter, "Effects of Decision-Making Procedure on the Quality of Individual and Group Decisions." Paper presented at the Speech Communication Association, November 1983.
5. R.Y. Hirokawa, "Communication and Group Decision-Making Efficacy," in *Small Group Communication,* ed. Robert S. Cathcart, Larry A. Samover, and Linda D. Henman (Dubuque, IA: Brown and Benchmark Publishers, 1996), pp. 109–109.
6. C.R. Shepherd, *Small Groups* (Scranton, PA.: Chandler, 1964), p. 88.
7. I.L. Janis, *Victims of Groupthink* (Boston: Houghton Mifflin, 1972).
8. B. Myers, *USA Today,* Friday, May 7, 1999, p. 6B.
9. B. Myers, *USA Today,* Friday, May 7, 1999, p. 6B.

3 Quality Participation in Groups

Scenario

Jane is required to take a Small Group Communication course as a general education requirement for her bachelor's degree. She hesitated to enroll in this course because her previous experiences working in groups were not positive. During the second week of the class, students were assigned randomly to learning groups for the remainder of the term. Jane's group consisted of four other students whom she did not consider to be her equal in intellectual capabilities, based on her intuition and first impressions. The other students sensed that Jane considered herself to be intellectually superior. Needless to say, the productivity of the group suffered throughout the term as a result of these perceptions.

Although the scenario presented might seem far-fetched, this situation occurs quite often when individuals become members of a zero-history group. A zero-history group is defined as a set of individuals brought together in a group context that have no prior work or social interactions with each other. The purpose of this chapter is to discuss how quality participation in groups is impacted by individual perceptions, varying theoretical or ideological perspectives, personality differences, and cultural variations of the members within the group itself. Members need to consider these factors in order to assure that the decisions made in the group context are high quality. Prior to discussing these issues, Field Theory will be reviewed as a theoretical framework that explains many of the behaviors that take place in the small group context.

Theoretical Framework: Field Theory

Kurt Lewin, one of the foremost social scientists of the twentieth century, developed a theoretical framework called *field theory* to assist in understanding how individuals interpret their immediate surroundings and situations based on previous experiences.[1] Lewin theorized that individual perceptions and reactions to situations, including small group communication situations, are a direct result of previous experiences that have been catalogued in the human memory, also called the "field of reference." Hence, the experiences from your past serve as perceptual and predispositional factors to assist you in interpreting a given present situation.

One example, documented in nearly every small group communication situation that we have experienced, pertains to students in learning groups who are assigned a specific project or assignment. Invariably, at least one of the students in the group has a negative predisposition toward working on graded assignments in a small group context. When the cause of this negative predisposition is investigated, by asking probing questions, students often report at least one small group situation that was dysfunctional or unproductive. Another common example shared quite often is an account of one or more students in a small group who do not participate in assigned activities. Thus, the remaining group members often complete whatever projects or assignments are required for the course without an equitable amount of effort from each group member. The result of this situation is often documented by the responsible group members reporting a resentment toward group members they think are irresponsible, thus justifying their predisposition to avoid such projects and assignments.

Although these perceptions may have a certain amount of validity, one of the objectives of the leader of small groups should be to create small groups situations that counteract this predisposition and reduce or eliminate negative perceptions of the group process. Strategies to offset this and similar scenarios that serve as stumbling blocks to quality participation in small groups will be discussed later in this chapter. The immediate objective is to review the potential impact that different perceptions, personalities, and cultures have on the quality of participation in groups.

Perceptions of Others

In the scenario at the beginning of the chapter, Jane quickly formed an impression of the other members of her group. Her impressions were based upon limited data about her peers. The other members of the group accurately perceived Jane's feelings of superiority. These initial perceptions tainted the interaction and reduced the effectiveness of the group.

In perceiving, or having thoughts about another person, people often note certain features, movements, and sounds and form a mental image. The process of perception is generally believed to accomplish two things:

1. People record a diversity of data they encounter in a form simple enough to be retained by their limited memory.
2. They mentally go beyond the data given to predict future events, and thereby minimize surprise.

These two accomplishments of perception, selective recording and prediction, become the basis for forming our impressions of other people. In forming our impressions of others, we observe their actions and expressive movements, we notice their voices, and we note what they say and do as they respond to us and other stimuli. From these data we make inferences about other people's cognitions, needs, emotions and feelings, goals, and attitudes. Our actions toward them and prediction of future interactions are guided by these judgments. Simultaneously, others are making judgments about us that will direct subsequent communications to us. If our judgments of each other are correct, effective interaction becomes possible. If, however, our observations or predictions of each other are incorrect, communication is hampered and difficulties may develop.

As we interact with people we see or hear them do certain things; from these observed behaviors we infer or guess that they have certain personality characteristics, motives, or intentions. For example, we may see them smile and conclude that they are "friendly." This process of inferring traits or intentions is known as *attribution* and has become the focus of much interest and study in social psychology.[2]

Consider the following example. A group member felt ill and abruptly left the group in the middle of discussion. At the next meeting the other members were asked why they thought he had left. Responses included various reactions: the member was angered over the poor quality of the discussion and left in disgust; he had an appointment; he thought he had arrived at a good stopping point; he was reacting emotionally to a comment made by a member of the group. None of the group guessed the true reason, but all were willing to make inferences concerning the behavior witnessed.

In the development and testing of attribution theory, research has tended to support the following principles: (1) Much of the behavior of others that can be observed is trivial or incidental and is not valuable for drawing conclusions regarding personality or intentions—we must be carefully tentative in the attribution process; (2) the observable behavior of others is often neatly designed to mislead or deceive us; and (3) their actions are often determined by external factors beyond their control and *not* by their internal states, personalities, or intentions. As a result of these limiting factors, we must use attribution with care; however, our experience tells us that in large measure it often works for us well. This is essentially true for attribution of general dispositions or intentions formed on the basis of numerous observations over extended periods of time.

According to field theory, each experience, and the learning that accompanies it, plays a vital role in helping individuals make accurate judgments of others. Small children learn this at an early age by developing an understanding of "how far to go" before a parent will lose patience and impose some sort of punishment. However, this same child may not accurately predict when her/his teacher will lose patience and impose some sort of punishment for unacceptable behaviors. As an individual matures and interacts with a variety of people in varying contexts the ability to accurately predict how to behave becomes almost second nature.

Intelligence as well as maturity should obviously be related to our skill in judging people.[3] Two kinds of capacity (relevant to our judgment of others) are correlated with intelligence: the ability to draw inferences about people from observations of their behavior and the ability to account for observations in terms of general principles or concepts. Investigators have been particularly concerned with *self-serving* bias, the tendency to see oneself as the cause of one's successes but to attribute failure to outside sources.[4] In one experiment teams were formed and given responsibility for governing a fictitious country presently in the midst of a revolution. At intervals new information was provided about the nation's economy, people's attitudes, and the state of revolution. Many decisions were called for, and since the outcomes were uncertain, the researcher varied either periods of consistent disaster or consistent success. After each period, the members of the teams were asked the causes of their success or failure. Overwhelmingly when the groups experienced failure, outside circumstances were at fault, but when their actions were successful, they rated themselves as being responsible for the outcome. This study has obvious implications for the results of all group discussions. Some of the most serious distortions in perception of new acquaintances come from their chance resemblance to people who were once important to us. Freud called this process *transference*. A gray-haired woman in a group may be seen as a mother-symbol; those who enjoyed childhood dependence on their own mothers expect a similar acceptance from her, and those who found their own mothers hateful will anticipate that kind of personal relationship and perhaps guard against it.

A dominant male may be a father figure against whom men who have never worked out their parental conflicts will rebel. An older man may be perceived as a godlike person who has the power to solve all our problems. These are familiar transference patterns, but there are many others. The young man with horned-rimmed glasses resembles a fellow we used to know; until we learned otherwise, we expected him to behave as our earlier acquaintance did. We may feel let down because he does not exhibit the lively sense of humor we imagined he would have, or we may feel relieved because he is not so critical as we had feared. Often we attribute to "intuition" those immediate flashes of feeling about new acquaintances that lead us to feel that they will prove trustworthy, malicious, superficial, or kind. Actually, those strong impressions can be shown on analysis to arise from some resemblance, in physique, speech, manner, or relative position, to someone whom we earlier knew as trustworthy, malicious, superficial, or kind.[5] First impressions, in addition to what they tell us about others, tell us about ourselves. A genuine dislike for an exhibitionistic person may suggest how strictly we forbid expression of our own exhibitionist drives, whereas a feeling of attraction to such a person may suggest that we would like to live out our own drives in this direction. Rather than dismiss the value of first impressions, we should attempt to determine the bases of our reactions and remain tentative in our evaluations.

In a quality decision-making group, individual predispositions and biases would be discussed and evaluated openly. Individual members would try to understand each other's opinions and be aware of their own biases. Unfortunately, however, this process of opinion exchange and readjustment does not always occur. Individuals cling to their initial biases, distorting the final group decision.[6]

To illustrate, James Davis has carried out extensive research on decision-making in juries.[7] In one study, more than 800 students were asked about their general beliefs in rape trials. From their responses, three different types of predispositions were identified: proprosecution, moderate, and prodefense. Groups with each category of bias were shown a videotape in which an accused rapist admitted the rape took place but argued that the woman not only consented, but also initiated the action. The woman testified that the man had misrepresented himself as a police officer and subsequently raped her. After witnesses on both sides gave testimony and lawyers gave summary statements, the students were asked to give their opinions as to the defendant's guilt.

The students' preliminary biases had a strong effect on their evaluation of the case. After 30-minute discussions, the six-person groups that indicated a proprosecution bias were likely to vote guilty while prodefense groups voted innocent. This is why lawyers take jury selection so seriously.

General Predispositions

In addition to the specific biases that we hold on particular issues, we may also have general predispositions that influence our interactions with other members of a group. Milton Rokeach has suggested that people function in a continuum of degrees of open- or closed-mindedness.[8] This approach identifies the characteristic way an individual receives and processes messages from others. Extremely closed-minded people are characterized as highly dogmatic and described as follows:

1. Likely to evaluate messages on the basis of irrelevant inner drives or arbitrary reinforcements from external authority, rather than on the basis of considerations of logic.
2. Primarily seek information from sources within their own belief system; for example, "the more closed-minded Baptists are, the more likely it is that they will know what they know about Catholicism or Judaism through Baptist sources."
3. Less likely to differentiate among various messages that come from belief systems other than their own; for example, an extremely politically conservative person may perceive all nonrightists as extreme liberals.
4. Less likely to distinguish between information and the source of the information and more likely to evaluate the message in terms of their perceptions of the belief system of the other person.

Essentially, "closed" people are ones who rigidly maintain a system of beliefs, who see a wide discrepancy between their belief system and those belief systems different from theirs, and who evaluate messages in terms of the "goodness of fit" with their own belief system.[9]

Conversely, the "open" person is likely to be more receptive to messages that are disagreeable and to be tolerant of differences. This person will be likely to contribute to a supportive climate in the group.

A slightly more elaborate classification of interpersonal predispositions has been developed by Karen Horney.[10] Horney was among the leading psychiatrists in asserting that neurotic difficulties must be seen as disturbances in interpersonal relationships. In her theoretical work, she classified people into three types according to their predominant interpersonal response traits: (1) moving *toward* others; (2) moving *against* others; and (3) moving *away from* others.

According to Horney's system, *going toward* others ranges from mild attraction to affiliation, trust, and love. Such a person shows a marked need for affection and approval and a special need for a partner, that is, a friend, lover, husband, or wife who is to fulfill all expectations of life and to take responsibility for good and evil. This person "needs to be liked, wanted, desired, loved; to feel accepted, welcome, approved of, appreciated; to be needed, to be of importance to others, especially to one particular person; to be helped, protected, taken care of, guided."[11]

Behavior identified as *going against* others ranges from mild antagonism to hostility, anger, and hate. Such a person perceives that the world is an arena in which, following Darwin, only the fittest survive and the strong overcome the weak. Such behavior is typified by a callous pursuit of self-interest. The person with this interpersonal orientation needs to excel, to achieve success, prestige, or recognition in any form. According to Horney, such a person has "a strong need to exploit others, to outsmart them, to make them of use to himself." Any situation or relationship is viewed from the standpoint of "what can I get out of it?"[12]

Behavior that is characterized as *going away* from others ranges from mild alienation to suspicion, withdrawal, and fear. With this orientation the underlying principle is that one never becomes so attached to anybody or anything that he, she, or it becomes indispensable. There is a pronounced need for privacy. When such people go to a hotel, they rarely remove the "Do Not Disturb" sign from outside their door. Both self-sufficiency and privacy serve their outstanding need, the need for utter independence. Their independence and detachment have a negative orientation, aimed at *not* being influenced, coerced, or obligated. To such a person, according to Horney, "to conform with accepted rules of behavior or to additional sets of values is repellant . . . He will conform outwardly in order to avoid friction, but in his own mind he stubbornly rejects all conventional rules and standards."[13]

Horney summarizes the three types as follows:

> Where the compliant type looks at his fellow men with a silent question, "will he like me?"—and the aggressive type wants to know, "how strong an adversary is he?" or "can he be useful to me?"—the detached person's concern is " will he interfere with me? Will he want to influence me or (will he) leave me alone?"[14]

Our approach is based largely on the thesis that people interact with others in order to obtain something from them: An individual's interpersonal needs can be satisfied only through others. To summarize, numerous personality factors, and their corresponding behaviors, must be taken into consideration in small group communication contexts. A clear understanding of these same factors can assist the members of a group both in understanding how to react to others, and in assessing their own behaviors.

Furthermore, a clear understanding of individual personalities may yield an enhanced ability to work with others in a small group context and achieve levels of participation that yield quality decisions.

Cultural Factors

In order to understand the part that culture plays in the small group context we must first define the term itself and discuss the importance it plays in defining the group. Prosser defines culture as "the traditions, customs, norms, beliefs, values and thought-patterning which are passed down from generation to generation."[15] In the process of defining our contemporary culture we have learned the importance of being inclusive, unbiased, and respectful of individuals representing various cultures. This notion is supported with formal laws and rules of non-discrimination as well as with an acceptable range of behavioral patterns. However, it is important to note that each person, group, organization, and collective social group or society develops its own set of core values. For example, one cultural value pervasive in the North American value system is inclusion, which seeks to provide any and all individuals an opportunity to participate in social processes such as decision-making.

Once values are well defined, individuals are better able to identify the accepted patterns of normative behaviors in any given context. These behavioral norms provide an individual with enough information to know what specific behaviors are appropriate or inappropriate in any given context. For example, as a new student on a college campus, it should become apparent that the institution values academic integrity. As a direct extension of this value system, the student is taught how to appropriately attribute ideas presented in a written assignment to the original author or source of information, thus providing a set of parameters of acceptable behavior. Therefore, students should learn, as members of the culture, how to appropriately communicate their ideas in written assignments.

In the small group context, professors typically support a value system of equal participation among all members assigned to learning groups. This culture of "equal participation" provides students with an understanding that the "norm" is to allow and encourage all members of the group to participate in the group decision-making process. However, those individuals who do not behave according to these norms of acceptable and expected behaviors, such as those individuals attempting to dominate decision-making discussions or attempting to avoid providing input in a group decision, should be reminded by the other group members that their behavior(s) fall outside the range of acceptability. Therefore, each group becomes empowered to maintain the integrity of a culture of participation and inclusion.

Inherent to the group decision-making process is the notion of *collectivism*. This concept has been referenced earlier in discussions about the importance of making decisions with input from all concerned or affected parties. Ideally, this notion suggests that decisions made will be acceptable to all parties impacted. If this is the case, the decision was made using a collectivist decision-making model. Collectivism, in terms of decision making, is best defined as incorporating the ideas and inputs from everyone whom the decision impacts. However, this cultural value has not always been the status quo. In fact, the norm used to be that one, or a few, individual(s) made most decisions in group contexts. Over time, it has been discovered that this model of individualism is less effective than the collectivism model, in terms of both the quality of participation and the quality of decisions. Therefore, the values of our culture, in general, are "shifting" to a paradigm of collectivism in the context of group decision-making.

An additional cultural factor to consider is *ethnocentrism*. Simply defined, ethnocentrism is the evaluation of another culture according to the values of your own culture. Thus, ethnocentrism is problematic in that the individual evaluating a culture is imposing the characteristics of her or his own value system and culture as the referent paradigm for evaluation. This presents a problem because an individual often fails to understand the cultural values supporting the normative patterns of behavior that are observed. In the small group context it is important to recognize that other cultures may exist when interpreting the behaviors of individuals within a group or other groups. Once an individual has a clear understanding of the predominant culture it will become much easier to interpret the behaviors of other individuals. Obvious cases of ethnocentrism occur in small groups when an individual gains membership to the group as a new member who happens to be from a culture outside the host culture (i.e., an international student). This student may have been socialized that it is not appropriate to openly communicate in the classroom. However, once this individual is enrolled in a group communication course he or she is required to participate in decision-making tasks. Insensitive students will misdiagnose this student's reticence as an indication of unconcern or apathy about the group's performance. In reality, the reticent student is quite concerned about the group's performance. Unless one or more of the group members understand the principles of ethnocentrism, the possibility exists for one or more of the group's members to confront the reticent student in an offensive manner that is culturally insensitive. Therefore, it is "best" for individuals to interpret situations, such as this one, by developing a clear understanding of a given person's culture prior to evaluating their attitudes or behaviors. A quality group is often composed of individuals from a variety of cultural backgrounds. Such groups have proved to be more effective in decision-making tasks, assuming that the group draws upon the wealth of knowledge and varying perspectives within the group.

Each of the aforementioned factors serve as predictors of the quality of participation in small group contexts. Consideration of these factors is important to assist groups in achieving quality decisions. The following case study illustrates the magnitude of the concepts discussed in this chapter.

Case Study

A large government agency in the United States adopted quality circles as an approach to encouraging employee input pertaining to improving day-to-day business activities. Individuals from throughout this government facility were encouraged to participate. As mentioned in previous chapters, the objective behind using employee participation programs is to give all people within the organization an opportunity to help improve the effectiveness of business activities and the quality of work life. Employees from throughout the company volunteered to partake in these group decision-making discussions. Procedurally, these groups meet on a regular basis—weekly or bi-monthly—in order to investigate the viability of implementing changes in policies or procedures recommended by fellow employees. The following case scenario outlines the decision making process of one such group.

This quality circle consisted of seven individuals employed in the maintenance division. The group consisted of five men and two women, with each individual representing different work teams within the organization. More specifically, only two of the men were maintenance workers with the rest of the group composed of two clerical staff members, one human resource employee, one custodian, and one individual from the purchasing department. Therefore, we can assume, by the varying work assignments alone, that the individuals in this group possess a variety of perceptions, personality factors, and cultural backgrounds. Theoretically, this should assist this group in making better decisions.

The first issue that was brought to the attention of this group was a complaint by the maintenance workers that there was an insufficient supply of repair manuals for the number of workers employed in the division. An initial fifteen-minute discussion by the group led to a premature conclusion, based on the strong assertions of the two maintenance workers in the group validating this assumption, to purchase two additional sets of manuals. One month later the same group received the same complaint—that there were not enough maintenance manuals in the division. This led the group to believe that the purchase of additional manuals might not be the answer to this problem.

Consider the following discussion questions to understand how this group might have proceeded in order to reach a better decision the first time this issue was brought to their attention:

- Did the group take a sufficient amount of time to investigate potential solutions to this problem?
- Should the perceptions of all individuals in the group have been taken into consideration?
- How should the group proceed in the future, prior to making decisions?
- Should the group consider input from all members prior to making decisions?

The ability to accept variations in perceptions, personalities, and cultures will enhance the quality of participation in decision-making groups. Therefore, individuals need to confirm that their perceptions of others are accurate, develop an understanding and appreciation of differing personality traits, and develop a clear understanding of the cultures their peers represent in order to be effective members of a decision-making group. The denial of importance of any of these factors can prove quite disastrous to the group process and the quality of group participation. Field theory provides a referent of understanding for prior group interaction situations. For example, our predisposition toward all of the aforementioned factors (perceptions, interpretations of personalities, and the interpretation of cultures) are determined by prior interactions and experiences. However, it is important to note that we should make every attempt to enter each new group situation with as few predispositions as possible in order to avoid allowing our biases, generated from our prior experiences, to skew our attitude in a favorable or unfavorable direction. The best rule to follow is to draw upon your wealth of experience and knowledge, yet do not allow negative experiences from the past create negative predispositions that can diminish the present group experience. Consider the following:

- Take sufficient time to consider the ideas of all group members.
- Consider that some group members may assert their opinions, as if they know the answer to a problem, while in fact they are either ill-informed or uninformed about the problem at hand.
- Pursue information prior to making a decision in order to have sufficient data to support your conclusion.

Response

The real problem was that the individuals using the manuals rarely returned them to the appropriate location in the shop, thus providing the impression that an insufficient amount of manuals existed. In reality, the problem was solved by clearly defining procedures requiring workers to return the manuals to the appropriate location in order for them to be easily found when the next worker needed to refer to them.

Chapter Summary

All that we are influences our behavior in a group situation. The total study of psychology would contribute only a portion of the data needed for any global generalizations. Nevertheless, we have attempted to focus attention on certain interpersonal functions influencing the behavior of all individuals in a group. A study of a group cannot be made if factors such as the following are disregarded:

1. The motivations of the people to engage in interaction: What are their needs, drives, and modes of fulfillment?
2. The individual's attitudes and value orientations that exist prior to the meeting and that characteristically influence their behavior: Is there dissonance influencing potential action?
3. The individuals and collective prejudices and biases brought to the group: Do they limit the decision-making potential?
4. The self-conceptions of individuals within the group: Is self-determination present? What levels of consciousness are present in the group?

5. The degree of individual openness and willingness to communicate honestly within the group: Are individuals able to disclose honest feelings rather than merely fulfill role expectations?

From these frameworks of interpersonal orientations we shall proceed in the next chapter to examine the characteristics of groups that influence group productivity.

APPLICATIONS

3.1 Analyze some of the groups to which you have identified yourself as belonging in terms of the priority of needs described in this chapter.

3.2 Within your group, share initial perceptions that have been changed as a result of your interaction. How has your communication changed as you have grown to know each other?

3.3 Analyze your participation in groups according to the cultural factors that are implicit in the American culture. Have you noticed variations in different groups?

REFERENCES

1. K. Lewin, *Field Theory in Social Science* (New York: Harper and Row), 1951, pp. 188–237.
2. B. Weiner, "Spontaneous Causal Thinking," *Psychological Bulletin,* 97 (1985), pp. 74–84.
3. D.K. Simonton, "Intelligence and Personal Influence in Groups: Four Nonlinear Models," *Psychological Review,* 92 (1985), pp. 532–547.
4. G.W. Bradley, "Self-serving Bias in the Attribution Process," *Journal of Personality and Social Psychology,* 36 (1978), pp. 56–71.
5. S. Streufert and S.C. Streufert, "Effects of Conceptual Structure, Failure and Success on Attribution of Causality and Interpersonal Attitudes," *Journal of Personality and Social Psychology,* 11 (1969), pp. 138–147.
6. See P.B. Smith, "Social Influence Processes in Groups," *Psychological Survey,* 4 (1985), pp. 88–108.
7. J.H. Davis, "Group Decision and Procedural Justice," in *Progress in Social Psychology,* vol. 1, ed. By M. Fishbein (Hillsdale, N.J.: Lawrence Earlbaum, 1980).
8. M. Rokeach, *The Open and Closed Mind* (New York: Basic Books, 1960), pp. 61–64.
9. Ibid.
10. K. Horney, *Our Inner Conflicts* New York: Norton, 1945).
11. Ibid., pp. 50–51.
12. Ibid., p. 65.
13. Ibid., p. 78.
14. Ibid., pp. 80–81.
15. M.H. Prosser, *The Cultural Dialogue: An Introduction to Intercultural Communication* (Boston: Houghton Mifflin, 1978), p. 5.

4 Characteristics of Quality Groups

Scenario

A group of mid-level managers assigned to different sales regions throughout the United States were sent on a two-day retreat to determine why sales have been steadily declining over the past six months. Throughout this two-day session each manager was very reluctant to reveal any "problems" hindering the effectiveness of her or his own sales force. Thus, no matter how hard the facilitator of the meeting tried to initiate productive and honest discussion between the retreat participants, the discussions that ensued were quite superficial and very few solutions to any problems were generated. Afterward, the participants wondered why they had been asked to attend this retreat.

This case example is not uncommon in business and industry. Groups are often brought together to discuss problems or potential issues of concern and fail to work together as a group to resolve problems. What's worse, companies often accept such group interaction outcomes as the norm and do not hold the individuals present accountable for their actions. However, the present economy and the adoption of cultures of quality have begun to expect individuals and groups to meet (or exceed) designated performance standards. In order to meet performance standards and expectations, it is important to understand the following:

- how to engage in quality group interactions and understand what factors contribute to quality groups (e.g., group size, cohesion, trust, factors of diversity)
- what behaviors group members must adopt during the decision-making process in order to be more effective (e.g., open communication, critical evaluation of ideas, defining individual roles within the group)
- the importance of holding groups accountable for group interactions and decisions.

As the scenario indicates, the members of the group were not interacting in a way to assure that the discussion process was effective, and the resulting outcomes were equally ineffective and unproductive. The members of the group were not working together in order to solve problems that prevail throughout the organization. This chapter will discuss how "best" to proceed in the group context in order to develop high quality groups.

Successes and failures in small groups can be measured using a variety of methods and performance standards. It is important to assess the characteristics of a quality group from both a process and outcome perspective. In this chapter we will consider: (1) characteristics that promote behaviors that assist the group in functioning in an appropriate and effective manner and (2) ways to evaluate the effectiveness of group outputs. The outcomes of group processes can be subjected to standards of accountability. The group must be evaluated to determine if the proposed/implemented solutions to problems are viable or effective.

The term "accountability" suggests that at some point in time the actions or plans developed by any one individual or group will be subjected to a set of standards to determine their viability or worth. Typically speaking, almost all of the behaviors of individuals and groups can be subjected to some standard or benchmark. Unless the actions of a group are intentionally and systematically subjected to some sort of evaluative criteria, group processes and outcomes can go unchecked, thus allowing the goals/objectives of a group to go unmet for an indefinite period. More specifically, individuals in a group must be held accountable to perform their assigned tasks, and the group members must feel a sense of shared goals and interdependence in order to maintain a sense of purpose.[1] Assuming that these two premises are met, we can assume that accountability exists within the group context.

Characteristics of Quality Groups

Although many characteristics of quality groups can be identified, the following attributes will be discussed in detail as predominant concepts that serve as valid prerequisites to a quality group: cohesion, task assignment, group size, trust and cooperation, and factors of diversity within the group.

Cohesion

Although the term *cohesiveness* is used widely, the definition and conceptualization cause problems. Cohesiveness refers to the overall attraction of group members to each other and the way in which they "stick together." Members have a sense of belonging and are dedicated to the well-being of the group. Indirectly, cohesiveness refers to group morale, teamwork, or so-called group spirit.[2] In a review of experimental group research, Bednar and Kaul went so far as to suggest that there is little cognitive substance to the concept of cohesion and that the term "be dropped from the empirical vocabulary and that more representative alternatives be found."[3]

Researchers addressing this conceptual problem have examined constructs thought to be related to cohesion. Stokes has suggested three such constructs.[4]

1. *Attraction to individual members of the group.* This factor was suggested earlier by Zaleznik and Moment, who stated the strong connectedness between norms and cohesion:

   Norms of behavior tend to be strong when members are attracted to and identify with the group. Work groups create conditions for identification simply because membership is economically important to the individuals. We do not lightly undertake to leave jobs and abandon existing work groups. When group members, in addition, have few other group memberships the value of the group is enhanced for them. This phenomenon is seen most clearly in minority group formations. Where ethnic barriers prevent free movement among groups in a society, the restricted opportunities for membership result in strong systems of norms because the attraction to the group is high for its members.[5]

2. *The instrumental value of the group.* A group will thus be cohesive or attractive to its members to the degree that they see it as meeting their needs and as being helpful to them. This construct has also been supported by previous research. If members of a group feel included, liked, and respected, they come to depend on the group for these reinforcements. As people with similar needs find similar reinforcements, a cohesive group develops. Even one dissatisfied member, however, may damage the morale of the entire group. In one study, groups of college students were assigned tasks relating to dart throwing. In certain groups a confederate was planted, who expressed the opinion that the task was trivial, dull, and impossible of accomplishment. These groups had significantly lower levels of aspiration and satisfaction than did the other groups.[6]

3. *Risk-taking behaviors that occur in the group.* Since cohesive groups are more likely to permit risk taking in the form of self-disclosure and expression of hostility and conflict than are less cohesive groups, it seems reasonable to suppose that these behaviors in turn may lead to greater cohesion.[7]

Stokes found a high multiple correlation of these three constructs with cohesion. He suggests:

Conceptualizing cohesion as a combination of the three constructs suggested in this article might have heuristic value. Perhaps understanding the relation of cohesion to outcome would be facilitated by a more precise operationalization of cohesion. It could be that certain aspects of cohesion are more important for certain types of groups. Therapy groups, for example, might require risk taking for positive outcome, whereas a problem-focused counseling or self-help group's success on outcome measures would depend more on members' finding one another attractive as individuals.[8]

A continuing conceptual problem with cohesiveness is that researchers have treated it as both a dependent and an independent variable. We feel attracted to groups whose members we like, and we tend to like individual members of groups to which we are attached.[9]

How is cohesiveness achieved? Groups maintain their norms and solidarity through systems of reward and punishment. Rewards come through satisfaction of individual needs already discussed. Punishments or sanctions occur when members deviate from group expectations. The sanctions may be direct or indirect. Isolation, withholding of communication, and denial of other satisfactions provide corrective feedback to non-conformist group members. Persons who deviate from the group norms are not likely to be accepted as friends by other members of the group. Schachter tested this assumption by inviting students to join a club organized to discuss topics of lively interest. Three participants attended each meeting; of the participants two conformed to the beliefs of the group while the other took a clearly deviant position. The deviant member was rejected, while the other two partici-pants were accepted. Rejection of the deviant was stronger in groups with high cohesiveness and where the deviancy concerned matters highly relevant to the purposes of the group. This finding is consistent with the expectation that cohesive groups develop stronger norms. The conforming members received a steady, but low, amount of communication from other members. A confederate, called by the group a "slider" (one who moves from deviance to conformity), received a large number of hints from fellow members to conform. As sliders moved toward conformity, the number of messages to conform diminished. They received the greatest number of messages to conform when the group attempted to change their views. When their deviancy became fixed, group members ceased communicating with the deviants in an unconscious attempt to isolate him or her.[10]

One of the major effects of cohesiveness is the groups's influence over its members. As Cartwright states: "There can be little doubt that members of a more cohesive group more readily exert influence on one another and are more readily influenced by one another.[11] Cartwright points to the research of Thibaut and Kelley, which shows that the power of a group over one of its members appears to depend on what the members expect to receive from the group as against what the members believe they can receive from any other available group. The individual, then, is more dependent upon a group that he or she considers the best available.[12] A positive personal consequence of increased cohesiveness seems to be greater acceptance, trust, and confidence among members, resulting in a sense of security and personal value. People feel free to disagree and even express hostility; sup-pressed feelings sometimes become a hidden agenda.[13]

A negative aspect of cohesiveness will be discussed subsequently. For now, we point out that when a cohesive group's need for unanimity overwhelms a member's realistic appraisal of alternative courses of action, *groupthink* evolves.[14]

The interrelationships between norms, conformity, and cohesion are obvious but should be viewed with caution. With different definitions and methodologies, the studies cannot easily be compared.[15] More of a multidimensional approach such as has been tried by Stokes will help us in the future to better understand these processes.

Task

Most groups have some task or external purpose that can provide a basis for evaluation of the effectiveness of the group. Groups may be superior at solving some kinds of tasks, while individuals may be better at other kinds. Steiner has developed a taxonomy of different group tasks and specifies for each a "prescribed process" that, if followed, will lead to maximal group performance.[16] He distinguishes among four types of work, each with different requirements:

1. *Additive tasks.* Shoveling snow and collecting charitable contributions are examples of additive tasks. Each member's product can be added to the others' to yield the total group product. The more people, the greater the productivity. Few decision-making groups encounter additive tasks.
2. *Conjunctive tasks.* Mountain climbers or members of a marching band perform conjunctive tasks. All members perform similar activities and all depend on each other for group success. Adding another member may not increase productivity; in fact, just as a group of mountain climbers can move no faster than its slowest member, a group engaged in a conjunctive task can only be as efficient as its least proficient member. In decision-making groups that delegate research responsibilities, the group can only be as accurate as its least reliable source of information.
3. *Disjunctive tasks.* Working on a complex mathematical problem in a group usually depends on the proficiency of the most competent member. There is no division of labor, and the product does not depend on the summed efforts of individuals.
4. *Discretionary tasks.* Most decision-making groups are dealing with tasks in which the offerings of one individual may be accepted or rejected, and the skills of various members may be combined in a variety of ways to yield a product. Members may combine their efforts in any way they wish. The group product depends on the manner in which efforts are coordinated. Rather than relying on one expert, the group depends on how the members' efforts are balanced and coordinated. A discretionary task is chosen by a group, if the task is perceived to be necessary or important. For example, group members can decide if a meeting room needs to be cleaned after each session; if so, someone will be designated to perform this task.

Steiner argues that for each kind of task, productivity depends on *process gain* versus *process loss.* For a committee to be effective, the time spent together must produce a product superior to the work of the members if they had worked individually. Does the process of interaction promote gain or cause loss? Process loss includes the time spent deciding how a group is to function.

One study has attempted to answer the question by comparing individual judgments to group judgments. Davis devised mathematical techniques for establishing how in practice a group combines its individual views to form a group project.[17] Working from a knowledge of preferred individual solutions to a problem and of a historical group's actual decision, various hypothetical decision rules were tested out. For example, the probability that jurors would change their verdict from guilty to not guilty, or vice versa, was closely matched to how large a majority initially preferred that verdict. While this decision reflected normative social behavior, the degree of certainty that the decision was correct correlated with the size of the minority.

Hackman and Morris have used a *Job Diagnostic Survey* to predict the potential of a particular task to induce high performance motivation.[18] They classify the factors influencing the task effectiveness under three headings:

1. The level and utilization of member knowledge and skill.
2. The nature and utilization of task performances and strategies.
3. The level and coordination of members' effort.

While these broad classificatory headings certainly include many of the relevant variables, Hackman and Morris concede that until we have a much clearer view of which types of tasks require which types of organizational structure and influence processes, attempts to enhance group performance will have to rest on diagnoses of each specific situation. They see a usefulness for three types of such attempts, in line with their headings above: (1) modification of the group's composition, (2) redesign of tasks, and (3) modification of group norms. However, they emphasize that inadequately thought-out interventions may make matters worse rather than better. Job redesign schemes, such as job enrichment, often fail through inattention to detail, while interventions focused on the interpersonal relationships within a group sometimes neglect task variables.

Groups must be conscious of whether or not assumed tasks can best be handled by the group as a whole or through individual efforts. Complex tasks and decisions allow members to compare views and develop a more accurate picture of reality than that of any individual member. Such interaction can also reduce biases and provide a check for accuracy. If the individual members have a strong desire for group success, if new goals are based on past levels of successful performance, if all members know that the group needs their best efforts, and if a mechanism for providing feedback on results is available, then a group's performance is likely to be better.[19]

The prospect of working together to solve a group problem may require a new pattern of interpersonal relationships. Enemies may have to work together, and friends may have to stay apart, until the task is completed. Sometimes even norms must be broken or changed. Group members must realize that to work effectively with another does not necessarily mean that they have to like everyone. Actors in a play may not be on close personal terms, but the joint needs of a successful theatrical production may require them to work together cooperatively. The group goal thus supersedes the varied individual goals. "I can receive positive reinforcements from the audience only if the total production is a good one." The satisfactions of an achieved group goal are not likely to be as high, however, as in situations when the success of others reinforces the individual.

In general, then, people are committed to the group task when they conceive and accept the group goals; commit their personal resources, skills, intelligence, and energy toward accomplishing it; and give its accomplishment higher priority than their own goals, the group's norms, and the existing pattern of interpersonal relationships among members, including their own popularity and personal comfort.

Group Size

The number of persons in a group affects both the communication participation among members and the quality of interaction. However, the relationship between the size of the group and the group's effectiveness is complex.

In his classic studies at Harvard, Bales counted acts of initiation by each member in groups of varying size. In groups of three or four, the initiation was spread evenly; as the group size was increased from five to eight members, the groups were dominated by the more aggressive members and the quiet ones participated less. With further increases in group size, dominance by aggressive initiators increased.[20]

Research by Slater has shown that the quality of the interaction varies with group size. Comparing ratios of groups of two to seven members over four discussion sessions, he found that as group size increased, the index of inhibition decreased and that, as members became better acquainted through the course of the meetings, the inhibition levels dropped more for the larger groups than for the smaller. He felt that, as group size increased, the possibility of alienating other people or feeling self-conscious became less and less severe. As he states:

> In the larger group, physical freedom is restricted while psychological freedom is increased. The member has less time to talk, more points of view to integrate and adapt to, and a more elaborate structure into which he must fit. At the same time he is more free to ignore some of these viewpoints, to express his own feelings and ideas in a direct and forceful fashion, and even to withdraw from the fray without loss of face.[21]

Members of five-person groups expressed complete satisfaction; no members reported their group as being too large or small. Larger groups felt themselves disorderly and their members too aggressive, competitive, and given to wasting time. The smaller groups (with fewer than five members) complained that they were too small and that members were prevented from expressing their ideas freely for fear of alienating one another.[22]

How does size affect group productivity? Gibb discovered that the total number of ideas increased with an increase in group size, but not in direct proportion to the number of members.[23]

In larger groups the members tend to stifle contributions as the more aggressive tend to dominate; the other members contribute less and complain that group direction is lacking. In addition, a group with more than six members may cope with its size by forming functional subgroups within itself.[24] Zander makes this practical suggestion: "A person assembling a decision-making group will do well to restrict the group's size because give-and-take is more rapid and widespread in a small group than a large one."[25]

Trust and Cooperation

As people work together in a group, they must rely on one another in order to achieve their mutual goal. Such confidence, even in risky situations, depends on feelings of trust.[26] Closely akin to trust and often included in research is the concept of cooperation. For example, in early research on these topics, Morton Deutsch determined:

1. As there is an increase in an individual's confidence that his trust will be reciprocated, the probability of his engaging in cooperative behavior will increase.
2. As the ratio of anticipated positive consequences over negative consequences increases, the probability of his engaging in cooperative behavior will increase.[27]

A great deal of research in this area is based on a theoretical model called the "Prisoner's Dilemma."[28] This model portrays a situation in which police are holding two men suspected of armed robbery. Since there is insufficient evidence for conviction, the men are offered a deal. If they both confess, they are promised the minimum sentence for armed robbery, two years' imprisonment. If, however, only one of the two confesses, the confessor will be considered a state witness and set free, while the other will get a 20-year sentence. If neither confesses, they can be charged only with possession of firearms, which carries a penalty of six months in jail. Without an opportunity for discussion, the two are locked up in separate cells, unable to communicate.

What should the prisoners do? Since six months in prison is obviously their preference, it makes sense that neither of them confess. "But can I trust my cohort to reach that same conclusion?"—"Can I trust him?"—"If he confesses, he goes free and I go to prison for 20 years."—"Maybe I'd better confess and either go free myself or get no more than two years."

Note the depth of the dilemma. Even if the two are able to communicate and reach a joint decision ("neither of us will confess"), their fate will depend on whether each feels he can trust the other to support the decision.

Decisions are typically based upon the degree of trust as group members attempt to determine what actions others will likely take. Consider all the "real-life" applications of this dilemma—in arms control, labor negotiations, and divorce proceedings. In a summary of 50 years of research on trust and cooperation, Deutsch concluded that in the cooperative situation there were greater coordination of efforts, less homogeneity with respect to amount of participation, more specialization, more rapid decision making, more achievement pressure, more effective communication, greater productivity, and better interpersonal relations. He stated:

> To the extent that the results have any generality, greater group or organizational productivity may be expected when the members of subunits are cooperative rather than competitive in their interrelationships. The communication of ideas, coordination of efforts, friendliness, and pride in one's group which are basic to group harmony and effectiveness appear to be disrupted when members see themselves to be competing for mutually exclusive goals. Further, there is some indication that competitiveness produces greater personal insecurity through expectations of hostility from others than does cooperation. The implications for committees, conferences, and small groups in general appear fairly obvious.[29]

We shall address this topic again when we discuss conflict in Chapter 6. Cooperation and trusting behaviors are the keys to the successful functioning of groups and impact upon numerous other behaviors.

Factors of Diversity

Quality groups most often benefit from a diversity of opinions and perspectives within the group. A main reason for the difference is that individuals bring variations in cultural backgrounds, value systems, and cultural norms to the group as a part of their "field of experience" (previously discussed in this text). But, regardless of their source, different viewpoints are critical to the group's ability to succeed in making quality decisions.

In recent years attention has focused on the influence of gender on the activities within a group. Baird reviewed a body of research and concluded that men tend to be more task oriented while women are more maintenance oriented, concerned for individuals. He reported that men tend to talk more objectively, while women tend to be more opinionated, more positive in responses, and more likely to withdraw from unpleasant interactions.[30]

In a later study Bradley reported that women who demonstrated task competency were shown friendliness and fewer displays of dominant behavior by male counterparts. She also reported, however, that such women were not particularly well liked.[31]

Such research must be evaluated in terms of the changing roles of women and men. Until recently large numbers of women had not held roles of leadership and decision making in the organizational context. As women moved into such roles, the male norm was the standard to which the women were made to adhere. Issues of power and control were seen to be in the masculine domain while maintenance concerns were feminine and secondary.

We have read considerable research that shows that an androgynous model of decision making—a balanced concern for task and relationships—is likely to be best suited for effective ongoing group interaction. Women, when given the opportunity, have learned quickly the skills of instrumental problem solving. To this point, men have been less adaptive and have changed little in expanding their communication competencies to include empathic listening, sensitivity to nonverbal messages, and greater responsiveness to metacommunication.

Lafferty and Pond have studied groups of five people working on a group survival task that can be scored in terms of accuracy of accomplishment. The most successful groups both in terms of final score and of average gain over individual scores were made up of five women. In declining rank of accomplishment were (2) groups of three females and two males, (3) groups of four females and one male, (4) groups of four males and one female, (5) groups entirely of men, and (6) groups of three males and two females.[32] Perhaps you can provide some inferential explanations of why the sexual makeup of the groups provides these results.

The American Management Association conducted a survey in 1999 of over 1,000 managers and executives, evaluating the impact of diversity on performance measures such as annual sales, gross revenues, market shares, shareholder values, net operating profit, worker productivity, and total assets. While there is still a long way to go before senior management in U.S. business actually reflects the diversity of U.S. society in terms of gender, race, and ethnicity, the survey did find diversity in senior management teams. Only 11 percent of the 1,087 surveyed organizations have top teams that are entirely made up of over-40 males of European descent. Two-thirds of the senior staffs have at least one woman; 62 percent have at least one person under 40 years of age; and 37 percent have at least one person of non-European heritage.

Women hold a greater percentage of senior management posts in service firms than in manufacturing companies. Women particularly predominate in sectors such as communications and business and professional services and have greater than average representation on senior management teams in finance, insurance, and real estate. These are the same business sectors that out-performed the manufacturing sector in every category of organizational performance listed in the survey. It is important to remember that correlation is not necessarily causation, but women have definitely seized the opportunities for advancement offered in the service sector and seem to be prospering there.[33]

Analysis of group behavior shows that often men and women behave differently in group activities. Men characteristically make more task-oriented contributions while women are more socially oriented or contribute to the social concerns of the group.[34] Although these trends may change, to date no research has validated any such change.

People of color have a higher degree of representation on senior management teams in smaller companies and in the service sector, which again tend to report better organizational outcomes than larger companies and manufacturers.

While managers under age 40 hold an average of 21 percent of senior posts among all respondents, they represent an average of 33 percent of senior managers in the communications sector. That sector reported particularly strong results in net operating profits and productivity gains.

In short, the communications industry, which includes telecommunications providers, broadcasters, and publishers, have senior management teams that are particularly hospitable to women and to young managers. This industry is also far above average in their report of increases sales, operating profits, and worker productivity.

Survey authors note that it is not the predominance of any one set of people, but rather that participation of managers of varying gender, ethnicity, age, and experience that correlates to strong organizational performance. Where subsets are large enough to provide statistical reliability, the presence of "some" such managers on the senior management teams generally correlates to better performance than does an indicated presence of "none." While more research is certainly needed, this study confirms what many who work or teach in diverse settings have long suspected. Diverse groups provide valuable opportunities for learning and for productivity in a variety of settings.[35]

Evaluating the Effectiveness of Quality Groups

In reference to the concepts reviewed in this chapter, quality groups typically have several important characteristics. First, the size of the group itself should be manageable, with an optional amount of members in order to achieve its goals and objectives, yet not overcrowded to the point of reducing communication effectiveness. Second, the members of the group need to make a conscious effort to remain motivated and maintain a level of commitment to the group. As mentioned, this can be accomplished by recognizing influences and potential threats from outside the group that will serve as motivational factors that employees can rely upon for sources of comparison and incentives. The third factor discussed was trust. It is obvious that one of the core values of a group is honesty. The residual resentments left over from an incident of deceit can linger in the group for months or years and can serve as an unnecessary detractor from group productivity, not to mention the reduction in interpersonal relations, group satisfaction, and a lack of motivation to collaborate on tasks. The fourth primary factor mentioned suggests that quality groups consist of individuals with various perspectives and opinions. These factors of diversity may stem from cultural, political, gender, or ideological differences. However, the important fact to note is that it is always advantageous for a group to consist of individuals with varying perspectives as an important resource for decision-making groups.

As teams become more popular, interest in group productivity has increased. Research has been conducted on such topics as team composition (how to select and train team members),[36] how to assess team performance,[37] and the use of technology to improve team performance.[38]

After a group has created a product, members often reflect on its quality and the process needed to create it. Identification with a group usually increases with group success and decreases with group failure.[39]

Some of the most definitive research identifying characteristics of effective decision-making groups was conducted by Randy Hirokawa. A study conducted in

1980 compared communication patterns between effective and ineffective deci-sion-making groups with the results indicating that effective groups spend consid-erably more time agreeing on group procedures prior to engaging in discussion and that these same effective groups discuss ideas presented within the group until agreement is reached, prior to pursuing other discussion topics.[40] In 1983, Hirokawa and Pace conducted a second study investigating effective group decision-making.[41] Hirokawa and Pace determined that groups that carefully evaluate the validity of information presented in a group yield higher quality decisions; that these same groups used decision-making criteria to carefully evaluate alterna-tive decision choices; and that high-quality decisions tended to be based on facts, assumptions and inferences "grounded" in more factual information available during a decision-making task. The last factor Hirokawa and Pace defined as a distinguishing characteristic of effective groups was the presence of an influential group member, respected by fellow group members, who exerts more positive influence facilitation comments rather than using negative comments to exert her or his influence in the group. This research provides excellent practical exam-ples of behaviors that should facilitate more effective group decision-making processes.

To summarize, all these factors must be carefully considered and monitored in order to increase the probability of positive group interactions and successful goal attainment in group contexts. It should be noted that each group is unique and will present varying circumstances and outcomes in relation to all of these factors. Therefore, it is essential to constantly monitor the group to be prepared to adapt any given situation in order to offset any difficulties or barriers to success that may arise. The following case study provides an illustration of these concepts in action for discussion.

Case Study

Each year, colleges and universities must be sensitive to the enrollment patterns of students on an annual basis in order to assure that the fees collected are sufficient to offer the necessary courses and co-curricular activities needed to provide a quality learning experience. The particular university described in this case offered four quarters of classes, year round. However, one of the professional schools on campus, without sufficiently consulting the other academic units, stopped offering regularly scheduled courses in the summer and replaced these courses with offerings coordinated by the School of Continuing Education. Needless to say, this development had a negative impact on the whole university because the total number of students enrolled in the university dropped. When asked in a meeting why this development occurred without proper consultation and how the school planned to rectify the situation, the response was: "This is what we wanted to do and the other schools will have to figure out, collectively, how to offset this reduction in enrollments." The other groups on campus were appalled at this response! A heated debate ensued, yet the enrollment problem was not immediately resolved.

Respond to the following questions, in reference to information provided in this chapter:

1. Do you think the size of the campus and the number of potential individuals involved in this type of decision are factors that can explain why this incident occurred?
2. What impact might this situation have on the level of cohesiveness in the group that meets regularly to discuss and make necessary plans for enrollments?
3. How might trust within the aforementioned group be impacted?
4. Could a "better" decision have been made with input from a variety of perspectives? Why?
5. What type of role (in general) was being enacted by the representatives from this professional school? How should the other members of the group respond?

Chapter Summary

It is probably evident to you how this case pertains to the concepts reviewed in this chapter. This situation is not as unique as we would like to think. One fact to consider is that the professional school, in this case, demonstrated little regard for other members of the group and the campus community.

However, with an appropriate response and effective group problem-solving skills the individuals can, and should be, held accountable for their actions to both the immediate group members and the organization as a whole. Additional chapters in this book will review conflict management and resolution skills that will help individuals respond to similar situations in a positive manner. It is not the predominance of any one set of people, but rather the participation of individuals of varying gender, ethnicity, age and experience that correlates to strong group performance.

APPLICATIONS

4.1 List the norms that you can identify as operative within your group. Have these norms changed during the course of your meetings?

4.2 How would your group conceptualize cohesion? What factors do you feel are important in promoting cohesion in a given group?

4.3 Discuss the variables of group size and gender makeup in the groups you have observed. Can you identify differences that would have appeared had the groups been larger, smaller, or with a different combination of women and men?

REFERENCES

1. J. Katzenbach and D. Smith, *The Wisdom of Teams* (Cambridge, MA: Harvard Business School Press, 1993).

2. S. Drescher, G. Burlingame, and A. Fuhriman, "Cohesion-or: An Odyssey in Empirical Understanding," *Small Group Behavior,* 16 (February 1985), pp. 3–30.

3. R.L. Bednar and T.J. Kaul, "Experimental Group Research: Current Perspectives," in *Handbook for Psychotherapy and Behavior Change,* ed. by S. Garfield and A. Bergin (New York: Wiley, 1978).

4. J.P. Stokes, "Components of Group Cohesion," *Small Group Behavior,* 14 (May 1983), pp. 163–173.

5. A. Zaleznik and D. Moment, *The Dynamics of Interpersonal Behavior* (New York: Wiley, 1964), p. 109.

6. D. Rosenthal and C.N. Cofer, "The Effect on Group Performance of an Indifferent and Neglectful Attitude Shown by One Group Member," *Journal of Experimental Psychology,* 38 (1948), pp. 568–577.

7. Stokes, "Components of Group Cohesion," pp. 165–166.

8. Ibid., p. 170.

9. B.H. Raven and J.Z. Rubin, *Social Psychology: People in Groups* (New York: Wiley, 1976), p. 253.

10. S. Schachter, "Deviation, Rejection, and Communication," in *Group Dynamics,* ed. by D. Cartwright and A. Zander (New York: Harper & Row, 1968), pp. 165–181.

11. D. Cartwright, "Nature of Group Cohesiveness," in *Group Dynamics,* ed. by D. Cartwright and A. Zander (New York: Harper & Row, 1968), p. 104.

12. Ibid. Based on J.W. Thibaut and H.H. Kelley, *The Social Psychology of Groups* (New York: Wiley, 1959).

13. A. Pepitone and G. Reichling, "Group Cohesiveness and the Expression of Hostility," *Human Relations,* 8 (1955), pp. 327–337.

14. I.L. Janis, *Victims of Groupthink: A Psychological Study of Foreign Policy Decisions and Fiascos* (Boston: Houghton Mifflin, 1972).

15. Drescher et al., "Cohesion—or," p. 27.

16. I.D. Steiner, *Group Process and Productivity* (New York: Academic Press, 1972).

17. J.H. Davis, "Social Interaction as a Combinatorial Process in Group Decision," in *Group Decision Making,* ed. by H. Brandstatter, J.H. Davis, and G. Stocker-Kreichgauer (London: Academic Press, 1982).

18. J.R. Hackman and C.G. Morris, "Group Tasks, Group Interaction Process and Group Performance Effectiveness: A Review and Proposed Integration," *Advances in Experimental Social Psychology,* 8, ed. by L. Berkowitz (1975), pp. 47–99.

19. A. Zander, *Making Groups Effective* (San Francisco: Jossey-Bass, 1982), pp. 65–66.

20. R.F. Bales, F.L. Strodtbeck, T.M. Mills, and M.E. Roseborough, "Channels of Communication in Small Groups," *American Sociological Review,* 16 (1951), pp. 461–468.

21. P.E. Slater, "Contrasting Correlates of Group Size," *Sociometry,* 21 (1958), pp. 129–139.

22. Ibid., pp. 137–139.

23. C.A. Gibb, "The Effects of Group Size and of Threat Reduction upon Creativity in a Problem-solving Situation," *American Psychology,* 6 (1951), p. 324 (abstract).

24. J.M. Innes, "Group Performance," in *Social Psychology,* ed. by G. Gardner (Sydney: Prentice-Hall, 1981), p. 165.

25. Zander, *Making Groups Effective,* p. 21.

26. K. Giffin, "Interpersonal Trust in Small Group Communication," *Quarterly Journal of Speech,* 53 (1967), pp. 224–234. Also see R.D. Heimovics, "Trust and Influence in an Ambiguous Group Setting," *Small Group Behavior,* 15 (1984), pp. 545–552.

27. M.A. Deutsch, "Trust and Suspicion," *Journal of Conflict Resolution,* 2 (1958), pp. 265–279.

28. A. Rapoport and A.M. Chammah, *Prisoner's Dilemma: A Study in Conflict and Cooperation* (Ann Arbor: University of Michigan Press), 1965.

29. M. Deutsch, "Fifty Years of Conflict," in *Retrospective on Social Psychology,* ed. by L. Festinger (New York: Oxford University Press, 1980), p. 481.

30. J.E. Baird, "Sex Differences in Group Communication," *Quarterly Journal of Speech,* 62 (1976), pp. 179–192.

31. P.H. Bradley, "Sex, Competence and Opinion Deviation: An Expectation States Approach," *Communication Monographs,* 47 (1980), pp. 105–110.

32. J.C. Lafferty and A.W. Pond, *The Desert Survival Situation* (Plymouth, Michigan: Human Synergistics, 1985).

33. For a copy of the complete study see www. amanet.org/research.

34. W. Wood, "Meta-analytic Review of Sex Differences in Group Performance," *Psychological Review,* 102 (1987), pp. 53–71.

35. Ibid., www.amanet.org/research.

36. R.L. Moreland, L. Argote, and R. Krishnan, "Socially Shared Cognition at Work: Transactive Memory and Group Performance," *What is So Social About Social Cognition?* ed. by J.L. Nye and M. Brower (Newbury Park, Ca.: Sage, 1996), pp. 57–84.

37. H.F. O'Neil, E.L. Baker, and E.J. Kazlaukas, "Assessment of Team Performance," *TEAMS: Their Training and Performance.* ed. by R.W. Swezey and E. Salas (Norwood, N.J.: Ablex, 1992), pp. 53–176.

38. A.B. Hollingshead and J.E. McGrath, "Computer-assisted Groups: A Critical Review of the Empirical Research." *Team Effectiveness and De-cision-Making in Organizations,* ed. by R.A. Guzzo and E. Salas (San Francisco: Jossey-Bass, 1995), pp. 46–78.

39. C.R. Snyder, M. Lassegard, and C. Ford, "Distancing after Group Success and Failure: Basking in Reflected Glory and Cutting Off Reflected Failure," *Journal of Personality and Social Psychology,* 51 (1986), pp. 382–388.

40. R. Hirokawa, "A Comparative Analysis of Communication Patterns within Effective and Ineffective Decision-Making Groups," *Communication Monographs,* Vol. 47 (4), November 1980, pp. 312–321.

41. R. Hirokawa and R. Pace, "A Descriptive Investigation of the Possible Communication-Based Reasons for Effective and Ineffective Group Decision-Making," *Communication Monographs,* Vol. 50 (4), December 1983, pp. 363–379.

5 Critical Thinking in the Quality Group

Scenario

Vice President Rayburn was absent when the University Executive Council discussed the proposed policy change on student waivers. Rayburn knew the history of the current policy and why some students were given special exemption. By proceeding without this crucial set of information, the hour-long discussion was wasted and the decision reached was in error.

In the ideal group, the intelligence and knowledge present would assemble into a collective IQ. We know that such ideals rarely occur. Because different members of the group have varying ideas, beliefs, and patterns of thought, the group must create an environment in which competing ideas are taken seriously and processed appropriately. Quality decisions are discovered by thinking, analyzed by thinking, organized by thinking, transformed by thinking, and assessed by thinking. Members of a group must be able to argue themselves out of their present way of thinking into ways that are novel and different if the group is to perform at a quality level.

Other people are needed to probe and question our thinking, to present alternative points of view, and to engage us to stimulate our best efforts. In this chapter we shall examine the processes intrinsic to sound critical thinking and alternative approaches that may expand the group's capacities.

Procedural Description of Critical Thinking

The most often cited steps in the problem-solving process stem from John Dewey's landmark book, *How We Think* (1910). Dewey identified five phases of the reflective thought process:

1. The *suggestions* phase in which the mind searches for possible solutions to a "felt difficulty."
2. The *problem* phase in which the difficulty is conceptualized as a question for which an answer must be found.

3. The *hypothesis* phase in which one suggestion after another initiates and guides the collection of factual material.
4. The *elaboration* phase in which cognitive constructs test the reasoning behind the ideas.
5. The *testing* phase of the hypothesis by overt or imaginative action.[1]

Later, Schiedel and Crowell analyzed the content of the interaction of five small groups evaluating a metropolitan newsletter.[2] The researchers' primary interest was the process used in the development of ideas in groups rather than testing the hypothesis that groups progress in a linear fashion through a sequential set of steps in reflective thinking. Their most interesting finding, as they saw it, was "the modification and synthesis of ideas, actions which would seem to comprise the very essence of the development of thought." More than half of the comments recorded were statements confirming, clarifying, or substantiating ideas already presented to the group; less than one fourth of the comments were devoted to initiating, extending, modifying, or synthesizing ideas. They concluded:

> This oral play on an idea and the verbalizing of concurrence are probably the ways by which a group gets its anchoring. Group thought seems to move forward with a "reach and test" type motion, that which seems to be elaborated at length with movements of clarification, substantiation, and verbalized acceptance. Little wonder that group thought takes practically half the total time.[3]

B. W. Tuckman proposed another theory of group development.[4] He identified four stages of group development: forming, storming, norming, and performing. This theoretical framework demonstrates that a group changes as it solves certain interpersonal issues and achieves certain tasks.

In the first phase, "forming," a group is primarily concerned with "Who's in charge?" And "What are we supposed to do?" And "To whom are we responsible?" Individuals tend to depend on the designated leader to provide all the structure, to set the ground rules, to establish the agenda, and to do all the "leading." As far as one's task is concerned, one must identify one's charge using the following questions as guideposts: What exactly has one been asked to do? What data does one already have to work with? What is the time frame within which one is to work? To whom is one accountable? What are the resources each member brings to the task? Too often, rather than providing for new members' dependency and orientation needs, groups just barrel along, taking up where the last meeting left off, with the frequent result that new members do not become effective on boards and committees for a long time.

The second phase, "storming," refers to the conflict experienced in groups as the members organize to get the work of the group done and to make decisions regarding who is going to be responsible for what; what are going to be the work rules and procedures (e.g., who will approach the candidates one would like to nominate to the board?); what are going to be the limits (e.g., how many buildings will it look at as possible facilities?); what is going to be the reward system (e.g., how many of the members ever thought of being rewarded for their work on the committee?); what are going to be the criteria by which they will know they have accomplished their task? A group's effectiveness depends on how well its members solve these interpersonal conflicts over leadership and leadership structure, power, and authority.

The third phase, "norming," refers to the stage of development during which members of the group begin to experience a sense of groupness or cohesion, a feeling of catharsis at having resolved interpersonal conflict and having "gotten their act together." They begin sharing ideas and feelings, giving feedback to each other, soliciting feedback, exploring actions related to the task (getting on with it!), and sharing information related to the task (through phone calls and formal and informal reports). They begin to feel good about their work and about being part of the group, and there is an emerging openness with regard to the task at hand. We have seen this happen on various committees on which we have served, and we have witnessed it in groups we have observed. There is a sense of flow, of something clicking, and this leads to brief indulgences in playfulness where people abandon the task and just enjoy being with one another. Everyone has probably been a meeting when this has occurred—everyone was joking, and every joke evoked hilarity; one never had such a good time.

The fourth phase, "performing," is the culmination of the work as a group: People are both highly task oriented and highly person oriented. The group's tasks are well defined; members have a high degree of commitment to common activity, and they are able to support experimentation in solving problems. A trusting climate makes it safe to take risks.

When people share a common problem, such patterns of interaction make logical sense; however, many real-life group discussions do not follow such a pattern. Frequently, they omit one phase or another. For example, in a meeting of a local school board, members argued strenuously on the relative value of three different suggested "solutions" to "the problem," only to discover (after generating negative interpersonal feelings) that different members of the group held different views on the nature of the problem. Members actually were considering the value of different solutions for different problems. In fact, the poor performance of the group in its decision-making behavior created a serious human-relations problem. Our purpose here is to suggest a procedure that makes logical sense, to be followed in practice as well as you can work it out with your group. The point to be remembered is that at any given moment in a decision-making group you need to know what you are doing. If at times you begin to feel you are in a light-weight skiff on a tumbled sea of more or less unrelated ideas or comments, the situation can be helped by reviewing the logical elements of problem solving and comparing your efforts to this quality pattern. Ideas and contributions should never be arbitrarily cut off or derogated; they should be considered as means to help the group move toward its goal, the solution of a mutual problem.

We suggest that the quality decision-making process logically consists of the following steps: (1) identification of a group problem, including determination of the nature of concern shared by the group members; (2) analysis of the nature of the problem, including contributing factors, restraining factors, and the degree of intensity of the difficulty; (3) critical evaluation of the possible ways of trying to resolve the difficulty; and (4) development of a plan for group action designed to implement the problem solution agreed on by the group. In the next sections we shall examine these steps in detail.

Identifying a Common Problem

To solve a problem the first step clearly is to gain an understanding of the problem. Without this step confusion can easily frustrate a group. Confusion on the nature of the problem can pull the group apart and keep it from ever reaching a solution. Remember: "If we aim at nothing, we are pretty apt to hit it." The unchecked assumption that everybody in a group understands the problem (i.e., sees it the way we do or has the same basic concern we do) is entirely unwarranted in the experience of most decision-making groups.

To identify a mutual concern, all group members must clearly state their personal needs regarding the topic area. In fact, it is an excellent practice to identify clearly our personal needs or expectations whenever we interact with others; if the other person or persons respond in ways you deem appropriate, this understanding can provide solid ground for a satisfying interpersonal relationship. Without such understanding life can be full of surprises and disappointments.

To clarify a mutual concern with others you start with tentative, trusting behavior, clearly stating your personal view of the situation and how you feel about it. Your comment may be something like this: "I see a need to reconsider course requirements for the English major, and I feel this need is very important." The key elements are "I see . . ." and "I feel . . ." These elements indicate a personal viewpoint (rather than the "only" viewpoint) and signify that another group member may see or feel differently.

At this stage your interpersonal manner, way of stating your viewpoint, and attitude toward other members can indicate a good, or poor, understanding of this phase of the decision-making process. You must state clearly and honestly your viewpoint and your feelings. By all means be genuine and sincere, but show your expectation that others in the group will do the same, comfortably disagreeing as necessary. Your manner of stating your viewpoint and feelings should be genuine and honest, but it should deliberately and overtly tell other members you can tolerate expressed differences of viewpoints or feelings.

As each group member in effect says "This is the way I see it . . ." and "This is how I feel about it . . ." the nature and degree of common concern can be diagnosed. If honesty prevails, it will become apparent whether a group can work well together on a given problem previously thought to be of mutual concern. All members must be prepared to discover that others do not share their view and concern. In fact, it may be discovered that there is no common concern at all. In such case it is better to discover this early rather than later; it can save time, energy and, possibly, interpersonal emotional wear and tear.

In determining the complementarity between your goal and the goals of other members of your group the question of capability must be raised. Are the other members of the group actually capable of helping you achieve your goal? Can you actually help them achieve their goals? If so, and if the perceived costs for you (and them) are less than the perceived values of possible rewards (for both you and them), then you may proceed to work together on that basis, as a group working toward the achievement of complementary goals. This basis for group interaction is a bit more complex than it is when members can clearly identify a mutual concern; consequently, complementary concerns should be verified with care and estimates of probable costs and rewards given careful attention.

Analyzing the Problem

Let us assume that members of your group have identified their individual concerns and that at least one broad, general area of mutual concern has been exposed. Let us also assume that this sharing of mutual concern has produced a feeling of cohesiveness in the group and that such sharing has set a tentative pattern for openly expressing one's ideas and needs. The next logical step will be to focus directly on the problem area.

As a group attempts to set a group goal, there are specific procedures that can facilitate the effort. The most useful procedure is to compare what exists with what is desired.

By definition a problem consists of a situation or condition in which what currently exists is not what you prefer. For example, an undependable car may be what you have, and a dependable one may be what you want. In some cases that which exists, such as a practice of racial discrimination in selling houses, may not be the condition that you believe *ought* to exist. Often people become impatient with one another in discussing what ought to be. Often they could more quickly and easily accept one another's descriptions of a condition they would like to have than pronouncements of what ought to exist. Stating what you want and how it differs from what is allows others to deal with you as a human being rather than as a questionable spokesperson for imperative and mutable laws on what ought to be.

In its simplest terms, the process of problem analysis consists of determining the difference between what you have and what you would like to have. However, the determination of this difference can be a difficult and complex procedure when it is performed by a group; varying personal views of the difference may be voiced, most of which have at least some real merit.

Each of the personal views must be clarified, understood, and evaluated to form the best possible group perception of the problem. This procedure should not be slighted, even though it takes time and often seems repetitious, slow, boring, or hopeless. The ultimate value lies in achieving the best possible insight into the nature of the problem as well as gaining optimum group member effort and cooperation in working toward the solution. Quality group action requires such group commitment.

To analyze a problem in detail properly we must determine the size or extent of the difficulty involved. It may eventually be found to be extensive. For example, a minority group in a large city may be faced with numerous social and economic conditions that require change, such as poor housing, few job opportunities, limited financial credit, poor facilities for education, few opportunities to gain needed experience, poor motivation to put forth great effort, and little expectation of achieving desirable ends; indeed, the scope of such problems may be tremendous. On the other hand, in the case of a family in which the mother is killed in an auto accident, the scope of the problem may not be very extensive. In both examples, however, the intensity of the perceived need may be very great; the amount of emotional investment on the part of members of both groups may, indeed, be severe.

Thus to analyze a problem, we need first to determine its scope. How large is it? How many people are involved? How many forces are at work? Are social, economic, or political forces involved? Or is it a matter of obtaining a little more money?

We have suggested that a problem situation is one in which there is a difference between the way things are and the way you want them to be. Lewin borrowed a concept—force-field analysis, introduced in Chapter 3—from the physical sciences and offered it as a way of understanding social problems. This technique is based on the principle that any sociopsychological situation is the way it is at any given moment because sets of counterbalancing forces are keeping it that way. The technique of force-field analysis seeks to identify these forces.[5]

Let's look at an example. A student-faculty committee agrees that a required course is not satisfactory, suggesting the degree requirement needs to be changed. What forces are involved? Some committee members may feel that the basis of the problem is blind adherence to tradition; other members see it as lack of acceptance of graduates by hiring officials in industry; others see it as arising from the difficulty of securing instructors with special training or experience; others see it as mainly stemming from the high cost of obtaining special instructional materials or equipment; and other members believe that the basic difficulty lies in a low morale or poor motivation among instructors to change their classroom methods. You can immediately think of other factors possibly involved in such a problem.

The point is that a consideration of various forces in a problem can be well worth your while. Unless you deliberately look for these forces, you and others in your group may surprise each other by the degree of confusion generated by some members who think that a problem is simple when others are making it so complex. The lamentable feature of such confusion frequently is that the group members started the analysis of the problem with a cohesive agreement on a mutual concern—that is, that a common problem exists—and what seemed like a battle half won has turned into a shambles.

What specifically can you do to avoid this confusion? You can ask your colleagues carefully and deliberately to make a list of those forces that are impelling change in the present undesirable condition and to make a similar list of those forces that are currently holding back or constraining change. Such forces may be diagramed as in Figure 5.1.

In the illustrative example of the problem of course requirements, your lists (in part) might look like these:

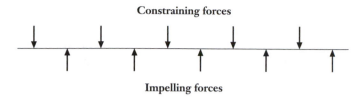

Constraining forces

Impelling forces

FIGURE 5.1 Constraining Forces and Impelling Forces

Impelling Forces
1. Inability of students to apply or use material learned.
2. Inability of students to grasp concepts presented.
3. Repetition of material previously learned by students.
4. Unimportance to hiring officials of material learned.
5. Etc.

Constraining Forces
1. Cost of new equipment for instruction.
2. Difficulty of finding specially trained instructors.
3. Resistance to change by school administrators.
4. Vested interests (e.g., the difficulty of finding new assignments for the present staff).
5. Etc.

Almost all problems have these basic components of *impelling* forces and *constraining* forces. Adequate analysis of a problem requires careful consideration of these two sets of forces, those impelling and those constraining. No solution that neglects either set can be optimal.

In actual fact we have been presenting a procedure for identifying what are commonly called the causes of a problem. Thus far we have avoided using the word because we have found it to be misleading. When people think of causes of a problem, their thinking frequently is overly simplistic. They tend to think that A caused B, a single cause (or at most two or three). Usually they identify only impelling forces as causes and neglect consideration of constraining forces. However, contraining forces are often more problematic than impelling forces. And as we have indicated, most problems that groups face are not simple but complex, involving numerous constraining and impelling components.

Full exploration and discussion of differing sets of values underlying each group member's view of a problem's intensity can help the group reach a better understanding of each member's attitude toward the problem. It can provide common ground for considering possible solutions. Such discussion may show that this group, at this time, cannot hope to agree on how quickly or at what cost a course of action should be adopted. If this is reality, the group needs to face it. At worst, they can agree that they cannot hope to reach agreement and they will have a basis for understanding why this is so. However, in most cases a discussion of the relevant value systems can produce mild changes by individuals in the direction of group agreement. In many cases common ground can be found, understanding of each other increased, and agreement reached on the general degree of intensity of the problem.

The major point to be made is this: it has been our observation that disagreement among group members more frequently occurs regarding the degree of intensity of a problem than on the facts of the situation being considered. If the disagreement is on intensity (based on differing values), no amount of "checking out the facts" can resolve this disagreement. In the face of such disagreement in a group, members who say "Well, let's just look at the facts" are headed for trouble. If they mean "Let's look at our interpretation of the facts based upon our sense of values," they should say so, and there is then some possibility of others understanding them, particularly if they will give other members the same opportunity.

In reality a disagreement over the intensity of a problem is not disagreement about facts of the problem situation, but about how much commitment one should have to one or another basic value or value system.

Critical Evaluation of Courses of Action

As we move from the familiar to the unknown, we are taking an intellectual step into the dark. We engage in such activities constantly in our daily lives. When we "decide" to eat at our favorite restaurant, for example, or even to show up at home for dinner, we are "predicting" on the basis of past experience that our needs probably will be satisfied better than if we went elsewhere.

The prediction of events involves reasoning; that is, identifying the reasons for believing that such events occur. The act of identifying and evaluating such reasons requires, first, knowledge of the relevant, or similar, past events; and second, a calculation of the likelihood, or probability, of similar events occurring under similar circumstances. If your group members can predict that selected conditions will very probably produce a set of desirable results, often the arranging of those conditions will help achieve the results.[6]

The essential core of the reasoning process is the identification of relevant similarities between events. This involves a classification of past events according to some pertinent set of characteristics. It also requires observation of these events, by yourself or by someone else, with special attention to these selected similar characteristics.

As you attempt to use the reasoning process it is likely you will raise questions concerning any specific proposed solution. Your questions probably will be similar to the following:

   1. Has a similar proposal been tried elsewhere?
   2. Was that trial successful; that is, did it solve a similar problem?
   3. Did persons similar to us put a proposal into operation?

4. Were there no costs or dangers that were not similar to those we can bear?
5. Has the proposal been tried in other similar situations with similar results?
6. Were each of these other situations similar in essentially relevant ways?

In this list of questions the importance of identifying relevant similarities between observed past events and the result desired from adopting a particular plan of action should be obvious. However, the principle is important, and an illustrative example may be useful. Suppose you are helping a friend with preenrollment for next semester. You need to know in advance which courses are interesting and valuable. You have had three courses with Professor Smith. Other students have commented on finding courses with Professor Smith highly interesting and valuable. From your experience and the reports of other students you begin to form a generalization: Professor Smith's courses are interesting and valuable to students.

Forming generalizations covering selected characteristics of events or conditions is called *induction;* this process is basic to critical thinking and the scientific method. It is the process by which we establish reliable knowledge about our world, in a manner both physical and social. As we use it we must be careful that we observe as many relevant similar events and conditions as possible.[7] The particular characteristics in questions (in the above example, "interesting" and "valuable") must be noted with great care; it is most helpful if some method of quantification can be devised to measure such characteristics. (How interesting were Professor Smith's courses; how valuable were they?)

The primary question in reasoning can be seen as one of relevant similarity: Is the unknown future event one of a set covered by the generalization we have formulated? In our example, will Professor Smith's course next semester be similar (in ways that matter to us: interesting and valuable) to those he has previously offered? We look carefully for information about these characteristics: Is next semester's course numbered and described the same as the one previously offered? Does Professor Smith tell us it is similar, that he plans to teach it the same way and cover the same material? In all relevant ways we try to make certain that the future event in question will be one of a set about which we have formed our generalization. Traditional scholars of logic have called this process *deduction.* They usually illustrate this part of the reasoning process as follows:

> All of Professor Smith's courses are interesting; course 530 is one of Professor Smith's courses; therefore, course 530 is interesting.

This paradigm is called a *syllogism;* we suspect that you have previously seen deductive reasoning illustrated this way. Actually, in this simplified approach the key issue of relevant similarity is neglected. What such reasoning can actually provide is this: Professor Smith's previous courses have been interesting.

Next semester Professor Smith will offer a course that appears essentially similar to a selected number of courses he has previously offered. Therefore, Professor Smith's course next year will probably be interesting.

Evaluating Proposed Solutions

The procedure for evaluating suggestions (even when operationally described) deserves special attention. In evaluating various suggested approaches, or plans of action, your group will be interested in achieving two objectives: (1) choosing the proposal that will be most satisfactory for your group and (2) obtaining members' agreement and commitment. This group commitment eventually will be necessary if you are to implement the chosen solution and make it work as envisioned.

Informal observation of task groups and practical experience in solving problems have made many people aware of three basic criteria that can be used to evaluate any proposed plan of action.

1. Will this proposal produce the desired changes in the current situation? Will it meet the need for changes as we have identified them?
2. Can we implement this proposal? Is it a workable suggestion?
3. Does this proposal inherently contain serious disadvantages?

These criteria have been found useful for evaluating proposals that involve plans of action or changes in current policies; that is, proposals that may be resolved by agreeing upon a plan of action or a change in existing policy. Such issues are called *policy issues* or *questions of policy.* For groups dealing with them the three criteria suggested above may be used to evaluate proposed changes in policy or plans of action. Let's look at each of these three criteria in some detail.

1. *Meeting the Need for Change.* This requires you to go back to the results of your force-field analysis and compare your impelling and constraining forces with the actual changes suggested by the proposal. Does the suggested plan of action actually propose a change in one or more of the impelling or constraining forces? We used the example of a student-faculty committee working on the problem of course requirements; one of the impelling forces was the inability of the students to apply or use the course material currently taught. The first criterion for evaluating a proposed change in policy could be met if the proposal changed the course material in such a way the concepts involved could be used in practical applications by the students. Of course, any proposal that changes a number of significant impelling or constraining forces will be evaluated as more desirable than a suggestion relating to only one of these forces. Thus each proposal must be evaluated in terms of its probable effect on each of the impelling and constraining forces earlier identified. It is easy to see that the quality of work done by your group as it produces an analysis of the problem will directly affect the way in which it is now able to evaluate various suggested proposals.[8]
2. *Implementing the Proposal.* Decision-making groups sometimes neglect this criterion. It is crucial because, if a proposal cannot be implemented, it is not practical. Care should be taken that suggestions are not branded impractical

without being given careful thought and consideration; sometimes plans that are new to a group are too quickly called impractical. Eventually it must be possible to implement any proposal of real value. In addition, implementation must be possible by your group. If such is not the case, you have identified a new problem for your group: How can your group influence people who can implement this proposal? Your group will have to deal with this problem, going the full route of force-field analysis, evaluating various proposals, adopting and implementing a plan designed to influence others who can take decisive action. Such an approach should be avoided if your group can think of any possible plan of action that it can implement without having to rely on influencing outsiders.

3. *Inherent and Serious Disadvantages in the Proposal.* This criterion requires you to look for inherent dangers or severe costs to your group. Inherent dangers usually consist of risks that your group cannot afford to take. For example, a student-faculty committee dealing with curriculum problems may evaluate proposed extension courses as inherently risky because of the difficulty of establishing the validity of such courses to the satisfaction of hiring officials, who may refuse to give proper consideration to such training. Costs are judged to be unreasonable if they are greater than the benefits that would be derived from the adoption of a given proposal or if they are greater than the costs of alternative proposals that can achieve the same results.[9] Government agencies in recent years have made the phrase "cost analysis" famous.

Implementing a Decision

After decision-making group members have reached agreement on the appropriate or best solution to a problem of mutual concern, they will need to give special attention to putting that solution into operation. A chosen solution does not ordinarily become operative just because a group approves it; individual group members must make sure that it is actually put into practice. It is at this point that so many "action groups" fail; many committees are remiss in making an effort to see that a prepared plan is *followed through* to completion.[10]

We shall deal with two issues: (1) developing a plan of action for your group members to follow and (2) mobilizing the resources external to your own group. In dealing with the first issue we shall assume that your plan is one that can be put into operation by your own group members without the help of people outside your group. For the second issue we shall suggest ways of implementing a plan that requires the help or cooperation of people who are not in your problem-solving group. These two approaches are significantly different, but at various times each one may be necessary.

In essence, a detailed plan of action is one that organizes the efforts of the members of your group. The objective is to arrange for the most capable member to do a needed job at the most appropriate time with the necessary equipment or material. Haphazard efforts or poor planning can result in poor group effort as well as a severe loss of interpersonal regard and trust. Lack of an effective plan of action for implementing a proposed solution to a problem can, in fact, result in the ultimate breakup of your group.

At the heart of any effort for developing a detailed plan of group action must be a strong *commitment* on the part of your members to the group effort. They must be willing not only to do their part individually but also to acknowledge the superior capabilities of other members in doing certain tasks and assuming certain roles. The key concept here is *interdependence* between group members; they must work together as a team, assuming individual responsibility as well as relying upon each other.

If your group members are highly committed to achieving a chosen solution to the problem, and if they are willing to work together as a team, you are ready to develop a detailed plan of action involving five steps:

1. *Identifying Specific Steps to Be Accomplished.* Detailed planning starts here. Various members suggest things to be done, one item at a time. A list should be kept by a member, preferably on a chalkboard or drawing table so that all can see. At some point you will need to be sure that all essential steps are identified. In addition, a chronological arrangement of these steps will be helpful. It is not uncommon for highly committed members to volunteer to perform some of these steps as they are being identified; such offers should be tentatively encouraged and reevaluated later in terms of the entire plan and its relation to an optimal use of the group's complete resources of time and energy.

    In making your final list of detailed steps to be accomplished, start with today: What needs to be done *now*? The immediate enthusiasm of the group should be put to work; nothing should be put off or delayed if it can be started at once. Your final list should conclude with a step that operationally completes, or finalizes, the changed state of affairs your proposal is supposed to achieve.

2. *Determining Required Resources.* As you complete your list of steps to be taken, you will need to identify equipment, machines, materials, and other resources needed in each step. The use of computers, office machines, offices, meeting places, and so on should be considered. Arrangements should be made so that at the appropriate time and place the required resources will be available. In some instances you will need to become informed as to where and how certain items can be obtained. These arrangements should be made a part of your detailed plan for implementing your chosen solution to the group problem and not be left to chance.

3. *Agreeing on Individual Responsibilities.* If there is high commitment to the proposed plan of action, the group members should find it fairly easy to assess individual interests and capabilities. Both personal desire and capability should be considered as individuals take on certain obligations. General group agreement should be obtained as individual responsibilities are determined; in essence the individual's responsibility should be to the group, not to one or two members or to theirself alone. As individual responsibilities are

determined, all involved should be acquainted with the overall plan as well as with the details of their area of responsibility. In addition, they should know how, when, and where they will obtain the equipment and material needed. They should also determine the amount of help, if any, they will need from other group members and should plan with them how their help will be used.

4. *Providing for Emergencies.* Our experiences show us that few plans, even when well developed, work perfectly without mishap. Accidents occur, unforeseen barriers are encountered, and some persons become ill or find that their capabilities were overestimated. Your overall plan should provide for such unforeseen emergencies; some group members should have the responsibility of handling such problems should they arise. In the military it is common to have some units in reserve, "just in case." Some people in your group should have the responsibility to anticipate and provide contingency plans for possible crises.

5. *Planning for Evaluation of the Proposed Plan.* An oil pipeline company had a policy to identify a problem, analyze it, select a plan of action, put the plan into operation, and go on to another problem. Only if a plan failed or worked poorly was it brought up again for further attention. However, a management consultant pointed out the value of systematically evaluating each "solution" after it was put into action. He suggested that the most appropriate time to plan or arrange for such evaluation was during the detailed planning of the program implementation. At this time procedures for evaluation could be built into the overall procedure; equipment for collecting performance data could be installed while other installations or modifications were being made. In this way total disruption and confusion would be reduced. The company adopted his suggestions and found them very useful.

We similarly recommend that your group include an evaluation of the proposed plan of action as one of the basic elements in implementing the plan. Seek information on the following items: (1) Did the predicted change actually occur; that is, did the proposal, when implemented, meet the need earlier identified by the group? (2) Did the plan, when implemented, cost no more (demand no more time, energy, or money) than predicted? (3) Were there any unforeseen risks or dangers after the plan was put into operation? A new policy or procedure cannot be properly evaluated until these questions are answered.

Case Study

In Troy, Michigan, people believed that they were given a difficult time when they applied for a loan from the Friendly Mortgage Company. Applicants faced a battery of forms, interviews, phone calls, and weeks to get an answer. As a result, Friendly, which does about $14 billion a year in mortgage loans, was losing business because applicants were often stalled.

With the introduction of new computer software, and more competitive pressure, the company wanted to become more "customer friendly" and overhaul its operating system. A team was formed to plan the overhaul. How should they proceed?

Response

When the team began it learned that no one had bothered to trace the path a mortgage application took from start to finish. By preparing a flow chart, the team found that a single application followed 17 steps involving 57 offices and up to 60 different forms. Over $600 was spent to process the paperwork in addition to employee salaries; as many as 20 people were involved in each decision.

The team's first step was to consolidate the duties of loan processing, underwriting, and closing into a single job handled by a customer loan specialist. That person would handle the application from start to finish, with dozens of forms replaced by an electronic system analysis. Other short cuts included eliminating pay stub verification from people with excellent credit records.

As a result, the process for securing a loan was greatly speeded up, resulting in far greater customer satisfaction. Each staffer now processes 18.5 loans a month, up from 6. The typical approval now takes 31 days, and the goal is 25. The number of centers was cut to 17, each of which processes 8,600 mortgages a month, up from 2,200. The number of customers who say they'll return has jumped to 45 percent.[11]

Chapter Summary

We have suggested an idealized format to aid decision-making groups in solving problems. First, groups are encouraged to compare the existing condition with the specific condition desired. This can be done by determining the scope of the problem, identifying the impelling and constraining forces, and noting members' perceptions of the intensity of the problems. Second, a realistic group goal must be set. Third, the group must obtain relevant information by evaluating the statements purported to be factual and determining the degree of acceptance of the statements by others.

In this chapter we have attempted to suggest appropriate ways of evaluating various proposed solutions to a problem when your group members have (1) previously agreed on an area of mutual concern and (2) made a careful analysis of the problem. We have admitted that many groups do not follow this sequence of consideration; however, we have held that groups can profit from looking at their problem-solving efforts in light of the logic of these sequential steps. The final section of the chapter has been devoted to suggestions for gaining the support of those outside your group when the resources of the larger community are required.

APPLICATIONS

5.1 Refer to the case study of the group made in the chapter. To what extent did the group follow the steps suggested in this chapter?

5.2 In groups in which you have participated, have appropriate efforts been made to obtain relevant information? What sort of research was characteristic of your experience?

5.3 Formulate a model showing the impelling and constraining forces of a group discussion that you have observed.

REFERENCES

1. J. Dewey, *How We Think* (Boston: D.C. Heath, 1910), p. 107.
2. T.M. Schiedel and L. Crowell, "Idea Development in Small Discussion Groups," *Quarterly Journal of Speech*, 50 (1964), pp. 140–145.
3. Ibid., p. 143.
4. B.W. Tuckman, "Development Sequences in Small Groups," *Psychological Bulletin*, 63 (1965), pp. 384–399.
5. K. Lewin, *Field Theory in Social Research* (New York: Harper and Row, 1951); see especially pp. 188–237.
6. P. Humphreys and D. Berkeley, "Handling Uncertainty Levels of Analysis of Decision Problem," *Behavioral Decision Making*, ed. by George Wright (New York: Plenum Press, 1985), pp. 257–282.
7. J. Bisanz, G.L. Bisanz, and C.A. Korpan, "Inductive Reasoning," *Thinking and Problem Solving*, ed. by R.J. Sternberg (San Diego: Academic Press, Inc., 1994), pp. 179–213.
8. R.S. Nickerson, *Reflection a Reasoning* (Hillsdale, N.J.: Lawrence Erlbaum Assoc., 1986), pp. 75–83.
9. M. Scriven, "Evaluation and Critical Reasoning: Logic's Last Frontier?" *Critical Reasoning in Contemporary Culture*, ed. by R.A. Talaska (New York: State University Press, 1992), pp. 353–406.
10. E.F. Harrison, *The Managerial Decision-Making Process* (Boston: Houghton-Mifflin, 1987), pp. 398–479.
11. M. Maynard, "Streamlined Mortgage Process Prevails," *USA Today*, May 7, 1999, p. 7B.

6 Promoting Cooperation and Positive Conflict

Scenario

Upon being hired as the CEO of a credit union, Mr. Gonzalez began to assess how well his senior managers worked together. After several months of observation he decided to begin a team-building process to promote cooperation between members of his senior management staff. An organizational consultant was hired to meet with the CEO and the staff in order to assess the need for team-building activities among the group of senior managers. In the course of a management retreat one of the managers, the chief financial officer (CFO), expressed discontent at his being required to attend; he felt the retreat would not accomplish anything and even refused to admit that the senior managers ever competed for resources, a well-documented problem which created a source of conflict among those in the group. By the end of the retreat the rest of the group felt they had accomplished setting ground rules for behaviors in order to work together in a cooperative fashion. However, the CFO did not share their sentiments, even though he responded as if he were in agreement. Ultimately, the CFO offered to resign from the credit union, citing that he did not feel he "fit in" with the rest of the management team. Although the CEO attempted to find a position in the company for the CFO, the offer to resign was eventually accepted. Follow-up meetings and retreats with the newly created management team provided evidence that much less tension existed within the group and that the senior management team was operating in a much more efficient manner.

Invariably, all groups experience some sort of conflict. The example cited above is based on a real life experience and is typical of relationships individuals experience within groups in the workplace, especially when the composition of the group changes. The ability to control and react to conflict situations in group contexts will determine, in part, how successful a group is in meeting its goals and objectives.

Starting on April 29, 1991, Los Angeles experienced one of the most violent and destructive urban riots in our country's history. Four white policemen had been acquitted of charges of assault against black motorist Rodney King; arson, looting, and killing were the result. Federal troops were called in to restore order. In the end, 52 people were killed, hundreds injured, and over a billion dollars of property destroyed.

During the riots, both of the authors of this text were faculty members at California State University, Los Angeles, located only five miles from downtown L.A. Throughout the crisis we were attentive observers to the issues of appropriate leadership and conflict resolution.

The word conflict often evokes a negative reaction or memory when mentioned to individuals. To many people it means quarreling, arguing, fighting, and the accompanying behaviors such as screaming and physical aggression. Jandt suggests that "conflict is not an external reality, but conflict is associated with an attitude determining perceptions and behaviors and behaviors held by members of a relationship."[1] One fact of life is that conflict is inevitable given that any two or more individuals possess differences in perceptions, attitudes, and expectations of others. However, we would like to suggest that conflict has positive dimensions in that innovative and creative solutions to problems may be the outcome of an "animated" interaction between two or more individuals. In fact, conflict can provide a precursor to interactions that question existing norms and practices and even an improvement in the quality of decisions a group reaches. This chapter reviews concepts of interpersonal and group conflict and explores the notion that conflicts, if resolved or managed appropriately, can enhance the effectiveness of decision-making groups.

An additional caveat to consider suggests that conflict situations often involve strong feelings and actions. In many cases intellectual judgments may give way to emotions. Thus, this material must be recognized as being context specific.

Interdependence and Conflict

One characteristic of the small group is *interdependence,* a concept derived from systems theory.[2] This concept suggests that each group member depends on the others, so members have the ability to influence each other. Such interactions are circular, with cause producing effect and effect turning into cause and feeding back to the original cause. Raven has, in fact, defined conflict as "any situation in which people are *negatively interdependent* with respect to goals, means, or both."[3]

Figure 6.1 illustrates this interdependence by means of a situation in which a group of graduate students prepare for their next meeting. Each graduate student has agreed to read five articles and be prepared to discuss them at the next class session. To the extent that they all want a good discussion, they will feel competition with other students and negatively interdependent concerning goals. If they

		Goals		
		Positive interdependence	Independence	Negative interdependence
Means	Positive interdependence	Subgroup division of labor; joint discussion at next meeting. (A)	Subgroup division of labor; noncurved exam at next meeting. (D)	Subgroup division of labor; curved exam at next meeting. (G)
	Independence	Everyone does own reading (multiple copies); joint discussion at next meeting. (B)	Everyone does own reading (multiple copies); noncurved exam at next meeting. (E)	Everyone does own reading (multiple copies); curved exam at next meeting. (H)
	Negative interdependence	Everyone does own reading (limited copies); joint discussion at next meeting. (C)	Everyone does own reading (limited copies); noncurved exam at next meeting. (F)	Everyone does own reading (limited copies); curved exam at next meeting. (I)

FIGURE 6.1 Raven's Model of Means-Goals Interdependence

From B. Raven, *Social Psychology: People in Groups* (New York: Wiley, 1976), p. 189.

anticipate being graded individually rather than comparatively, their goals will be independent.

Note in Figure 6.1 that the means and goals interdependence relationship is illustrated using the graduate student example cited above.

Kemp proposes that group members creatively handle conflict in the following ways:

1. Productive conflict arises because group members are so bound together that their actions affect one another; that is, they have accepted the fact that they have become interdependent.
2. Conflict occurs because people care. Often group members who have great creative differences share a very deep relationship. Because they care about one another and the group as a whole, they are willing to make, if necessary, a costly emotional response to help improve a situation.
3. Each member has different needs and values. These differences become evident and produce conflict unless the members repress their individual differences and assign the direction of the group to an authority figure.

Sometimes, members allow themselves to be taken over by such a leader, rather than accept the fact of their differences.[4]

Members of the animal kingdom, when confronted by an aggressive opponent, have several options: they can submit to the aggressor; they can take flight; or they can stay and fight. In human terms, to submit would be to become submissive, allowing someone to dominate you; to take flight would be to become independent by leaving the group or relationship; to fight means to remain interdependent and work through the conflict either positively or negatively. Let us consider how conflict interactions impact the group and individuals in the small group context.

Within Group Conflict

No matter how many members make up a group, as few as 3 or more than 20 people, those members will most likely experience situations that lead to conflict. Conflicts *within* the group may be the result of interpersonal or task-oriented conflict. The source of the conflict is not pertinent to this concept. The fact remains that most groups experience conflict situations that are created and perpetuated by those within the group.

Numerous sources of internal group conflict exist. Perceived changes within the group, ranging from changes in leadership roles to group structure to task activities to the arrival of new group members, may provoke conflicts. These conflicts may be inevitable; the nature of the predispositions of the group members will determine how these conflicts are handled, from an interpersonal perspective. In fact, how a group reacts to conflict may be determined by the reaction of only one group member. Conflicts within groups may be described in many ways. The following information describes some of the conceptual definitions of conflict as they pertain to small groups.

Types of Conflict

Conflicts in groups may be classified in many ways. Kowitz and Knutson suggest that *informational conflict* is "when members of a group disagree about the substance of group discussion."[5] These same conflicts may also be due to differing interpretations or perceptions of the same information. *Procedural conflict* may occur when group members do not agree how the group should proceed in the decision-making process.[5] Thus, one fraction of a group may decide to proceed one way while the other members of the group stage a significant protest in favor of proceeding differently. An additional factor pertinent to the perpetuation of conflict scenarios in groups is the amount of ego-involvement an individual has regarding a specific decision being discussed. In fact, research by Sereno and Mortensen suggests that less resistance or conflict in reference to an idea, especially one leading to change, will occur if an individual's level of ego-involvement is minimized, with ego-involvement being defined as the amount of concern or relevance an issue has to an individual and that person's commitment and willingness to take a stand on a particular issue.[6] Individuals possessing a high level of ego-involvement are often described as willing to argue and "dig their heels in" during an argument. While this response can be frustrating to the other members of a decision-making group, quite often the decisions made are of higher quality due to careful evaluation of ideas discussed during the decision-making process.

During the group discussion process, each individual group member will express many ideas. While group members often reach simple agreements and consensus, it is also possible to have misunderstandings. An interesting scenario occurs when two or more individuals agree with each other but perceive that their ideas are in conflict. Beebe and Masterson refer to such incidents as *pseudo-conflicts* because individuals actually agree but, due to poor communication or mispercep-tions, think that they are in disagreement.[7] Quite often these discussions, assuming members of the group persist in attempting to understand the source of a conflict, result in both parties stating something to the effect of "Hey, we really agree on this topic, although I initially thought we didn't." While pseudo-conflicts are common, they are usually only damaging to effective decision making if the group is not persistent enough to pursue the source of conflict, which, at least in these cases, is due to misperceptions of a conflict when one does not actually exist.

The *outcome* of a conflict situation is often defined as *win-win*, *win-lose*, and *lose-lose*. These three outcomes can be defined as follows: *win-win* suggests that both parties of a conflict are fully satisfied with the outcome; *win-lose* suggests that the solution to a conflict favored one party over the other, leaving the second party in a compromising position; and a *lose-lose* outcome suggests that neither party really benefited from the resolution of the conflict and, in fact, both parties somewhat accepted a solution having one or more aspects that could be considered negative to both of the groups goals and objectives. Johnson and Johnson suggest that when groups negotiate with the objective of maximizing the outcome in their favor the negotiations are *distributive*.[8] This term suggests that one group will be in an advantageous position over the other group due to an unequal distribution of resources as an outcome of a negotiation process. The outcome of distributive negotiations is equivalent to win-lose conflict resolution strategies. Similar to win-win conflict resolution strategies, groups can negotiate from an *integrative* perspective by sharing resources and approaching problems, and solutions to those same problems, with outcomes that satisfy both parties. Stephen Covey, author of the best-selling book *The Seven Habits of Highly Effective People,* provides an additional approach to negotiation called the *win/win or no deal* approach.[9] This negotiation strategy provides the option for both parties to withdraw from the negotiation process if a solution is not acceptable or if one party feels the outcome of an agreement will eventually result in the creation of an adverse relationship. Thus, Covey suggests that the *no deal* option encourages both parties to be open from the beginning and encourages people to consider that anything less than a win-win solution is unacceptable. Furthermore, this scenario has often resulted in individuals developing mutual respect for each other, even when an initial agreement is not reached.

In reference to distributive negotiations, this approach to conflict resolution has the potential to cause problems for task-oriented groups. Among the problems are the following:

- Development and perpetuation of "we-they/us-them" and "superiority-inferiority"complexes within the group. The group may splinter into factions or subgroups if this distributive behavior becomes the group norm.
- In groups with internal competitive pressures, individuals tend to overestimate their contributions and unrealistically downgrade the work of others.
- Under competitive pressures group members think they understand one another when in fact they do not. These distortions in perception may cause areas of agreement to go unrecognized.[10]

Labor-management negotiations characteristically use a distributive approach of interaction between groups. Labor parties often win at management's expense. An alternative model in this negotiation situation would be to use an integrative approach, which would explore ways that both parties might equally gain. We shall discuss this possibility in greater detail when we suggest alternative modes of handling conflict in the "promoting cooperation" section of this chapter.

On the other hand, conflict of the integrative type can have positive benefits for the group. However, only when members feel comfortable in the group can conflict safely emerge. Basic problems cannot usually be resolved without some conflict because of the different values, feelings, and perceptions of the members. For a conflict to center on issues, rather than on personalities and exaggerations, an acceptance of individual differences and some degree of mutual trust is a prerequisite. While distributive situations are based on a win-lose premise, the integrative approach provides an opportunity for win-win solutions and agreements leading to higher levels of satisfaction with decision-making outcomes.

Group conflict has the potential to bring out the best in a group or literally tear the group apart, as well as realizing outcomes somewhere in the middle. The overall social structure of the group may determine which occurs. As sociologist Lewis Coser states: "Conflict within a group frequently helps to revitalize existent norms; or it contributes to the emergence of new norms. In this sense, social conflict is a mechanism for adjustment of norms adequate to new conditions."[11]

In a study of conflict in organizations, Kabanoff found the cause often to be structural incongruencies in the distribution of influence. While acknowledging other variables, he found major causal factors:

For example, if interpersonal relations are poor between two persons in an interdependent work system, the felt hostility may push the parties involved toward assertive influence modes while their interdependence pushes them toward cooperative modes. The outcome may be a joint function of these two "forces" or may reflect the "dominant" relationship in the conflict. A high level of hostility may dominate the choice if interdependence is relatively slight, but the reverse may be true if interdependence is very high.[12]

An implication of this study is that conflict is intimately linked to potential influence relations and tactics within small group context. If both parties concur to minimize their differences, interpersonally, they are more likely to work cooperatively and effectively.

Conflict Between Groups

Considering the fact that numerous groups coexist within contexts such as cities, organizations, neighborhoods, and geographic regions it is common for individuals and groups to be in conflict for recognition or resources (to name a few common conflict sources). These conflicts can be either diffused or perpetuated, depending upon the nature of the relationship(s) of the individuals within each group. A common occurrence in an organization is to witness two or more groups competing for a limited amount of resources. This scenario can either create a healthy competition for resources or a climate of distrust and politically motivated activities.

Whether we are aware of it or not, our future goals and fortunes are greatly affected by the states of harmony or conflict between groups. Problems of intergroup relations include conflict between political groups, religious groups, economic groups, labor and management, and young and old, as well as across international boundaries.

A classic study of conflict between groups was conducted by Sherif and Sherif.[13] They studied groups of young boys, aged 11 and 12, at campsites under experimentally manipulated conditions. All of the boys were from similar socioeconomic backgrounds and none had a history of behavioral problems, such as violent or aggressive behaviors. The boys were randomly divided into two groups and were not told of this arrangement until competitive games pitting the two groups against each other began. A series of mutually frustrating events arose naturally in the course of these competitive activities. Stealing and burning of the opposing group's flag, raiding cabins, and name calling resulted. As a result of these experiments the researchers validated the following hypotheses:

1. When members of two groups come into contact with one another in a series of activities that embody goals that each group urgently desires but that can be attained by one group only at the expense of the other, competitive activity toward the goal changes with time into hostility between the groups and among the members.
2. In the course of such competitive interaction toward a goal available only to one group, unfavorable attitudes and images (stereotypes) of the out-group come into use and are standardized, placing the out-group at a definite social distance from the in-group.

3. Conflict between two groups tends to produce an increase in solidarity within the groups.
4. The heightened solidarity and pride in the group will be reflected in an overestimation of the achievements of fellow members and in a lower estimation of the achievements of members of the out-group.
5. Relations between groups that are of consequence to the groups in question, including conflict, tend to produce changes in the organization and practices within the groups.

The Sherif and Sherif study results indicate that overt differences are unnecessary for the rise of intergroup hostility, social distances, stereotyped images, and negative attitudes in a group of "normal" young males.[14] In other words, it is not necessary to have evidence of differences in physical appearance, language, or culture to serve as catalysts for conflict situations. Sometimes the presence and perpetuation of mere perceptions, even those that are contrived, are sufficient enough to initiate and intensify conflict between groups.

Promoting Cooperation

Under what circumstances will cooperation emerge in a group? This question has intrigued social scientists for a long time. We know that people are not angels, that they tend to be selfish and look after themselves first, yet we also know that cooperation does occur and that our civilization is based on it. Exchange theorists assume that people will attempt to gain as much as they can at minimum cost. As people receive satisfaction from mutually pleasurable exchanges, rules develop to ensure continuation of such exchanges.

Problems arise when people disagree on what constitutes equitable exchange, what the costs and rewards actually are. And, as we observed in Chapter 4, discussing the "Prisoner's Dilemma," how much can you trust another person both to report honestly and to do what they promise to do?

Axelrod has developed a *cooperation theory* based upon his investigations of individuals who pursue their own self-interest without assistance from a central authority forcing them to cooperate.[15] The pursuit of self-interest when behavior is not guided is greater in a group using the win-lose alternatives implicit in a situation.

Axelrod's theory grows out of the Prisoner's Dilemma model. The Dilemma is actually an abstract formulation of very real situations in which what is best for *each* person individually leads to mutual defection, whereas *everyone* would have been better off with mutual cooperation.[16] Players too often merely take turns at exploiting each other. Axelrod attempted to find the most reasonable and predictable way to promote cooperation.

Professional game theorists were invited to participate in a computer tournament based on the Prisoner's Dilemma. Scholars from different academic disciplines designed programs that exemplified a *rule* to select the cooperative or noncooperative choice for each move; knowledge of all previous moves was built into the program. The winning entry, *tit for tat,* was submitted by Professor Anatol Rapoport of the University of Toronto. This program was not only the simplest, but the best. *Tit for tat* simply starts with a cooperative choice and thereafter does what the other player did on the previous move. For example, if one player chooses green and one chooses red, the red choice wins. If both choose red, they both lose, while if they both choose green, they both win. With tit for tat the player establishes that, in each subsequent round, they will replicate the choice of the opponent in the previous round. Thus, if you vote green in the first round, the other player votes green in the second round. Axelrod summarizes the basis for its success:

> What accounts for tit for tat's robust success is its combination of being nice, forgiving and clear. Its niceness prevents it from getting into unnecessary trouble. Its retaliation discourages the other side from persisting whenever defection is tried. Its forgiveness helps restore mutual cooperation and its clarity makes it intelligible to the other player, thereby eliciting long-term cooperation.

The remaining problem is that trial and error is slow and costly as people learn how to achieve rewards from cooperation. Within the small group, conditions should promote mutually rewarding strategies based on reciprocity. As Gergen and Gergen have commented, "The most promising means of increasing cooperation may be the improvement of communication."[17] Reciprocity in the interdependent group should suggest, "If I help you to win, I win too." Johnson and Johnson suggest that groups can develop normative behavioral patterns while attempting to resolve conflicts or negotiate.[18] For example, if a group responds to a group with a similar level of reward or harm the *norm of reciprocity* prevails. Additionally, when groups receive equal levels of reward or punishment it is referred to as the *norm of equity.* However, it is up to both groups negotiating a conflict scenario to set the tone of interaction and agree on normative patterns of behavior. It should be noted that once these patterns of behavior, also referred to as *contractual norms,* have been agreed on neither party should violate this agreement, unless they choose to intentionally sabotage the negotiation process.

Deutsch suggests that conflicts can be either of a destructive or a constructive nature.[19] A conflict is considered destructive if the parties involved are dissatisfied with the results and feel they have lost something attributed to the conflict itself. Conversely, if the participants in a conflict are satisfied with the outcome the conflict is considered constructive. It is also important to note that when a conflict is considered to be optimally constructive all of the participants are fully satisfied with the outcome.

At the intergroup level Sherif and Sherif used what they called *superordinate goals* to bring the boys in the "robbers cave" experiment out of the state of conflict. The operating principle was that "if conflict develops from mutually incompatible goals, common goals should promote cooperation."[20] Camp activities were planned in such a way that desirable goals could not be achieved by the efforts of only one in-group; both groups were forced to cooperate toward the common goal. One such goal involved repairing a sabotaged water-supply system. Others included coopera-tively raising money to obtain a movie that both groups wanted to see and moving a stalled food truck. All the tasks were accomplished by the cooperative efforts of the two groups.

After the boys had participated in these cooperative activities, sociometric tests were again administered. The results revealed that attitudes toward members of the out-group had clearly changed. While the friendship choices remained primar-ily within each in-group, the choices of out-group member friends had increased, and there was less total rejection of out-group members. As Sherif says:

> Our findings demonstrate the effectiveness of a series of superordinate goals in the reduction of intergroup conflict, hostility, and their by-products. They also have implications for other measures proposed for reducing intergroup tensions.
>
> It is true that lines of communication between groups must be opened before prevailing hostility can be reduced. But, if contact between hostile groups takes place without superordinate goals, the communication channels serve as media for further accusations and recriminations. When contact situations involve superor-dinate goals, communication is utilized in the direction of reducing conflict in order to attain the common goals.[21]

The identification and utilization of superordinate goals seem to have genuine effectiveness in reducing intergroup conflict.

The principle of superordinate goals can easily be demonstrated by describing effective learning groups, either students or workers in a training seminar, and the goals the group members agree to at the onset of a learning activity. Using the concept of collaborative learning, structuring activities that require individuals to work together in a group, learners can define their level of desired group perform-ance. Usually groups pursue a high level of performance, quite often striving for perfect or near-perfect performance. However, in order for the group to function at such a high level each group member is required to pursue an equally high level of performance and understanding of the material to be learned. Most often one or more members of the group will not perform or contribute to the group learning activity at a level of competency high enough to support the original goal. Given that everyone agreed to a certain standard of performance at the outset of the activity, it is usually much easier to regain cooperation from the member whose individual performance was temporarily substandard. Thus, the utilization of a superordinate goal has the ability to keep the group, and it's members, focused on a specific goal while maintaining a cooperative team-based group dedicated to reaching a desired goal.

Managing Conflict

Kowitz and Knutson suggest that conflict should not always be viewed as a negative occurrence within the small group context.[22] In fact, they are proponents of the theory that conflicts serve a positive function. Rather than viewing conflict as a behavior that must be resolved they suggest that conflict should be managed. For example, during the course of an argumentative discussion it might be necessary to procedurally keep the conflict positive by avoiding or eliminating dysfunctional or destructive comments. Furthermore, allowing functional conversations to occur should yield higher quality decisions. Therefore, one objective of decision-making groups should be to include the creation of a group climate that allows critical discussions yet makes sure these same discussions keep a positive tone. To summarize, Baird concurs with Kowitz and Knutson by suggesting that:

> Conflict need not always spell trouble, nor should it always be avoided or kept under wraps. Although conflict can have a negative effect, we need to look at it more often as a dynamic, positive force for change. When managed properly, it can achieve positive and productive results. It's essential to learn how to handle conflict effectively because it affects work efficiency, job satisfaction and cost containment.[23]

Therefore, despite all of the negative images and stereotypes of conflicts, we should begin to recognize that conflicts can serve a very positive function and assist the group in achieving higher quality decisions due to the fact that discussions were much more carefully evaluated using positive and constructive criticism. For example, this principle prevails when student learning groups diligently work through conflict situations in classes. Groups experiencing conflict discussions that can keep those same discussions constructive typically perform better on assignments than groups that either avoid conflict or poorly manage conflict discussions.

Case Study

Universities typically consist of academic departments and schools or colleges made up of those same departments. Whenever a department proposes a new degree program it is typically authored by one or more faculty members from within the same academic unit. On occasion an interdisciplinary group of faculty and administrators will create a new degree program. One such incident occurred when a group of faculty members attempted to develop a "minor" in the content area of Information Studies. Although all of the individuals present (each from different departments) appeared to like the conceptual ideas included in this proposal, it quickly became apparent that those present possessed many differences in their theoretical and practical approaches to designing this degree program. An additional factor pertains to the question of resources. More specifically, which department will receive the units for all courses students enroll in over the years to come. As the series of discussions regarding this topic progressed, the individuals became more and more contentious and eventually this group stopped meeting altogether. The next academic year a new administrator was asked to revisit the discussion of creating a degree program in this same content area. Once the committee began to meet this administrator sensed a significant amount of conflict that had not been resolved or effectively managed. Several of the current committee members were present during the dysfunctional meetings of the previous year. To make matters even more challenging, the new administrator became the facilitator of these discussions, with some of the individuals present still harboring resentments toward the proposal and the committee members from the previous year.

Discussion Questions

1. How best might the facilitator of this conflict proceed?
2. What factors should be considered to promote a positive discussion?
3. What types of conflict might prevail in this scenario and how might the facilitator respond to each of them?
4. How might the group promote cooperation?
5. What type(s) of conflict currently exists?
6. What type of conflict resolution/management strategy do you recommend using? Why?

Chapter Summary

Although conflict is inevitable, it may be positive in some instances, negative in others, and irrelevant in still others. Within a decision-making group a distributive approach to conflict problems leads to distrust and competition, whereas an integrative approach promotes openness and cooperation. Between groups, sustained conflict over mutually desired goals attainable to only one group provokes hostile and aggressive acts, social distance, negative stereotypes, and also internal group solidarity and changed relationships. Establishing superordinate goals provides a framework of cooperation among rival groups and has the potential to effectively reduce negative conflicts.

Cooperation leads to coordination of effort, productivity, good human relations, and other positive benefits. Competition leads to distrust and insecurity. The implications for all groups are readily apparent. Covey's "win-win or no deal" approach is unique and important to note. This premise allows individuals an opportunity to determine if they can work together or not. If not, or a conflict cannot be resolved, it is perfectly acceptable for either or both parties to break off negotiations or disassociate with each other in the workplace. Besides presenting an excellent methodology to avoid conflicts, this approach avoids creating or perpetuating bad feelings between two parties that, under different conditions, might have felt compelled to work together despite the recognition of incompatible differences. Such approaches to conflict management can only make the workplace a more effective and productive work environment.

APPLICATIONS

6.1 Describe a situation in a small group in which a conflict arose between those present. How did the group members respond?

6.2 How might individuals in a small group avert conflict and promote cooperation?

6.3 Groups attempting to work together often experience between group conflicts. How might groups learn to work cooperatively?

6.4 Describe how members of a group might "manage" conflict within the group.

REFERENCES

1. F.E. Jandt, *Conflict Resolution Through Communication* (New York: Harper and Row, 1973).
2. L. Von Bertalanffy, *General Systems Theory* (New York: Braziller, 1968).
3. B. Raven, *Social Psychology: People in Groups* (New York: Wiley, 1976).
4. C.G. Kemp, "The Creative Handling of Conflict" in *Perspectives on the Group Process*, ed. by C.G. Kemp (Boston: Houghton Mifflin, 1970).
5. A.C. Kowitz, and T.J. Knutson, *Decision Making in Small Groups: The Search for Alternatives* (Boston: Allyn and Bacon, 1980).
6. K.K. Sereno and D.C. Mortensen, "The Effects of Ego-Involved Attitudes on Conflict Negotiation Dyads," *Speech Monographs*, 36 (1969), pp. 8–12.
7. S.A. Beebe and J.T. Masterson, *Communicating in Small Groups: Principles and Practices* (New York: Longman, 1997).
8. D.W. Johnson and F.P. Johnson, *Joining Together: Group Theory and Group Skills* (Boston: Allyn and Bacon, 1997).
9. Stephen R. Covey, *The 7 Habits of Highly Effective People* (New York: Fireside, 1989).
10. R.R. Blake and J.S. Mouton, "Reactions to Intergroup Competition Under Win-Lose Conditions," *Management Science*, July, 1961.
11. L. Coser, *The Functions of Social Conflict* (New York: Free Press, 1964).
12. B. Kbanoff, "Potential Influence Structures as Sources of Interpersonal Conflict in Groups and Organizations," *Organizational Behavior and Human Decision Processes*, 36 (1969), pp. 128–129.
13. M. Sherif and C.W. Sherif, *Social Psychology* (New York: Harper and Row, 1969).
14. Ibid., *Social Psychology*.
15. R. Axelrod, *The Evolution of Cooperation* (New York: Basic Books, 1984).
16. Ibid., *The Evolution of Cooperation*.
17. K.J. Gergen and M.M. Gergen, *Social Psychology* (New York: Harcourt Brace Jovanovich, 1981).
18. Ibid., *Joining Together*.
19. M. Deutsch, "Conflicts: Productive and Destructive," *The Journal of Social Issues*, 25 (1969), pp. 7–41.
20. Ibid., *Social Psychology*.
21. M. Sherif, "Superordinate Goals in the Reduction of Intergroup Conflicts," *American Journal of Sociology*, 63 (1958), p. 356.
22. Ibid., *Social Psychology*.
23. J.E. Baird, *Positive Personnel Practices* (Prospect Heights, IL: Waveland Press, 1982).

7 Task Formats of Quality Groups

Scenario

"There are four people in my business who should be working together better," said Claudia Daniels, production manager of a bicycle company. "Unfortunately our organizational chart makes them look like four apples hanging out on a limb. The structure doesn't say they have to work together, but that's what their jobs require them to do." These four people—the raw material's purchaser, the production planner, the market forecaster, and the distribution manager—are all affected by what each one knows and does. Daniels knows that if they can't function as a team, then the narrow profit margin vanishes.

This scenario is true in all walks of life—from film crews to certified accountant audit teams. All require capable individual specialists who have acquired the motivation and ability to work together effectively on teams. In business, permanent groups or boards of directors are complemented by numerous groups assigned to temporary tasks in order to stimulate innovation, creativity, and increased productivity. How can you prepare and equip yourself with the necessary team-building skills? In this chapter we will discuss the expectations of such groups, the formats available, and ways to develop a high-performance team.

Teamwork-Defining Characteristics

We have to look no further than a championship sports team or a symphony orchestra to appreciate the results of teamwork. As with other groups, the ability to work together is guided by a common vision and clarity of purpose. In the middle 1990s many initiatives of "reengineering" and TQM failed because groups were overwhelmed and lacked proper direction.

To participate in a quality way, all members of the team must be clear about the group's core purpose. Why does this group exist at all? The answer to this question provides a navigation mark for thinking about goals, structures, priority of activities, and allocation of resources. Each individual will have ideas about how to proceed with the project, and they will differ with each other. Major problems result when the members of the team differ significantly and are not vectored in a similar focus.

A group must agree on a shared goal in order to become cohesive or a "team." This common direction, focus, and goal must be identified through group discussion and ultimately be accepted by all members. In terms of scientific principles we know what happens when forces are marshaled in the same direction, and what happens when they are in opposition. Similar reactions occur when group members are either together or at odds. Ideally, it would be best for the group to describe this goal succinctly in a sentence. While this goal may be modified by members' consent, it provides the connectiveness that transforms a collection of individuals into a team.

The team's performance is then based on the successful integration of all the groups' resources toward the identified goal. Thus, a corporate team may be made up of representatives from research and development, manufacturing, sales, and public relations. The special knowledge of each member must be clearly communicated and integrated into the database and functions of the team. The total capability of the team should transcend the sum of the parts (or members of the group) and provide a new level of thinking, planning, and acting that can be considered high quality.

This model of teams, formed with individuals from various backgrounds of knowledge, is often referred to as a *multifunction* or *cross-functional team*. From your own work experience, consider the many functions required and the personnel in charge of performing the functions. If a product is concerned, functions such as engineering, manufacturing, marketing, and accounting must be performed and can be identified as necessary components in quality decision-making. Among the various types of multifunctional teams are product development teams, project teams, process teams, or focus groups.

Charles Garfield, a scientific member of the Apollo 11 mission team, says that such teams can be developed "essentially by getting people from different functional areas into a room with a facilitator. The facilitator helps break down departmental barriers."[1] Coordination is important to ensure clarity of goals and purpose. The team should then take over.

Several advantages have been cited for multifunctional teams. They tend to work quickly and have little tolerance for topics not germane to the task; they promote a better understanding of the problem, and different perspectives within the group can promote greater creativity. In addition, complex problems can be solved by teams demonstrating both personal expertise and a willingness to accept the contribution of people from diverse perspectives.[2] A company that assembles a team from different departments garners a totality of perspectives and a chance to test ideas across the full organization. Business consultants have observed: "Clusters of unlike minds create novel ideas."[3]

A team is a group with an agreed-on goal, in which the technical skills and personal abilities of the members are complementary. A quality team has the properties of a more ordinary team but to an enhanced degree. Each member is both a specialist and a team member skilled at performing functions needed by the task and relating effectively with the other members. Teams are often appointed by and held accountable to a higher body. Members are more likely to be appointed rather than volunteers, and when the goal is reached, the team may cease to exist.

Strategic Planning

One typical assignment to a multifunctional team is strategic planning. Peter Drucker defined planning as "the management function that includes decision and action to insure further results."[4] The substance of planning is the choices that are made through a group planning process. Since many organizations engage in strategic planning, we will discuss the process as evidenced by quality groups. Specifically, strategic planning refers to the specification of organizational goals and the development of a time-phased set of tasks for attainment.

Step One: Vision, Mission, and Belief Statements

As with most groups, the first step is one of definition and delineation. Vision has been variously defined as:

- A coherent and powerful statement of what the organization can and should be in the future.[5]
- A clearly articulated desired end state that applies to all organizational elements. It is memorable and inspirational.[6]
- A preferred future state description that is rooted in reality but focused on the future.[7]

Discussing this vision should force the group to share perspectives, values, and challenges that can focus the group on the potential future. A specific time frame may be established, such as, what should we be in the year 2020?

The vision that the group accepts can lead to the development of a *mission statement*. When effective, it is a short statement that answers the question, What business should we be in? Its greatest use is to provide clarity and focus to the group's activities; it can and should be used as a criterion in helping to decide what specific objectives and strategies the organization should pursue and those it should not. Most businesses would consider components such as: customers and markets; type of business or ownership; products/services; a desired image; growth and profits; quality and service; geography; and competition. In a sales situation, the product and market are keys to the statement and define the scope of the business. Products are often used generically to denote services as well as tangible items. Examples of mission statements follow:

THE MISSION OF THE ZOOM COMPANY IS TO PROVIDE A MODERATELY PRICED, HIGH QUALITY, AND READILY AVAILABLE LINE OF BICYCLES TO MEET THE NEEDS OF CONSUMERS IN THE MIDWEST PORTION OF THE UNITED STATES.

THE DOWNS COMPANY IS COMMITTED TO THE DEVELOPMENT OF QUALITY PARTNERSHIPS WITH ITS CUSTOMERS, EMPLOYEES, AND SUPPLIERS FOR THE PURPOSE OF ENSURING LONG-TERM PROFITABILITY AND PROVIDING SECURITY AND OPPORTUNITY FOR EMPLOYEES AND SHAREHOLDERS. EMBRACING THE PHILOSOPHY OF CONTINUOUS IMPROVEMENT,

- THE COMPANY FOCUSES ON SERVING THE NEEDS OF BOTH ITS CUSTOMERS AND SUPPLIERS AND MAINTAINING ITS POSITION AS MARKET LEADER IN THE CONTINENTAL UNITED STATES THROUGH THE IMPLEMENTATION OF CREATIVE AND INNOVATIVE BUSINESS PRACTICES. ALL TRANSACTIONS ARE GUIDED BY THE PRINCIPLES OF INTEGRITY.

DAVIS AIRCRAFT STATED AS ITS MISSION: "TO BUILD AND SELL THE BEST AIRCRAFT AND AEROSPACE PRODUCTS IN THEIR CLASS, THROUGH

- CONTINUOUS QUALITY IMPROVEMENT, EFFECTIVE USE OF RESOURCES, AND THE FULL INVOLVEMENT AND CONTRIBUTION OF DAVIS EMPLOYEES, IN ORDER TO INCREASE MARKET SHARE, CUSTOMER SATISFACTION, AND PROFITABILITY."

Step Two: Situational Analysis

The situational analysis must precede effective strategic plans. We cannot, of course, control all external factors, but we can survey them to see how they can be used to create an advantage. We must therefore analyze the market; determine the competition; and map the general environment.

In order to plan, certain assumptions must be made about the future market. The sales and marketing departments, for example, will be handcuffed without some sort of starting point. The analysis must answer these questions: How rapidly is the market expanding? Who is currently responding to the market? Your product may be untested in the marketplace, and you may have to rely on a judgmental forecast. Research will be necessary to allow the group to make an educated guess. In this market analysis we are looking for trends that will supply a firm foundation for our plans. Trends in the marketplace tend to steer fairly straight lines once set in motion unless influenced by other environmental factors.

We must take a good hard look at the intended market: Who is currently supplying the needs? How intense is the competition? It might be useful to list the competition including their percentage shares of the market. We must then determine the key success factors that appear to be operating in the industry and determine the sales leaders. Such topics as brand name recognition, creativity advertising, comprehensive distribution centers, and low cost may be keys to sales success.

Analysis of the environment characteristically includes categories such as new technology, governmental regulations, political issues, economic forecasts, and social trends.

Step Three: Establishing Goals and Timetables

What do we want to see accomplished and when do we want it accomplished? This phase of discussion will attempt to answer these questions. In this phase the team will determine specific accomplishments that the organization/group intends to achieve by a specified date.

For example, to serve an older group of people who ride bicycles, our company might plan to have for distribution a three-wheel model produced at a rate of two thousand a day by the year 2006. This goal has been driven by our environmental analysis and our mission statement. The goal can be further articulated through the steps necessary to get the bicycle into production and the timetable for marketing.

Step Four: Objectives and Tasks

With the goals established, next we must determine who will take the steps and who is responsible to see that they are met satisfactorily. Specific assignments and accountability are essential to the success of the plan.

Individuals or subunits may be required to develop strategies for achieving the target, a step-by-step timetable, a budget, and any personnel requirements. Action plans may be formulated in such a way as to provide progress reports and feedback.

People need to know what their deadlines are, who's responsible for various tasks, and what it will take to get the tasks accomplished. At the end of each meeting, it is a good idea to debrief the action to be taken and the people responsible. Each team member will leave the meeting knowing what is to be done, who is doing it, when it will be accomplished and what resources are needed.

Step Five: Implementation, Control, and Reward

What should we do if things go wrong? How and when will we know? What is the incentive to get there? We should remember that strategy is the *how* of accomplishing an objective. There are usually many ways of doing this; for example, if our objective is to increase profits, strategies could include raising prices, cutting costs, increasing volume, introducing high margin products, or some combination of these actions. Contingency planning should be done in case outcomes don't happen as predicted.

Strategic planning helps a group or organization look toward the future and develop a coherent and defensible basis for decision making. Groups can research decisions in light of future consequences, establish priorities, and develop effective strategies. When a team, rather than individuals working independently, develops a plan, not only are the strategies more comprehensive, but the team buys into the solution that supports their implementation. A quality strategic planning process has the following characteristics:

1. It is flexible. It fits the organization and is user-friendly.
2. It is participatory. The process involves executives, managers, supervisors, and staff at all levels. Further, it is not left to planners; everyone plans.
3. It clearly defines responsibilities and timetables. It is carried out by those who have the responsibility within the organization for achieving objectives but is coordinated by a central figure, someone who has the "big picture."
4. It energizes an organization. It produces understanding and common purpose throughout an organization.
5. It remains aware of the environment in which it functions. It obtains perspectives from many levels and sources, both within and outside the organization.
6. It is realistic about goals, objectives, resources, and outcomes. While not attempting to avoid all risk, it recognizes such constraints as public accountability, visibility, short-term horizons, personnel issues, overall fiscal conditions, and budgetary trends.
7. It is convincing. It develops and conveys compelling evidence for its recommendations. (This characteristic is especially important in linking the strategic plan to an agency budget request.)

Functional Teams

As organizations agree upon major goals, teams in a unit or department will be required to work together effectively. Total quality programs rely on the stimulation that one person gives to another. We shall now examine some of the functional teams present in many modern corporations.

Supply Chain

Characteristic of many organizations is the supply chain, where all of the operations from ordering raw materials to the delivery of the finished products occur. Often the supply chain is a complex process, involving from five to a dozen functions in which group efficiency is critical to success. The supply-chain team may also involve customers or suppliers who are concerned with matters such as improved scheduling, better inquiry handling, lower cost, inventory reduction, and process simplification. Better customer service and on-time delivery are characteristic indicators of success.

When Hong Kong moved from British jurisdiction to that of mainland China, an American-based company established a workshop to deal with the transition. Fifteen people came from nine different countries including people from Asia, Europe, South America, and Australia as well as the United States. Their assignment was to plan the set-up of the manufacturing plant for the distribution of raw materials and finished products throughout the world working with the new government. Each person knew a specific part of the process, but the total plan required everyone's input and knowledge. These people had never met before and were separated by differences in culture, language, and work background. In two days, however, they were able to draw up a plan that has since proved effective.

Even though the operations in production may be quite different, the overlap is so significant that such functional teams serve constructive purposes. The best work requires that each individual understand how they fit into the organization with the others and be allowed to contribute ideas for improvement.

Sales and Marketing

Sales and marketing people characteristically are required to interact and discuss the processes and forces at work in markets and customer's companies. Often complex issues are required to be solved in a short time. Examples of goals include adjustment of marketing plans to problems in the sales field, new competition, and response to unfavorable public relations. Sales and marketing teams are often able to discuss the processes that influence the total organization and resolve opposing ideas in a neutrally satisfying way. Creativity often must be encouraged by a receptive atmosphere.

Customer Service

Teams concerned with customer service perform a number of functions required to maintain high quality. Often the problem is that some unit or individual does not feel that they play a role in customer service until a problem emerges. Often such teams must work with speed to solve problems that customers view as significant. Modern organizations have placed a higher status on such service functions and have defined ways to measure quality.

The Registrar's Office at a major university recently underwent such a meeting of all people involved in working with students from admissions, student loans, and student records. Students had complained that they were having to fill out information items repeatedly in slow and unresponsive lines. The team was able to find ways to enhance the process and eliminate unnecessary steps by the students and redundancies in the system.

Information Systems

Within the organization people often need to form teams to consider how information is gathered, stored, and disseminated. Often a wide number of business functions with different priorities and needs for different information must plan on how to work together. Common computing systems need to establish priorities for major projects. In an effective team, the diversity of views can be used to stimulate creativity rather than to create barriers. Systems users and service providers must have a mutual understanding and an ownership in the course of action.

Administration

An organization suffers if the goals, objectives, and performance measures are not precise and clearly articulated. Administrative groups may be removed from customers or the public that they are serving and have to take extra efforts to gather appropriate information. In the modern organization customers and other stake-holders must see that administrative processes reflect clear objectives and measures. Managers of various departments must be able to function as a team if the organization is to achieve its overriding goals.

Improvement Groups

Sometimes groups are assigned the task of determining the best ways to improve the quality of work or the level of productivity. The analysis of the way we go about making decisions is a fertile topic for discussion. Can the group improve by discussing its decision-making process? Janis and Mann have presented a framework for groups to analyze their decision-making processes.[8]

1. *Develop a balance sheet.* The balance sheet procedure was designed as a technique for fostering vigilant decision making. When a complex decision is at stake, a group should develop lists of positive and negative factors before making a final decision. This procedure was tested by Janis using Yale seniors facing career choices prior to graduation, by eliciting alternatives and probable outcomes (gains and losses). Typically, at the beginning of an interview, the students were asked to describe all of the alternatives they were considering and to specify the pros and cons for each. Then they were shown a balance-sheet grid with empty cells as shown in Figure 7.1. They were asked to fill out a sheet for the most preferred alternatives and asked to reexamine each cell on the balance sheet, trying to think of considerations not yet mentioned.

This procedure was also shown to be effective in a group situation involving a decision to remain physically active,[9] and in studies of occupational choice con-

Alternative # _____	Positive Anticipation +	Negative Anticipation –
1. Tangible gains + and losses – for self		
2. Tangible gains + and losses – for others		
3. Self-approval + or Self-disapproval –		

FIGURE 7.1   The Balance Sheet Grid. Alternative Forms.

ducted in Germany.[10] The list should not be developed with the aim of proving whether a decision is good or bad. Rather, the group should simply try to generate as many ideas, pro and con, as possible.

   2. *Role play the decision outcome.* Once a group decision appears to be a reasonable and preferred one, the group should envision the consequences by role playing the people affected by the decision. Janis and Mann have adapted these techniques from emotional experiences in groups promoting personal change, for example, requiring heavy smokers to play roles of persons told by their physicians that they have lung cancer.[11] The technique requires a person to take the role of someone who learns vividly and dramatically the consequences of complacency.

Role playing may encourage the group to foster a more comprehensive appraisal of pros and cons by anticipating emotional as well as logical personal responses. The group may also be better prepared for dealing with negative feedback when the decision is implemented. Occasionally the group may feel that more information is needed before a final decision is made.

   3. *Obtain decision counseling.* When a group has been in existence a long time, the ways of making decisions may be questioned. If the group feels that it has not always made the best possible decisions or finds the process difficult, an outside counselor might observe the group impartially and furnish new insights.

Brainstorming

Brainstorming was developed by Alex Osborn over 40 years ago for use in his advertising agency.[12] The technique employs four basic rules:

   1. *Criticism is ruled out.* Adverse judgement of ideas must be withheld until later.
   2. *"Free-wheeling" is welcomed.* The wilder the idea the better; it is easier to tame down than to think up.
   3. *Quantity is wanted.* The greater the number of ideas, the more the likelihood of winners.
   4. *Combination and improvement are sought.* In addition to contributing ideas of their own, participants should suggest how ideas of others can be turned into *better* ideas, or how two or more ideas can be joined into still another idea.

The primary objective is to free group members temporarily from inhibition, self-criticism, and criticism of others, in order to produce more imaginative alternative approaches to a specific problem. The problem should be carefully specified and all evaluation withheld. Somebody with secretarial ability should record *all* suggestions, and a spirit of fun and excitement should be encouraged. At a later session the group should evaluate the various suggestions produced.

After a large number of suggestions, sometimes as many as 100, have been presented, there is nearly always the need to clarify many of them. When they were first suggested, their potential value may be clouded. In some cases their relevance will need to be explored. This clarification process will need to be carried out when all group members are present. The original author of a suggestion will often be the best equipped to explain its potential value; however, just because the brainstorming session is over, creative thinking should not be shut off. In many cases a suggested alternative can be modified, added to, or otherwise enhanced by a person other than its original author. Creative thinking, once started, should be encouraged and continued.

A number of informal experiments briefly described by Osborn support the view that the use of brainstorming in groups increases the production of valuable ideas. In addition, he reported many indications of its wide acceptance. Various other studies have shown that brainstorming was superior to methods in which critical evaluations were not delayed, in that the total number of ideas was greater and that, as the quantity of ideas was increased, the number of *valuable* ideas was increased proportionately.[13]

A field experiment in brainstorming was conducted by Balchan to test Osborn's technique using his directives.[14] She studied variables such as group size and the method of recording ideas presented: on a chalkboard with the list visible to the group, on a notepad by a designated secretary, and on a tape recorder. Two different tasks were assigned: one was "contrived," using the problem, "How many ways can you find to use a Pringle Potato Chip container?"; the other was "real" and formulated to generate alternative ideas to solve the problem identified by the group. The same leader was used in all conditions of the experiment, and groups were given the same instructions and led through a training session using Osborn's suggestions for idea creation. There were five significant findings:

1. Participants in small groups contributed a greater mean number of ideas per person than did participants in large groups.
2. Although all participants were satisfied with their involvement and with their own participation, responses from the small groups indicated a greater satisfaction.
3. Participants in the board method indicated greater satisfaction with their productivity than did the participants in the secretary or oral methods.
4. The real task was significantly more meaningful to participants than the contrived task.
5. All of the groups contributed most of their ideas in the first 5 minutes of the 15-minute brainstorming sessions.

This issue should not be confused with the questions of whether brainstorming in groups produces more ideas or more valuable ideas than an equivalent number of persons working alone; on this particular question experimental findings are inconclusive.[15] However, there appears to be considerable evidence in support of the value of the brainstorming technique to groups working on a problem that requires a group decision. For such groups we advocate the use of brainstorming to uncover approaches that otherwise might be neglected.

The brainstorming technique should not be used until a problem has been well defined: Uninhibited creativity combined with ambiguity can produce a general sense of confusion. In addition, a group should recognize full well that uncovering a lot of good ideas does not eliminate the need to evaluate them later in order to select the best one. Careful evaluation of alternatives must always follow a brainstorming session.

It has been our experience that a 20- to 30-minute brainstorming session can be not only profitable to a problem-solving group but also a lot of fun. There is a sense of freedom from ordinary restraints, the challenge to think of something clever or new, the excitement of discovery, and the good-natured, temporary acceptance of apparently ridiculous suggestions. In many ways a brainstorming session can inadvertently satisfy a need to increase group cohesiveness at a particular time that should not be overlooked.

No idea should be abandoned immediately just because it is apparently ridiculous; it should be given careful and serious consideration to realize its possible potential. For example, one of the authors helped a country club steering committee attack the problem of obtaining new members. One suggestion was to pay prospective members $10 to attend a free dinner. The committee, after some joking, came to see that a $10 payment plus the cost of the meal totaled less than $20; the dues were more than $200; if one prospect in 10 could thus be led to join the club, there would be an initial net income. For the better part of a year this approach was used as the primary instrument in a successful drive to increase the club's membership. To some prospects the suggestions seemed to make no sense; but on the other hand, what did they have to lose? Where else could they make $10 by eating a free meal?

Case Study

The success rate for kidney transplants performed at the Medical Center in Albany, New York, was one of the best in the country in 1998; however, patients spent an average of 15 days recovering compared to the national average of 8. Longer recovery discourages cost-conscious health maintenance organizations from sending patients to this hospital. Also longer hospital stays increase the patients' risk of infection.

A team was formed of doctors, nurses, and administrators with the goal determined to help get people up and out of the hospital as soon as possible.

Response

The team decided to plot and review each step of the transplant procedure. A "pathway" was established that showed the speediest ways from one step to the next. Nurses were empowered to decide when a patient is ready to move on to the next step, while the doctors can spend more time in surgery rather than making routine decisions. Previously patients had to wait on average 18 hours for a doctor to review progress and approve the next step. Also, the hospital asked people to visit the outpatient center the day before surgery rather than having to be admitted to the hospital. Follow-up treatments are also given at the outpatient center, and patients over 50 miles from their homes are provided hotel rooms, which are less expensive and have fewer germs than hospital rooms.

As a result, the hospital stays were reduced to 8 days in 1999, the national average. The one-year survival rate of patients increased from 87 percent in 1994 to 97 percent in 1999; costs were cut $10,000 per patient, or about 25 percent; re-admission rates were reduced by 50 percent. As Dr. John Moran, a reviewer of the program from another Center, stated: "They took an excellent program and made it better."[16]

Chapter Summary

A team is a process, not a thing. A team is a group that is able to think, act, and lead as a unit. More than the sum of its parts, a team should be able to think more expansively and creatively than the individuals who make it up.[16] Collaboration and teamwork allow people to compensate for someone's weakness with another's strength.

Teamwork involves working on different tasks and in different formats using such techniques as brainstorming; such assignments as strategic planning and implementation of functional and cross-functional teams require effective communication and a recognition of an organization as a system. In closing, we share 10 guiding questions that should make team meetings more efficient and effective.

1. Why hold the meeting? The answer to this question—or the lack of one—will dictate the need for the meeting.
2. What is the expected outcome? This answer determines the focus of the meeting and acts as a benchmark for the actual outcome.
3. What type of meeting is it? Members should be informed as to whether the meeting is to solve problems, share information, gather data, or make decisions.
4. Based on the type of meeting planned, have the right people been included? The right people with the right information are essential.
5. Has sufficient time been allocated? Assign times for each part of the meeting plan and use the time accordingly.
6. Was an agenda distributed with enough lead time? Participants will be better prepared if the agenda—including start and stop times, a purpose, and desired outcomes—has been distributed far enough ahead of the meeting so they know what to expect.
7. How will the team deal with agenda items? Members need to understand group processes so they can act efficiently and productively.
8. Who does what? The various roles need to be decided and rotated among members.

9. How will decisions be made during the meeting? In a team, every opinion is valued, and teams usually reach a decision through consensus.
10. Who will make the final decision? Everyone should know.[17]

APPLICATIONS

7.1 Form a team with the goal of developing a mission statement for a real or imaginary product or service.

7.2 Develop a model strategy plan for promoting the product or service. Utilize a designated observer to give the team feedback on the process.

7.3 Select a simple problem and practice the techniques of brainstorming described in this chapter.

REFERENCES

1. "Talking with Dr. Charles Garfield About Empowering Your Team," *Working Smart,* June 1992, p. 7.
2. Andrew J. DuBrin, *The Breakthrough Team Player* (New York: AMACON, 1995), pp. 89–99.
3. Thomas R. Harvey and Bonita Drolet, *Building Team Building People* (Lancaster, PA: Techonic Publishing Co., 1994), p. 158.
4. Lionel L. Fray, *How to Develop the Strategic Plan* (Boston: American Management Assoc., 1987), p. 1.
5. Thomas R. King, *Teams and Techniques for World Class Improvement* (Franklin, PA: Thomas R. King, 1996), p. 19.
6. Stephen J. Wall and Shannon Rye Wall, *The New Strategists* (New York: The Free Press, 1995), p. 120.
7. M. Hensey, *Collection Excellence* (New York: American Society of Civil Engineers, 1992), p. 20.
8. I.L. Janis, and L. Mann, "A Theoretical Framework for Decision Counseling," in *Counseling on Personal Decisions*, ed. by I. L. Janis (New Haven, Conn.: Yale Univ. Press, 1982), pp. 47–72.
9. L.M. Wankel and C. Thompson, "Motivating People to be Physically Active: Self-persuasion vs. Balanced Decision Making," *Journal of Applied Social Psychology*, 7 (1977), pp. 332–340.
10. S. Jeromin and E. Kroh-Puschel, "Occupational Choice: Information Behavior in Decision Aids," in *Studies in Decision Making*, ed. by M. Irle (Berlin: de Gruyter, 1985), pp. 737–787.
11. I.L. Janis and L. Mann, "Effectiveness of Emotional Role-playing in Modifying Smoking Habits and Attitudes," *Journal of Experimental Research in Personality*, 1 (1965), pp. 84–90.
12. A.F. Osborn, *Applied Imagination* (New York: Scribner, 1957).
13. S.J. Parnes and A. Meadow, "Effects of Brainstorming Instructions on Creative Problem-Solving by Trained and Untrained Subjects," *Journal of Education and Psychology*, 50 (1959), pp. 171–176; A. Meadows, S.J. Parnes, and H. Reese, "Influence of Brainstorming Instructions and Problem Sequence on a Creative Problem-Solving Test," *Journal of Applied Psychology*, 43 (1959), pp. 413–416; J.K. Brilhart and L.M. Jochem, "Effects of Different Patterns on Outcomes of Problem-Solving Discussion," *Journal of Applied Psychology*, 48 (1964), pp. 175–179.
14. E.M. Balchan, "Group Brainstorming Field Study: Effect on Size, Recording Method, and Task, on Productivity and Participants' Reactions," unpublished doctoral dissertation, University of Michigan, 1980.
15. See, for example, D.W. Taylor, P.C. Berry, and C.H. Block, "Does Group Participation When Using Brainstorming Facilitate or Inhibit Creative Thinking?" in *Problems in Social Psychology*, ed. by C.W. Backman and P.F. Secord (New York: McGraw-Hill, 1966), pp. 299–309.
16. "Hospital Speeds Recovery Time," *USA TODAY*, May 7, 1999, p. 7B.
17. W.H. Schmidt and J.P. Finnigan, *Race Without a Finish Line* (San Francisco: Jossey-Boss, 1992).

8 Leadership in the Quality Group

Scenario

In her first year at college Joanne became a member of a sorority pledge class. This group of young women progressed through college as a cohort group experiencing and sharing many fun activities and sponsoring community-based projects. By the end of her junior year Joanne was recognized as a leader among her peers. As a result, she was nominated to serve as the president of the sorority during her senior year. Joanne was very flattered by the nomination, agreed to run for office, and was elected president of the sorority. Throughout the previous three years Joanne was recognized as a very charismatic individual who was a tireless worker and respected for her innovative ideas and intelligence. However, as an innovator Joanne was also known for not always following the rules defined by the Greek Council or the National Chapter Office. On the other hand, Joanne's vice president, Gail, was a very rules-oriented and detail-driven individual. At times the inevitable occurred when Joanne and Gail would engage in lengthy debates during chapter meetings and executive committee planning sessions. While both of these individuals were highly respected among their peers, the majority of the sorority members sensed tension between Joanne and Gail and often felt frustrated during meetings when protracted arguments occurred between the president and vice president.

The scenario presented is not uncommon. In fact, the context could easily be changed to describe two corporate managers working for a Fortune 500 company. This scenario shows that the enactment of leadership roles are very important to the success of a group, satisfaction of group members, and the quality of group interactions. The concept of leadership has received a great deal of attention in various research disciplines. While a review of more traditional approaches to group leadership is provided in this chapter, we also provide a review of current leadership practices and expectations of leaders in contemporary organizations, especially those companies who have adopted team-based approaches to managing corporations.

Review of Traditional Approaches to Group Leadership

The following sections review several areas of research in group leadership. While many of these studies and approaches to leadership have similarities, each paradigm of thought also makes a unique contribution to our knowledge about group leadership. We also would like to note that although theories of leadership have changed over the past 100 years, several of the original concepts and theories prevail and are still considered relevant in reference to today's approaches to team-based leadership. Therefore, an understanding of the evolution of thought in the area of group leadership is important.

Traditional leadership researchers focused on the attributes, both perceived and actual, of individuals. For example, a group of adults was asked to list the behaviors of effective leaders they had witnessed. The group offered the following list:

- shows knowledge
- is confident
- is analytical
- delegates
- provides structure
- is hardworking
- is energetic
- is honest

- leads by example
- is creative
- is flexible
- provides feedback
- keeps focus on the task
- is group centered
- listens carefully
- is willing to make decisions

How do you respond to this list? Are there other behaviors you would add to the list or ones you feel are suspect?

Scholars and researchers have been extremely interested in the phenomenon of leadership. Bernard M. Bass revised and expanded the *Handbook of Leadership,* originally compiled by Ralph M. Stogdill.[1] This sourcebook summarizes and interprets more than 5,000 books and articles on the dynamics of leadership. It is highly recommended as a reference for exploring in greater detail the rich resources available on this topic; in this chapter we shall merely be able to give an overview of these theories and suggest general findings of the research.

Leaders, like groups, vary in their characteristics. Different situations and circumstances require different functions to be performed if a group is to move closer to its goal. We view leadership as a role that provides for vital group needs by exerting influence toward the attainment of group goals. Leadership, according to this definition, is a process. It is present no matter who the individuals are who are taking leadership roles or what their influence is.

Characteristics of Leaders

What kind of person is most likely to become a leader? A number of researchers have attempted to identify the traits of people who are generally regarded as effective leaders. For example, as long ago as 1915 investigators who were looking at the relationship between leadership and *height* found that executives in insurance companies were on the average taller than subordinates, university presidents were generally taller than presidents of small colleges, and railway presidents were taller than station agents. Such single variable studies are now easily dismissed because of their lack of sophistication. Researchers then turned to internal traits.

Studies of personality traits of leaders indicate that people in leadership roles are more self-confident than other people, are better adjusted, and show greater empathy and interpersonal sensitivity than other people.

> Bass summarizes his analysis of more than 200 studies on traits of leadership as follows: The leader is characterized by a strong drive for responsibility and task completion, vigor and persistence in pursuit of goals, venturesomeness and originality in problem solving, drive to exercise initiation in social situations, self-confidence and sense of personal identity, willingness to accept consequences of decision and action, readiness to absorb interpersonal stress, willingness to tolerate frustration and delay, ability to influence other persons' behavior, and capacity to structure social interaction systems to the purpose at hand.[2]

This evidence that leaders have different traits from nonleaders must be interpreted with caution. Exceptions to all these general trends can be found, and having these traits does not guarantee that a person will assume positions of effective leadership. Causality is also subject to scrutiny. Possibly, if you are elected to a position of leadership, your self-confidence will increase, you will be better adjusted, and you will become more sensitive to others.

In a study of the selection and performance of leaders, researchers at the New Jersey Institute of Technology discovered a high correlation between the number of verbal comments made by a group participant and the participant's anticipation that few or numerous comments indicated leadership potential. In a controlled experiment that allowed the researchers to know in advance the correct answers to a group problem, there was no correlation between the quality of the leader's prediscussion solution and the likelihood of their being selected as a leader. They state: "Thus, we see that it is the relatively verbose person who becomes leader, not the person with the most knowledge about the problem the group would try to solve."[3]

Styles of Leadership

The classic dichotomy of contrasting styles of leadership has been the *authoritarian-democratic*. In an extensive study of groups of children in summer day camps, White and Lippitt were concerned with the effects on productivity and on membership satisfaction of three different styles of leadership, which they called authoritarian, democratic, and laissez-faire.[4] Adult leaders were trained to be proficient in these leadership styles. The distinctions in leaderships are shown in Table 8.1.

TABLE 8.1 Leader Behavior in Three "Social Climates"

Authoritarian	Democratic	Laissez-faire
1. All determination of policy made by leader	1. All policies a matter of group discussion and decision, encouraged and assisted by leader	1. Complete freedom for group or individual decision; minimum of leader participation
2. Techniques and activity steps dictated by the authority, one at a time, so that future steps are always largely uncertain	2. Activity perspective gained during discussion period; general steps to group goal sketched and, when technical advice needed, two or more alternative procedures suggested by leader	2. Leader supplying various materials, making it clear they would supply information when asked, but taking no other part in discussion
3. Particular work task and work companion of each member ususally dictated by leader	3. Members free to work with anyone; division of tasks left up to group	3. Complete nonparticipation of leader
4. Dominator tending to be "personal" in praise and criticism of work of each member; remaining aloof from active group participation except when demonstrating	4. Leader "objective" or "fact minded" in praise or criticism, trying to be regular group member in spirit without doing too much of the work	4. Leader infrequently spontaneously commenting on member activities, unless questioned; no attempt to appraise or regulate course of events

Source: R. White and R. Lippitt, "Leader behavior and member reaction in three 'social climates,'" in *Group Dynamics,* 3rd ed., ed. by D. Cartwright and A. Zander (New York: Harper & Row, 1968), p. 319.

The major results were the following:

1. Democratic leadership led to more and better productivity than did laissez-faire leadership.
2. Autocratic leadership led to more productivity than did democratic leadership over a short period of time (in the long run democratic leadership tends to higher productivity). On the other hand, the quality of work was consistently better in democratic groups, compared with that in autocratic groups.
3. When autocratic leaders were absent, the group tended to "fall apart"; this did not happen in democratic groups.
4. Members of democratic groups were more satisfied than members of laissez-faire groups; most of the members were more satisfied with democratic leadership than with autocratic leadership, although a few were more satisfied under autocratic leaders.

5. There was least absenteeism and fewest dropouts under democratic leadership.

6. Autocratic leadership was characterized either by the greatest incidence of hostility and aggressiveness among members or by the greatest apathy, depending on the group. On the other hand, autocratic groups displayed the least "talking back" to leaders.

Similarly conceived studies have applied similar conceptual schemes to the study of effective supervisory and administrative behavior. The conclusion seems inescapable that, to the extent that group members participate in the making of decisions that affect them, they will have greater productivity and greater satisfaction.[5]

Jack Gibb has equated the authoritarian style with defensive behavior. Defensive leaders believe that the average person cannot be trusted, so their role is to supervise and control. They rely on subterfuge and manipulation through extrinsic rewards. A cycle of fear and distrust is created. As Gibb states:

Defensive leaders use various forms of persuasion to motivate subordinates toward the organization of goals, but often the results are either apathy and passivity or frenetic conformity. Persuasion is a form of control and begets resistance, which may take many subtle forms. Open and aggressive cold war between teachers and administrators, for instance, is an obvious form. More common—and less easy to deal with—is passive, often unconscious resistance such as apathy, apparent obtuseness, dependent demands for further and more minute instructions, bumbling, wheelspinning, and a whole variety of inefficiencies that reduce creative work.[6]

As an alternative to such defensive leadership, Gibb suggests:

The key to emergent leadership centers in a high degree of trust and confidence in people. Leaders who trust their colleagues and subordinates and have confidence in them tend to be open and frank, to be permissive in goal setting, and to be noncontrolling in personal style and leadership policy. People with a great deal of self-acceptance and personal security do trust others, do make trust assumptions about their motives and behavior. The self-adequate person tends to assume that others are also adequate and, other things being equal, that they will be responsible, loyal, appropriately work-oriented when work is to be performed, and adequate to carry out jobs that are commensurate with their levels of experience and growth.[7]

An additional factor to consider is an open style of communication. It is suggested that openness thus begets openness. An experiment attempted to determine the effects of different leader verbal styles on group members. Leaders were trained to be either speculative (open) or confrontive. Confrontive-led members perceived their leaders to be charismatic, strong, and powerful and tended to intimidate members during the group's formative stage. In the speculative-led groups, members spoke more and saw their leaders as peers. While the leader style in this experiment had an effect on the group process, no correlation was found with the members' satisfaction scores or the types of leaders on members' self-concept scores.[8]

Situational Leadership

A number of social critics suggest that had World War II not occurred, history would have ignored Winston Churchill. He was considered dogmatic, authoritarian, impatient, and opinionated. In the crisis of war, however, England needed such a leader to inspire the people in a single-minded mission. Thus, these critics believe it was a case of history making the man, rather than of the man making history. This perspective illustrates the *situationist concept*, which posits the view that most people have the potential to serve as leaders if the conditions and circumstances favor their unique talents.

An example of research on this topic was conducted by Arthur Hastorf, who was interested in seeing whether shy, quiet people who are often unnoticed in groups have the potential for leadership.[9] After observing groups of four students discuss a case study (from behind a one-way mirror), the individual whose participation was next to the lowest in each group was selected for the experiment. During the experimental phase the subjects were told that shielded panels in front of each of them would display either a red or a green light, as determined by human relations experts in the observation room. The green light was a signal to talk more, and the red light suggested silence. The shy person was thus able to be encouraged to talk more and the more talkative members encouraged to participate less. As expected, the quiet person's contributions increased substantially.

A subsequent phase of the study dispensed with the lights, and the participants were allowed to talk as much as they pleased. During this final discussion, the new leader did not relinquish his position. This study suggests that most people have some leadership potential and, given the opportunity and encouragement, can learn to take command. As new leaders without experience emerge, people are likely to be skeptical of their potential, but the situationist would predict that the leader will be viewed as more capable after taking leadership.

The best-known proponent of situational leadership effectiveness is Fred E. Fiedler with his *Contingency Model of Leadership*.[10] This model specifies the kind of situation in which a leader with a high LPC (Least Preferred Coworker) score will be more effective than a leader with a low LPC score, and vice versa. The score is obtained by having individuals rate a person using opposite-meaning word pairs (e.g., very neat and not neat), referred to as semantic differential scales. A leader is thus asked to think of the coworker with whom they could work least well. The ratings for each item are scored, using a scale from 1 to 8, and added together. A leader who is quite critical in rating their least preferred coworker will obtain a low LPC score, while a lenient leader will obtain a high LPC score.

From considerable research, Fiedler observed that a high LPC leader tends to have close interpersonal relationships with people and is more person-oriented than task-oriented. The low LPC leader is committed to task objectives, often at the expense of people. The precise behavior of the two types of leaders varies depending on the situation.

In Fiedler's model, the relationship between leader LPC scores and leader effectiveness depends on a complex situational variable with multiple components. The variable is called either *situational favorability* or *situational control,* defined by the extent to which the situation gives a leader influence over subordinate performance. Situational control is usually measured in terms of three aspects:

1. *Leader-member relations.* A leader who has the loyalty and support of the group can rely on members to comply enthusiastically with directions, while a leader who is disliked may have group members ignore directions or subvert policies.
2. *Task structure.* A task is highly structured when a detailed description of the product, service, or goal of the group is available to determine how well the work has been performed. If the task is unstructured, the leader cannot easily determine how well group members are performing.[11]
3. *Position power.* A leader with substantial position power is able to administer rewards and punishments as incentives for compliance, while leaders without such power must rely on other means of influence.

Fiedler has found that leader-member relations are the most important determinant of situational control, followed by task structure and finally by position power. When the situation is either very high or very low in situational control, leaders with low LPC scores will be more effective than leaders with high LPC scores. In the intermediate area, leaders with high LPC scores will be more effective. Fiedler has proposed an explanation for this relationship, suggesting that the particular motive hierarchy of some leaders makes them more likely to use the kind of leadership behavior appropriate for that situation.[12]

Fiedler's model and the methodology of validation studies have been severely criticized in the last few years. Critics suggest that the LPC score is speculative and inadequately supported. The causal links are questionable, without strong justifications for an arbitrary system of weighing variables.[13] The debate continues, and more research is being conducted in an attempt to determine the model's validity and utility.

Task and Maintenance Functions

An early analysis of the leadership duties of business executives made by Barnard in 1938 suggested that two dimensions must be considered: achievement, or the performing of the group task, and efficiency, or keeping the members satisfied.[14] These two dimensions parallel the functions of task and maintenance described in Chapter 2.

The leadership functions related to task accomplishment include helping set and clarify goals, focusing on information needed, drawing on available group resources, stimulating research, maintaining orderly operating procedures, introducing suggestions when they are needed, establishing an atmosphere that permits testing, rigorously evaluating ideas, devoting oneself to the task, attending to the clock and the schedule, pulling the group together for consensus or patterns of action, and enabling the group to determine and evaluate its progress. The group maintenance functions of leadership include encouraging participation by everyone in the group, keeping everyone in a friendly mood, responding to the emotional concerns of group members when appropriate, promoting open communication, listening attentively to all contributions, encouraging with positive feedback, showing enthusiasm and good humor, promoting pride in the group, judging accurately the changing moods of the group, and providing productive outlets for tensions.

The performance of both task and maintenance roles, then, is essential if a group is to move toward its goal. These roles are constantly being filled, adequately or inadequately, through the participation of group members. To some degree, therefore, all good members help in fulfilling these necessary leadership roles.

Robert Blake and his associates refined the theoretical view of leadership as it relates to managerial behavior in industry with the Managerial Grid.[15] This grid contains two dimensions, concern for people and concern for task accomplishment. On the basis of questionnaire surveys and responses to value statements, Blake categorized people as follows: the "bureaucrat," unconcerned with either dimension, people, or tasks; the "country-club manager," interested in people but not in tasks; the "taskmaster," high on tasks but low on people; the firm but fair "compromiser"; and the "ideal," concerned greatly with both tasks and people. Blake believes that it is possible to attain a maximal concern for both production and people simultaneously.

Some task groups are so concerned with what they are doing that they ignore problems of maintenance, sweeping them under the rug. Conversely, other task groups are so concerned with creating a warm, acceptant atmosphere and analyzing personal functioning that they allow the development of frustrations in the area of task accomplishment. Groups need a balance of both task and maintenance functions if they are to be effective. In most groups, especially those with a formal leader, these functions must be assumed by the leader if they are to lead effectively. Failure in either category will give rise to an unofficial or informal leader who takes over neglected roles.

In leaderless groups the two functions are assumed typically by two different people, a "task specialist" and a "maintenance specialist." The task specialist is seen as having the best ideas and plays an aggressive role in moving the group toward a solution of its problems; this person may, however, thereby incur hostility.[16] The maintenance specialist is highly liked and is concerned with solving the socioemotional problems of the group, resolving tensions and conflicts within the group and preserving its unity.[17]

Extending Blake's Managerial Grid model, Hersey and Blanchard developed a situational leadership theory based upon the variable of follower "maturity."[18] Maturity is defined as "the capacity to set high but attainable goals (achievement motivation), willingness to take responsibility, and education and/or experience."[19] Measurement is made regarding a particular task to be performed and may differ

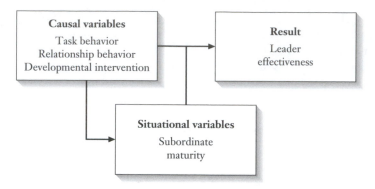

FIGURE 8.1   Causal Relationships in Situational Leadership

from subordinate to subordinate and task to task. According to their theory, as subordinate maturity increases to a moderate level, the leader should use more relationship-oriented behavior and less task-oriented behavior. As subordinate maturity increases further, the leader should decrease the amount of both types of behavior because workers become self-sufficient and require less attention pertaining to relationship and task behaviors.

The causal relationships implied by the theory are shown in Figure 8.1. The leader can alter the maturity level of subordinates by using developmental interventions consisting of reduced directives and delegating greater responsibility. If the subordinate responds positively, the leader reinforces with praise and encouragement. This theory and model has also been seriously criticized in terms of the absence of validation studies and the omission of other significant situational variables.[20] However, it makes a positive contribution with its emphasis on flexible, adaptable leader behaviors.

Research by Sandra Ketrow supports an attributional theory of leadership. She found that people judge as leaders those who match an implicit set of valued leadership behaviors. Subjects in her study chose procedural specialists most often as leaders, but viewed task-oriented specialists as most influential in a small-group decision-making discussion.[21]

Schultz has confirmed that leaders can be predicted based on members' ratings of communication function. Leadership is thus defined by those functions that move a group toward its goals: setting goals, giving directions, and summarizing. Leader competence was determined by actions related to goal setting or direction giving.[22]

Group-Centered Leadership

In contrast to the theories just cited, in which the leader serves to motivate, direct, and evaluate the group's outcome, Bradford contends that better results can be attained through a group-centered approach.[23] According to this view of leadership, the group as a whole must share the responsibility for its effectiveness, and maintenance functions are considered as important as task-oriented functions. Bradford summarizes the contrast between traditional and group-centered leadership as follows:[24]

Traditional Leadership

1. The leader directs, controls, polices the members, and leads them to the proper decision. Basically it is the leader's group, and his/her authority and responsibility are acknowledged by members.
2. The leader focuses their attention on the task to be accomplished, brings the group back from any diverse wandering, and performs all the functions needed to arrive at the proper decision.
3. The leader sets limits and uses rules of order to keep the discussion within strict limits set by the agenda. He/she control the time spent on each item lest the group wander fruitlessly.
4. The leader believes that emotions are disruptive to objective, logical thinking and should be discouraged or suppressed. He/she assume it is their task to make clear to all members the disruptive effect of emotions.
5. The leader believes that they should handle a member's disruptive behavior by talking to the member away from the group; it is the leader's task to do so.
6. Because the need to arrive at a task decision is all-important in the eyes of the leader, the needs of individual members are considered less important.

Group-Centered Leadership

1. The members, including the leader, own the group, or meeting. All members, with the leader's assistance, contribute to its effectiveness.
2. The group is responsible, with occasional and appropriate help from the designated leader, for reaching a decision that includes the participation of all and is the product of all. The leader is a servant and helper of the group.
3. Members of the group should be encouraged and helped to take responsibility for the group's task productivity, its methods of working, its assignment of tasks, and its plans for the use of the time available.
4. Group members and the leader recognize feelings, emotions, and conflict as legitimate facts and situations demanding as serious attention as the task agenda.
5. The leader believes that any problem in the group must be faced and solved within the group and by the group. As trust develops among members, it is much easier for an individual to discover ways in which their behavior is bothering the group.
6. With help and encouragement from the leader, the members come to realize that the needs, feelings, and purposes of all members should be met so that an awareness forms of being a group. Then the group can continue to grow.

Bradford recognizes that group-centered leadership requires considerable skill on the part of both leader and group members. Traditionally oriented leaders may be afraid to risk sharing control or dealing openly with emotions. Even in the absence of strong validation checks under experimental conditions, personal experience leads us to favor and encourage the group-centered approach. While all groups do not have the maturity to employ such an approach, we believe that this style of leadership will promote greater trust and commitment to the group. The interpersonal skills and sensitivity to the well-being of others can be developed if the risks are taken and appropriate time is available.

Leadership Behaviors

In keeping with the task/maintenance functions of leadership, specific leadership behaviors can be identified that enhance the group-centered approach. The following list is a composite drawn from the work of Bales,[25] Bradford,[26] and Benne and Sheats.[27]

Task Orientation

1. *Initiating-structuring:* to present a problem to the group, to propose an objective and get the group's approval, to introduce a procedure for the group to use in solving a problem or making a decision, to develop an agenda listing topics to be discussed and issues to be decided, to suggest that the group is ready to proceed to a different activity, to direct the discussion back to the task after it has wandered off track, to recess or end the meeting.
2. *Stimulating communication:* to seek specific information from group members, to ask members for their opinions, to encourage members to contribute their ideas, to provide specific information yourself.
3. *Clarifying communication:* to reduce confusion or clear up a misunderstanding by asking a member to elaborate what they have said, by restating in a different way what someone has said, by asking a group member how they interpreted another member's comment, by interpreting ideas and defining terms, or by integrating separate ideas to show how they are related.
4. *Summarizing:* to review what has been said or accomplished so far, to review ideas and facts offered during a lengthy period of discussion, to list or post ideas as they are suggested and ask the group to review them.
5. *Consensus testing:* to check on the amount of agreement among group members regarding objectives, interpretation of information, evaluation of different alternatives, and readiness to reach a decision.

Maintenance Orientation

1. *Gatekeeping:* to regulate and facilitate the participation of group members, to suggest ways of increasing participation, to encourage contributions by quiet members and prevent dominant members from monopolizing the discussion.

2. *Harmonizing:* to smooth over conflict between members or mediate it by suggesting compromises, to reduce tension with humor, to ask members to reconcile their differences in a constructive manner, to discourage personal attacks, insults, and threats.

3. *Supporting:* to be friendly and supportive to group members, to be responsive to their needs and feelings, to come to the aid of a member or help the person save face, to show appreciation for the contributions of members.

4. *Standard setting:* to suggest norms and standards of behavior (e.g., objectivity, fairness), to encourage the group to establish norms, to remind the group of norms that it established previously, to point out implicit group norms and check how members really feel about them.

5. *Process analyzing:* to examine group processes in order to identify process problems and dysfunctional member behavior, to point out process problems to the group, to ask members for their perception of the group meetings (e.g., effectiveness of communication, degree of trust, amount of cooperation, effectiveness of procedures, etc.).

Recent Perspectives on Leadership

While prior sections reviewed several theories and concepts pertinent to studying group leadership, the following information outlines some of the contemporary perspectives described in leadership literature and business practices.

Leadership Emergence

Quite often a group leader is appointed by an individual or a governing body. Although the individual appointed may well be the best candidate to lead a group toward the completion of a designated task, the other group members may be "put off" by the imposition of someone as their leader. For example, if the corporate vice presidents chooses a team leader to head up a special task force on diversity in the workplace based solely on an understanding of current labor laws, the other group members may be quite dissatisfied because they know how incredibly insensitive and interculturally inept this person really is. The flaw in this scenario is, at least in part, that aspects other than expert knowledge were not considered when selecting this individual as group leader. Therefore, the group's success may be much improved if the members of the group are permitted to select a leader, from within the specified group, to fulfill this specialized task.

One process outlining the selection of a group leader is referred to as *leadership emergence*. Bormann's study of temporary groups suggests that emergent leadership occurs when "the group selects its leader by the method of residues."[28] Simply stated, this suggests that as the group members become more familiar with each other and continue to work together over time the members will identify who they think can best lead this particular group toward the completion of a specific task. Typically, members will be eliminated one at a time as they either choose not to pursue the leadership role or commit some sort of error, such as violating a significant group norm, and are eliminated by the other group members as a potential leadership candidate. Hackman and Johnson suggest using the following strategies if you want to be considered as an emergent leader:[29]

1. Participate early and often
2. Focus on communication quality as well as quantity
3. Demonstrate your competence
4. Help build a cohesive unit

According to Fisher and Ellis those choosing not to be considered for the leadership role may engage in the following behaviors in order to be eliminated from consideration:[30]

1. Absence from meetings (as often as possible)
2. Contribute little to the conversations
3. State you are willing to do as you are told
4. Be overly assertive or aggressive in the early meetings
5. Volunteer to serve in a support function such as a recording secretary or treasurer
6. Assume the role of a joker or give the impression you are not very serious
7. Act as if you are knowledgeable in all areas
8. Indicate your dislike of leadership roles

While an appointed leader may be very effective, the fact remains that the group may not actually consider them the leader per se because they will defer many leadership tasks to the person they feel is best suited to be the group leader. Trice and Beyer accurately capture the essence of the leadership emergence concept by suggesting: "Emergent leaders are almost automatically likely to be able to influence their groups' cultures because their informal origins mean they already represent group beliefs, values, and norms" and "Emergent leaders thus reflect, amplify, and channel social impulses that arise from their followers and their situations."[31] Thus, if given an option, it may be prudent to allow leaders to naturally emerge from within the group rather than taking the risk of imposing the role upon an individual who may lack either enthusiasm or skills to perform the leadership role in an effective manner.

Principled Leadership

Larson and LaFasto use the term *principled leadership* to describe effective group leaders.[32] They suggest that principled leaders are able to "transform" situations and people to maximize efforts and improve group outcomes. The concept of transformative leadership has been discussed by several management theorists. Three specific factors pertaining to principled leadership are: (1) establishing a vision, (2) creating change, and (3) unleashing talent. Research indicates that the last factor, unleashing talent, suggests that three categories of expectations exist in order to be an effective leader: (1) identification of what the team should expect from the team leader, (2) identification of what the team leader expects from the team members and what the team members expect from each other, and (3) utilization of leadership principles and behaviors that establish a supportive decision making climate and encourage members to take risks. Lastly, principled leaders are individuals who allow others to provide answers and solutions to problems. Thus, the conceptual framework of principled leadership provides additional factors and behaviors to consider implementing in order to be a more effective group or team leader.

Team Leadership

The advent of quality circles (QCs), total quality management (TQM) groups, and continuous quality improvement (CQI) teams as group-based decision-making bodies in business and industry confirms the need to understand how to be a better team leader. Katzenbach and Smith suggest that groups consist of members sharing information, making decisions, and sharing ideas but they are often not evaluated collectively for the work they perform.[33] On the other hand, a team is a group of individuals who are expected to work together to produce some sort of outcome that will be evaluated as a collective effort. Examples of team projects include selecting a new computer software program, hiring committees, and strategic planning groups, to name a few. Research suggests that team decisions, based on a thorough evaluation of information and the utilization of effective decision-making processes, are almost always more effective and produce higher quality outcomes.

Larson and LaFasto suggest that a successful leader will promote the development of team-building skills in order to improve team performance.[34] They identified the following eight strategies, which they feel lead to an enhancement in team performance:

1. Establish clear and inspiring team goals
2. Maintain a results-oriented team structure
3. Assemble competent team members
4. Strive for unified commitment
5. Provide a collaborative climate
6. Encourage standards of excellence
7. Furnish external support and recognition
8. Apply principled leadership

Assuming that these principles are followed, an individual should be a much more effective team leader.

An additional example of effective team leadership is provided by organizations that have incorporated self-directed work teams (SDWTs) into their infrastructure. Basically, a SDWT consists of a group of individuals who are fully responsible for a job (e.g., developing a new product). Thus, this team will consist of people capable of designing, manufacturing, marketing, and distributing a product. This means that not only are these groups self-directed, they are considered to be self-sufficient. In terms of leadership, the members of a SDWT are empowered to perform their jobs and share in the enactment of the leadership role. Therefore, SDWTs encourage and motivate employees to perform up to their potential and also serve as a training ground for future leaders.

Case Study

Upon graduating from college with a degree in Computer Information Systems, Helen is employed by one of the largest computer manufacturing corporations in Silicon Valley. As a new employee Helen is assigned to a design team. The leader of her team, Bob, is very quiet and introspective. Helen finds that she continually must pursue Bob and ask a multitude of questions regarding corporate policies, procedures, performance expectations, etc. Although Bob is the team leader, you, as the Production Manager, suspect that he is not doing a great job as the team leader. After three frustrating months of employment, Helen comes to you seeking advice and support.

Questions

1. How would you define Bob as a leader?
2. Has the company done an adequate job selecting leaders? Why or why not?
3. Describe how you think individuals working on Bob's team interact with each other.
4. What might you do to intervene in this situation to improve the effectiveness of the group and enhance the group leadership that you perceive to be missing?
5. How might you determine if there is another individual in this group who might serve as the leader?

Chapter Summary

Leadership is certainly an important consideration in the relative success or failure of any group. In this chapter we have surveyed approaches to the study of leadership by looking at characteristics of effective leaders, styles of leadership, situational and contingency factors, and suggested group-centered leadership as a goal to be pursued.

In essence we concur with Bernard Bass, who summarized his monumental survey of the research and theory on leadership as follows:

The real test of leadership lies not in the personality or behavior of the leaders, but in the performance of the groups they lead. Groups, when free to do so, appear to select as leaders members who create the expectation that they will be able to maintain goal direction, facilitate task achievement, and ensure group cohesiveness. Whether objectives are long-term to develop the group or short-term to maximize current performance will make a decided difference. The behaviors furthering task accomplishment are not necessarily the same as those fostering cohesiveness. Some leaders are extremely effective in furthering task achievement. Others are exceptionally skilled in the art of building member satisfaction and intermember loyalty, which strengthen group cohesiveness. The most valued leaders are able to do both.[35]

Contemporary research has focused on the important process of leadership emergence, principled leadership, and team leadership—distinguishing the difference between groups and teams. As previously mentioned, organizations continue to expect employees to work in groups and on project teams. The ability to fully understand the dynamics and interactions between the members of a group and how best to serve as the leader for any given group will prove invaluable to your career and aspects of your personal life that include working with others to achieve specific goals.

APPLICATIONS

8.1 As a group, identify two prominent leaders in industry or government. Define the predominate leadership style of each individual and provide evidence to support your perceptions.

8.2 Select one person you know, or have known, in a leadership role. Describe how this person enacts their leadership responsibilities during situations that can be considered normal. Compare the aforementioned behavior with this person's response to a crisis situation, in their capacity as a leader.

8.3 From previous experiences in small groups describe how one member of the group emerged as the leader. Be sure to describe the predominant behaviors group members engaged in throughout this leadership emergence process.

REFERENCES

1. B.M. Bass, *Stogdill's Handbook of Leadership* (New York: The Free Press, 1981).

2. Ibid., p. 81.

3. S.R. Hiltz, M. Turoff, and K. Johnson, "The Effects of Human Leadership and Computer Feedback on the Quality of Group Problem Solving Via Computer," paper presented at the International Communication Association, May 1984.

4. R. White and R. Lippitt, "Leader Behavior and Member Reaction in Three Social Climates," in *Group Dynamics*, 3rd ed., ed. by D. Cartwright and A. Zander (New York: Harper & Row, 1968), pp. 318–335.

5. See, for example, K. Giffin and L. Ehrlich, "The Attitudinal Effects of a Group Discussion on a Proposed Change in Company Policy," *Speech Monographs*, 30 (1963), pp. 337–379.

6. J.R. Gibb, "Dynamics of Leadership," *Current Issues in Higher Education*, a publication of the American Association for Higher Education (1967), p. 27.

7. Ibid., p. 31.

8. S. Barlow, W.D. Hansen, A.J. Fuhriman, and R. Finley, "Leader Communication Style-Effects on Members of Small Groups," *Small Group Behavior*, 13, No. 4 (November 1982), pp. 518–531.

9. A.H. Hastorf, "The Reinforcement of Individual Actions in a Group Situation," in *Research in Behavior Modification,* ed. by L. Krasner and L.P. Ullmann (New York: Holt, Rinehart and Winston, 1965).

10. See, for example, F.E. Fiedler, *A Theory of Leadership Effectiveness* (New York: McGraw-Hill, 1967). See also F.E. Fiedler and L. Mahar, "A Field Experiment Validating Contingency Model Leadership Training," *Journal of Applied Psychology,* 64 (1979), pp. 247–254.

11. F.E. Fiedler, "The Contingency Model and the Dynamics of the Leadership Process," in *Advances in Experimental Social Psychology,* ed. by L. Berkowitz (New York: Academic Press, 1978), pp. 62–65.

12. Ibid., pp. 59–112.

13. L.H. Peters, D.D. Hartke, and J.T. Pohlmann, "Fiedler's Contingency Theory of Leadership: An Application of the Meta-analysis Procedures of Schmidt and Hunter," *Psychological Bulletin,* 97 (1985), pp. 275–285.

14. C. Barnard, *The Functions of the Executive* (Cambridge, Mass.: Harvard University Press, 1938).

15. R.R. Blake, J.S. Mouton, and A.C. Bidwell, "The Managerial Grid: A Comparison of Eight Theories of Management," *Advanced Management Office Executive,* 1 (September 1962), pp. 12–16, 36.

16. R.F. Bales, "The Equilibrium Problem in Small Groups," in *Working Papers in the Theory of Action,* ed. by T. Parsons, R.R. Bales, and E.A. Shils (Glencoe, Ill.: Free Press, 1953).

17. J.W. Thibaut and H.H. Kelley, *The Social Psychology of Groups* (New York: Wiley, 1959).

18. P. Hersey and K.H. Blanchard, *Management of Organizational Behavior* (Englewood Cliffs, N.J.: Prentice-Hall, 1977).

19. Ibid., p. 161.

20. G.A. Yukl, *Leadership in Organizations* (Englewood Cliffs, N.J.: Prentice-Hall, 1981), pp. 143–144.

21. S.M. Ketrow, "Valued Leadership Behaviors and Perceptions of Contribution," paper presented at the Speech Communication Association, San Francisco, November 1983.

22. B. Schultz, "Predicting Emergent Leaders: An Exploratory Study of the Salience of Communicative functions," *Small Group Behavior,* 9, No. 1 (1978), pp. 109–114.

23. L.P. Bradford, *Making Meetings Work* (La Jolla, Calif.: University Associates, 1976).

24. Ibid., p. 13.

25. R.F. Bales, *Interaction Process Analysis* (Reading, Mass.: Addison-Wesley, 1950).

26. Bradford, *Making Meetings Work.*

27. K.D. Benne and P. Sheats, "Functional Roles of Groups Members," *Journal of Social Issues,* 4 (1948), pp. 41–49.

28. E. Bormann, *Discussion and Group Methods: Theory and Practice* (New York: Harper and Row, 1975).

29. M.Z. Hackman and C.E. Johnson, *Leadership: A Communication Perspective* (Prospect Heights, IL: Waveland, 1996).

30. B.A. Fisher and D.G. Ellis. *Small Group Decision Making,* 3rd ed. (New York: McGraw-Hill, 1990).

31. H.M. Trice and J.M. Beyer, *The Cultures of Work Organizations* (Englewood Cliffs, N.J.: Prentice Hall, 1993), p. 289.

32. C.E. Larson and F. M. LaFasto, *Teamwork: What Must Go Right/What Can Go Wrong* (Newbury Park, CA: Sage, 1989), p. 123.

33. J.R. Katzenbach and D.K. Smith. "The Discipline of Teams," *Harvard Business Review* (March-April, 1993), pp. 111–120; J.R. Katzenbach and D.K. Smith, "The Wisdom of Teams" (Boston: Harvard Business School Press, 1993).

34. Larson & LaFasto, *Teamwork.*

35. Bass, *Stogdill's Handbook of Leadership,* p. 598.

ADDITIONAL REFERENCES

1. W. Bennis and B. Nanus, *Leaders: The Strategies for Taking Charge* (New York: Harper and Row, 1985).

2. K.J. Gergen and M.M. Gergen, *Social Psychology* (New York: Harcourt Brace Jovanovich, 1981).

3. C.A. Gibb, "Leadership," in *The Handbook of Social Psychology,* ed. by G. Lindzey and E. Aronson (Reading, Mass.: Addison-Wesley, 1969).

9 Using Technology in the Quality Group

Scenario

The immediate need to meet and discuss a new marketing strategy for the sale of products over the Internet was crucial for the sales managers of an international software company. However, the ability to convene a meeting with everyone in the same room was impossible since each of the managers works in a facility located in a different state. The solution is to convene a meeting using teleconferencing. The result was a meeting that could be arranged within hours and conducted in less than one hour. Although this meeting was short, the decisions made allowed this company to develop a new marketing plan. This new marketing plan proved successful, increasing sales of software on the Internet by 40 percent.

The scenario described above is not uncommon. In fact, quite often during each working day people use various mediated technologies to meet and share ideas despite the fact that they may be in varying locations, even dispersed throughout the world. Technologies such as e-mail, teleconferencing, and desktop videoconferencing are a few of the mediums that will be discussed in this chapter.

While we feel compelled to note that current technologies mentioned in this chapter will most likely be vastly improved or become outdated or obsolete shortly after this book is published, we have provided a typology describing the technologies commonly used to facilitate mediated group interactions. The three basic domains of technology used are: (1) visual-based technologies, (2) audio-based technologies, and (3) text-based technologies. Visual-based technologies include desktop videoconferencing, a well-established medium that typically does not provide the highest quality of audio and video outputs but has proved to be quite functional. A newer visual-based technology is IP Video, capable of providing real-time digital signals of a much higher quality than desktop videoconferencing systems. Audio-based communications systems have proved to be quite reliable, using existing telecommunications networks as the medium for teleconferences between members of a group or task force. The obvious detractor to audio teleconferencing is the absence of visual signals and nonverbal cues of the group members during an interaction. The third category of technology-based interaction systems, text-based technologies, simply provides group members opportunities to share ideas and data with e-mail messages, bulletin boards, and chat rooms (to name a few examples). Obviously, text-based technologies present limited interaction abilities for discussion participants, with the exception of providing an opportunity to carefully and critically analyze the text of each individuals' comments while participating in a discussion session. Although at times it may not be critical for discussion participants to have an opportunity to see or hear the nonverbal cues of their fellow group members, the ability to do so often yields a higher quality interaction. Conceptually, visual-based technologies provide the discussants with a more "media rich" interaction. To summarize, the decision to use a particular technology system to facilitate group interactions is often dependent on the availability of each of these systems and the ability to sustain the usage costs for each type of technology. Lastly, group members must learn to adapt to the technology used to facilitate interaction in order to assure that the use of these mediums does not detract from the quality of the interaction or the decisions reached by the group.

The ability to use technology to facilitate meetings when individuals are unable to meet face-to-face is important in today's working world. One factor to consider is that the use of mediated technologies to convene a meeting reduces, to some degree, the amount of human contact that people have during group discussions and decision-making processes. To date, despite advanced technologies used to interact in the business world, it is inevitable that some portion of the human contact and dimensions of interpersonal communication will be compromised with reliance on mediated technologies. However, the loss of human contact is offset by the conveniences afforded to individuals using such technologies to facilitate and expedite the constant and immediate transactions of ideas in order to make decisions on a day-to-day basis.

The Advent of New Technologies

New technologies developed over the last 25 years have significantly changed how people in groups communicate. Examples of such technologies include e-mail, voice mail, computer bulletin boards and computer conferencing (e.g., chat rooms), desktop video teleconferencing, interactive TV, IP video, intranets within organizations, and the internet and Web-based communication networks. While each of these technologies have varying attributes, they all facilitate communication between individuals and individuals in groups despite the fact that each person may be in a different location, including states or countries. In fact, each of the aforementioned technologies facilitates timely communication between individuals.

One fact remains true regardless of the medium used to communicate: the message itself will be modified in comparison to face-to-face communications. The reduction or elimination of face-to-face communication reduces or eliminates the existence of nonverbal communication. Given that scholars such as Mehrabian suggest that nonverbal communication provides as much information, if not more, than the verbal message being communicated by an individual, the reduction or elimination of the nonverbal component of a message can be a significant detractor to accurately understand the message being conveyed.[1] Rice suggests that, dependent on the medium of communication used, varying levels of communication cues will be present while Walther suggests that without the presence of nonverbal cues it is difficult for group members to initially form impressions of each other, although over time members of computer-mediated groups gradually developed impressions of each other that nearly equate to the impressions formed in face-to-face groups.[2,3] Another factor to take into consideration is that text-based messages can easily be edited prior to sending them, while responses to messages in a face-to-face communication interaction are immediate and unable to be edited. In fact, Adkins and Brashers suggest "In a computer-mediated environment, language is especially important because the information exchange process is conversational, yet a sender can only encode a textual message."[4] Therefore, the presence of nonverbal messages adds dimensions of communication that provide additional meaning to messages conveyed from other individuals. However, it should be noted that while communication within the group is mediated, researchers such as Straus and McGrath have found little difference in the quality of communication between computer-mediated and face-to-face groups.[5]

Developing Effective Communication Networks

Several researchers in the 1980s began to investigate the impact that mediated communication has in the workplace.[6,7] Rice and Love suggest that we must continue to investigate how to develop and maintain relationships with others while using mediated communication technologies.[8] Berge recognizes that electronic discussion groups are playing an increasingly more important role in communication and decision-making processes in organizations. In fact, Berge suggests that electronic discussion groups assist group members in retrieving and exchanging information, bring individuals together to share ideas regardless of geographic difference, and have the potential to eliminate constraints dictated by attempts to schedule face-to-face meetings.[9] Despite what we currently know about the effects of mediated communication in group contexts, further research needs to be conducted in order to identify what constitutes quality communication in mediated groups.

Traditional groups meeting face-to-face typically consist of 20 percent of the participants doing 80 percent of the talking due to intimidation, apprehension, or status differentials between people in the group.[10] With the use of technology all group members have equal participation rights and status differentials are reduced to a minimum, encouraging all group members to participate on an equal basis.[11] In fact, Adrianson and Hjelmquist found that face-to-face communication in groups tends to yield higher levels of conformity and opinion change than communication in computer mediated groups.[12] Research by Adkins and Brashers suggests that individuals using powerful language—defined as being assertive and avoiding qualifier statements such as "don't you agree?"—are perceived as higher in credibility, attraction, and persuasiveness.[13] Thus, the use of language, rather than perceptions of an individual based on face-to-face interactions, becomes a significant predictor for the impact an individual's contribution to a decision-making process can have on other group participants.

Mediated decision-making groups are often described as being quite different from face-to-face decision-making groups in terms of interaction patterns and group productivity. In terms of interaction patterns group members are not required to take turns when ideas are being shared asynchronously, meaning that the discussion and sharing of ideas between individuals does not occur simultaneously, and ideas are shared without any interruptions.[14] Also, group members' ideas can be chronicled for everyone to read at a later point in time. The fact that everyone's comments and ideas are available for review may lead to a reduction in responses due to a fear of being negatively evaluated. The fact that typing information takes additional time to create and share new ideas also may be a detractor to group members fully sharing their ideas in mediated group decision-making activities. On a more positive note, mediated group discussions often have the ability to remove an individual's status from the process, thus encouraging all members to communicate on an equal basis and hopefully avoiding such negative factors as groupthink.[15] Furthermore, if given sufficient time for discussion, research suggests that mediated discussion groups will reach consensus.[16]

Effective communication networks suggest that certain premises of quality communication will be adopted while communicating electronically in a small group context. Theoretically, we assume that individuals communicating in a group context have adopted some of the principles of systems theory as fail-safe mechanisms designed to reduce miscommunication. Two systems theory concepts pertinent to effective communication in groups are *openness* and *interdependence*. Openness suggests that the individuals within the group will freely share ideas and perspectives pertaining to the topics being discussed at any given time. The concept of interdependence pertains to mediated discussion groups because in order for groups to systemically make the best decisions all of the individuals involved need to work with each other, being dependent on the other group members to contribute ideas based upon varying perspectives and areas of expertise. Grenier and Metes provide the following quote, which underscores the importance of working together on group projects despite working in a distributed network context:

> In the new work model, professionals had to share data even if they were incomplete and not as good as they would be if "we only had a few more days (weeks, months) to work on it." People had to remain convinced that their reputations and credibility would not suffer because, in the interest of sharing early, they released incomplete or erroneous data.[17]

Also, simple interaction rules should be adhered to, such as clarifying that everyone is in agreement by consistently restating and reconfirming decisions before they are implemented.

Technically speaking, mediated discussion groups will also be more effective if the communication network/medium being used is user-friendly, efficient, and individuals are easily accessible via the creation of user groups, such as listservs, in order to expedite the dissemination of information and ideas pertinent to the decision-making process. Furthermore, Sharples suggests that we should consider how the medium of communication affects the quality of work life; assuming the impact is positive, the adoption and use of technology will become widespread.[18]

Technology and Mediated Instruction

The use of mediated communication has become increasingly widespread over the past 20 years. Instruction has been presented to students in traditional classrooms and corporate learning environments via televised instruction, videotaped lectures, networked video conferencing, computer instruction, and Web-based instruction, to name a few formats. Each of these technologies have varying strengths in terms of presentation formats and the quality of instruction provided to the learners. Currently, the trend is to use computers as the medium for instruction, often including decision-making activities as one of the learning exercises. Although much of the research has been conducted in college classrooms, the results of numerous studies also pertain to corporate education and training environments.

A common outcome of contemporary learning experiences includes using a computer to interact with peers and the instructor of a course in a variety of learning contexts, giving students the opportunity to share ideas and decision-making processes.[19] As early as 1989 Phillips and Santoro report adapting a traditional group discussion course to incorporate computer-mediated communication.[20] The course was offered to over 500 students across four consecutive semesters. Using this format of instruction it was found that students contacted their professors more often and evaluated these courses with high approval ratings. In terms of group productivity, demonstrated learning by students in the mediated course equaled or exceeded students in traditionally taught courses. Although Phillips and Santoro recognize that the use of computer-mediated instruction does have shortcomings, this teaching and learning format was adopted as a regular component of their campus curriculum.[21]

Bresler suggests that computer-mediated communication (CMC) is a medium that affords students the opportunity to express themselves differently than they do using other modes of communication.[22] CMC is recognized as a gratifying activity for students to engage in because they have the unique opportunity to be heard and have their ideas recognized with feedback from peers and learning cohorts. During a mediated group discussion activity students will typically respond to the comments from a peer when they feel it is appropriate to comment. Furthermore, it has been suggested that CMCs "democratize" discussions between individuals by allowing both bright and slow students an equal opportunity to compose a response and be recognized for the contributions they make throughout the process of interacting as a group in order to complete projects and assignments.

Santoro recognizes that individuals can use interactive messaging as a form of synchronous communication, often referred to as a "chat" function or discussion.[23] In this case all parties communicating must be on-line at the same time allowing all individuals access to a client server so they can simultaneously communicate. Although individuals often use "chat rooms" for recreational purposes, individuals in task-oriented groups can also use this technology to simultaneously share ideas with each other on the Internet. Groups using chat rooms or similar means of technology are often referred to as individuals interacting with the assistance of a Group Decision Support System (GDSS). Groups using GDSS have shown to be quite effective in achieving their goals via vigilant interactive decision-making processes.

Face-to-face groups have been compared to computer-mediated task groups in various research studies.[24] Results suggest that computer-mediated groups focus more on the task at hand than groups meeting face-to-face. This may be interpreted as those meeting face-to-face have more opportunities to become distracted during the group interaction process. Additionally, CMC groups have been found to produce more decisions than their counterpart face-to-face groups.[25] Lea and Spears suggest that in order to reduce miscommunication between individuals communicating electronically participants should not be anonymous or isolated from each other.[26] The ownership of an individual's ideas has an impact on the input they make and the accuracy of that input. In fact, although researchers initially suspected that the use of mediated communication would lack a relational dimension, evidence has been found that users adapt and develop their own "language" of social and emotional expressions. Thus, the theory that a lack of nonverbal cues will diminish the effectiveness of mediated communication has not been supported. For instance, using an exclamation point at the end of a message is considered raising your voice slightly, from a textual analysis perspective, and writing a message in all capital letters followed by an exclamation point is considered the equivalent to screaming or yelling out a response. The development and utilization of such text-based cues allows individuals the opportunity to emphatically present their ideas using mediated channels of communication. Overuse or excessive use of text-based cues in electronic communication is referred to as flaming. Some e-mail users are quite offended by this behavior and will let the author of such messages know that their communication has been rude or offensive.

The impact of technology on the learning process has also been well documented. Hiltz studied the virtual classroom, defined as a learning environment with enhanced software programs that allows students to engage in collaborative learning activities.[27] Students reported that the use of a virtual classroom provided them better access to educational activities and was, overall, a better mode of instruction in terms of learning. A similar study by Gregor and Cuskelly studied the use of a bulletin board and e-mail as a communication medium to discuss case study group exercises in graduate courses.[28] A significant majority of these students (80 percent) felt that e-mail was a very helpful tool for their learning experiences, that it seemed to make their instructor more accessible, and that they prefer to use e-mail as a communication medium for future studies. However, with this group they report social interaction among the students and between the students and the instructor as low, an outcome opposite to most research accounts of e-mail use in an educational context.

Research by McComb suggests that modes of mediated instruction, specifically CMCs, have the potential to extend learning outside of the classroom by making instructors and outside expert resources more readily available.[29] McComb's research also confirms that the use of mediated communication fosters the development of caring relationships between students and instructors. Lastly, computer-mediated communication provides students with an opportunity to equalize control and power in learning relationships that they develop with their peer learners. Thus, students are encouraged to take initiative and increase control and responsibility for their own communication and participation in learning activities. This outcome is considered outstanding because it teaches young adults to be responsible for the contributions they make to work or school-related projects. Therefore, the utilization of mediated modes of communication appears to have had a significantly positive outcome on the learning opportunities for students in both graduate and undergraduate classrooms.

Case Study

Within the state university system there are 11 separate institutions, each with Schools of Business. In recent years applications to the MBA programs at these institutions have dwindled, in part, due to the strong U.S. economy as well as the economic decline in several of the Asian nations. For the past year the deans of each Business School, and their respective department chairs, have been discussing this problem and various potential solutions. However, despite several meetings none of these Schools of Business developed a solution to this problem. In frustration, one of the deans decided to host a teleconference including representatives from each institution.

Although all of those involved in the discussion agreed that a serious problem existed, a solution had not been reached. In fact, the drop in enrollments nationwide was discussed quite often at national and regional conferences. Prior to the teleconference each dean was asked to develop and submit potential solutions to this problem. Unfortunately, all of the Schools did not provide ideas or potential solutions to the problem prior to this electronic meeting. Therefore, without a response from each institution it became apparent that not all of the Schools were equally committed to resolving this problem.

The dean whose idea it was to convene the meeting served as the facilitator for this discussion session. During the teleconference it became apparent that a consensus could not be reached. The participants did agree on three potential solutions during the allotted time for the teleconference. However, the participants decided to divide into three groups and continue these interactions using bulletin board discussion groups, e-mail, and teleconferences. Three months after the initial teleconference the group as a whole had not yet reconvened.

Questions

1. How should this group reconvene, as a whole, in order to reach a solution to this problem?
2. What should the participants do in order to reach a consensus?

Chapter Summary

While high quality decisions have traditionally been made by groups of individuals meeting face-to-face, contemporary practices have continually become more reliant on the use of varying technologies as the medium to facilitate group interactions. Although the reliance upon technology will inevitably continue, current technologies are still incapable of fully simulating face-to-face communication between individuals. For example, it is difficult to fully comprehend the nonverbal cues of individuals during mediated interactions. These nonverbal communication cues complement what an individual communicates verbally and often serve as more accurate indicators of a person's attitudes and intentions.

Despite some obvious shortcomings, Santoro suggests that the use of computer-mediated communication has transformed the way countless people work, learn, and exchange ideas.[30] It has been suggested that as many as 13 million people in 1993 telecommuted to work via a computer network on at least a part-time basis. In fact, the federal government has encouraged businesses to allow their employees the opportunity to telecommute, whenever possible and practical to the nature of business being conducted. National trends indicate that the number of telecommuters has continually increased since 1993, assuming that the individuals being offered the opportunity to telecommute have the discipline to work in an environment with little or no structure and supervision.

Given the constant upgrades of existing technologies and the perpetual onslaught of innovative technological developments, our society should anticipate that the use and reliance upon mediated modes of communication will continually increase. To date, individuals and groups have adapted to the use of these technologically enhanced modes of communication. However, the need for continued studies and corrective actions are pertinent to assure that processes such as group decision making continue to be enhanced by the utilization of technology-based assistive devices. One of the most important factors to attend to is the attempt to humanize interaction between individuals in order to maintain an effective domain during interactions that are technologically mediated. Despite any negative factors attributed to mediated communication, the fact remains that the use of technology, assuming it is used correctly, has the potential to significantly enhance group interaction-opportunities and decision-making skills.

APPLICATIONS

9.1 As a group, create a question to discuss on-line. Engage in an "electronic discussion" in order to reach a consensual decision. Afterward, meet face-to-face to discuss differences in the on-line decision-making process in comparison to face-to-face interactions.

9.2 Discuss how the reduction of nonverbal cues available for interpretation during face-to-face discussion might impact individuals engaging in on-line or mediated discussions. How might individuals and groups offset the reduction of nonverbal cues in order to assure decisions made are high in quality?

9.3 Discuss how technology has been infused into current learning curriculums. How has technology changed learning processes and instructional activities?

REFERENCES

1. A. Mehrabian, *Silent messages: Implicit communication of emotions and attitudes* (Belmont, CA: Wadsworth, 1981).

2. R.E. Rice, "Computer-mediated Communication and Organizational Innovation," *Journal of Communication*, 37 (1987), pp. 65–94.

3. J.B. Walther, "Impression Development in Computer-mediated Interaction," *Western Journal of Communication*, 57 (1993), pp. 381–398.

4. M. Adkins and D.E. Brashers, "The Power of Language in Computer-mediated Groups," *Management Communication Quarterly*, 8 (1995), p. 289.

5. S.G. Straus and J.E. McGrath, "Does the Medium Matter? The Interaction of Task Type and Technology on Group Performance and Member Reactions," *Journal of Applied Psychology*, 79 (1994), pp. 87–97.

6. S. Kiesler, J. Siegel, and T.W. McGuire, "Social Psychology Aspects of Computer-mediated Communication," *American Psychologist*, 39 (1984), pp. 1123–1134.

7. J. Siegel, V. Dubrovsky, S. Kiesler, and T. McGuire, "Group Processes in Computer-mediated Communication," *Organizational Behavior and Human Decision Processes*, 37 (1986), pp. 157–187.

8. R.E. Rice and G. Love, "Electronic Emotion," *Communication Research*, 14 (1987), pp. 85–108.

9. Z.L. Berge, "Electronic Discussion Groups," *Communication Education*, 43 (1994), pp. 102–111.

10. D. Kirkpatrick, "Here Comes the Payoff from PCS," *Fortune*, 1992, March 23, pp. 93–102.

11. J. Nunamaker, A.R. Dennis, J.S. Valacich, D.R. Vogel, and J.F. George, "Electronic Meeting Systems to Support Group Work," *Communications of the ACM*, 34 (1991), pp. 40–61.

12. L. Adrianson and E. Hjelmquist, "Group Processes in Face-to-face and Computer-mediated Communication," *Behaviour and Information Technology*, 10 (1991), pp. 281–296.

13. Ibid., "The Power of Language in Computer-mediated Groups."

14. Ibid., "Group Processes in Computer-mediated Communication."

15. S. Barnes and L.M. Greller, "Computer-mediated Communication in the Organization," *Communication Education*, 43 (1994), pp. 129–142.

16. B.A. Olaniran, "Group Performance in Computer-mediated and Face-to-face Communication Media," *Management Communication Quarterly*, 7 (1994), pp. 256–281.

17. R. Grenier and G. Metes, *Enterprise Networking: Working Together Apart* (Bedford, MA: Digital Press, 1992), p. 199.

18. M. Sharples, "A Study of Breakdowns and Repairs in a Computer-mediated Communi-

cation System," *Interacting-With-Computers*, 5 (1993), pp. 61–77.

19. S.A. Kuehn, "Computer-mediated Communication in Instructional Settings: A Research Agenda," *Communication Education*, 43 (1994), pp. 171–183.

20. G.M. Phillips and G.M. Santoro, "Teaching Group Discussion Via Computer-mediated Communication," *Communication Education*, 38 (1989), pp. 151–161.

21. Ibid.

22. L. Bresler, "Student perceptions of CMC: Roles and experiences: II," *Journal of Mathematical Behavior*, 9 (1990), pp. 291–307.

23. G.M. Santoro, "The Internet: An Overview," *Communication Education*, 43 (1994), pp. 73–86.

24. S.R. Hiltz, K. Johnson, and M. Turoff, "Experiments in Group Decision Making: Communication Process and Outcome in Face-to-Face Versus Computerized Conferences," *Human Communication Research*, 13 (1986), pp. 225–252.

25. J.S. Valacich, D. Paranka, J.F. George, and J.F. Nunamaker, "Communication Concurrency and the New Media: A New Dimension for Media Richness," *Communication Research*, 20 (1993), pp. 249–276.

26. M. Lea and R. Spears, "Computer-mediated Communication, De-individuation and Group Decision-making," *International Journal of Man-Machine Studies*, 34 (1991), pp. 283–301.

27. S.R. Hiltz, "Correlates of Learning in a Virtual Classroom," *International Journal of Man-Machine Studies*, 39 (1993), pp. 71–98.

28. S.D. Gregor and E.F. Cuskelly, "Computer Mediated Communication in Distance Education," *Journal of Computer Assisted Learning*, 10 (1994), pp. 168–181.

29. M. McComb, "Benefits of Computer-mediated Communication in College Courses," *Communication Education*, 43 (1994), pp. 159–170.

CHAPTER

10 Process Measures of the Quality Group

Scenario

As Ed walks into the meeting, a sensor at the door scans the information on his name tag and transmits it to a computer that provides a readout on a large monitor at the front of the room. Numbers on the readout advance steadily like a taximeter, calculating the cost per minute of each participant's time. With 10 people present and each earning on average $45,000 a year, the meeting is costing about $300 an hour. With such meetings costing thousands of dollars in personnel costs, is it any wonder that companies are asking whether these investments are worth it?

In this chapter we shall examine ways to determine if the group processes and outcomes of the meeting can be measured in ways that provide answers to this question.

Benchmarking

Drawn from Asian practices, quality performance has relied heavily upon the practice of "benchmarking." David T. Kearns, the CEO of Xerox, has defined benchmarking as: "The continuous process of measuring products, services, and practices against the toughest competitors or those companies recognized as industry leaders."[1]

Drawn from the term for a surveyor's reference point, benchmarking serves as the standard against which a company or a group can be measured. This business practice can be adapted to the group process as we choose activities and outcomes to measure.

Types of Benchmarking

Consider how we unconsciously benchmark in our everyday lives. Suppose something bad happens to you, such as failing a test. What do you do? Many students will look around to find someone else who has had a similar experience. What did they do in the course to improve and cope? Others will look to successful models: students who did well on the test. What did they do differently that helped them succeed?

For members of a group, the essence of benchmarking is to assess their own situation, identify comparable groups that are dealing with similar problems or tasks, find out what they are doing, and use these groups as a basis to determine if the original group can improve its processes.

There are generally four types of groups that can be identified for benchmarking:

1. Internal benchmarking analyzes existing practices *within the group.* Having someone serve as an outside observer of the group can assist in the collection of data regarding process. Internal questionnaires can identify feelings such as satisfaction, degrees of involvement, and perceptions of the group.
2. Comparison benchmarking looks externally to identify how other *similar groups* are performing. Observations of such groups with agreed on targets of key elements in the process can provide interpretation data. If the observed group is willing to cooperate, questionnaires may also be employed.
3. Outstanding groups may be identified as *models.* Just as industries look for the "best-in-the-class," a group may also identify a group to be emulated. Such groups may provide insights on ways to achieve better results.
4. *Normative* benchmarking may be secured from the body of literature on groups. Many measures of group process have established normative indices that can let you know how a group compares to other groups "on the average." Leadership functions, participant roles, and interpersonal behaviors can be coded and analyzed.[2] One such useful instrument is the Interaction Process Analysis developed by Robert Bales.

Steps in the Benchmarking Process

The benchmarking process is designed to ascertain how "we" compare to another group. The following steps provide a logical sequencing:

1. The group must determine what factors are desired for the comparison. There are so many variables in the interaction of any group, that strategies decisions must be made to focus on elements that are deemed most significant.
2. The type of benchmarking, as discussed in the previous section, must be identified. With what group or groups do we wish to compare?
3. Data is collected for which the benchmarking comparisons will be made. Observation charts, interviews, surveys, and questionnaires are among the tools that you may choose to utilize.
4. The data is analyzed, and a report is formulated focusing on the key findings.
5. Based on the findings, the original group should establish goals and objectives that can lead to improvement.[3]

Teachers routinely divide classes into small groups of five to seven students, asking each group to observe an on-going, outside-of-campus, or community, group in action. This assignment means that students must attend routine "business" meetings in which problems are discussed and decisions made.

Observing Group Behavior

It is not always easy to interpret observed behavior, even when the data gathered are fairly specific; frequently, it appears that more than one interpretation is reasonable. For this reason, after our student groups have observed and collected data on their out-of-class groups we require them to present a report to the entire class and discuss their interpretations with their fellow students. We request the following five items be covered in these reports:

1. A brief description of the nature (goals, memberships, special regulations) of the observed group.
2. Identification of some aspect of group problem-solving interaction that can be improved (occasionally our students observe a group that, in their opinion, does everything very well).
3. Evidence (data) to support point 2.
4. Specific learning derived from the observed group.
5. Support from established authorities in the field or from published research that provides creditability for their recommendations (point 4).

In Chapter 4 we discussed the task and maintenance orientation of people in groups and the impact of their behavior. As groups are systematically observed, these categories of behaviors can provide focus for the data gathered.

Task-Oriented Behavior

A. Lack of Identification of Group Task or Problem
   1. Lack of mutual concern—or lack of any concern
   2. Inability to overcome confusion regarding group task, or problem
B. Inability to Analyze a Problem
   1. Failure to compare what *is* with what is *desired*
   2. Lack of information on *causes* of a problem (i.e., forces increasing need for a change from status quo)
   3. Lack of information on *restraining* forces (i.e., forces resisting desired change)
   4. General lack of factual information regarding a problem (i.e., too much reliance on unverified opinions, guesses, suppositions, etc.)
C. Inability to Evaluate Proposals
   1. Lack of identification of possible solutions (i.e., inexperience in area; lack of creative thinking)
   2. Poor identification of criteria by which the group could evaluate various proposals: (a) Does it meet the problem as analyzed by group? (b) Is there any evidence it could really work? (c) Are there any serious disadvantages (e.g., costly, or dangerous)?
   3. Inability to agree on the best possible solution
D. Inability to Implement Group Decision when Reached
   1. Inability to sort and allocate relevant group resources

2. Inability to agree on individual group members' responsibilities
3. Inability to persuade others (outside the group) to give support, approval, assistance, etc.

Interpersonal Behaviors

A. Interpersonal Needs Not Met
  1. Personal needs for inclusion not met, poor spread of participation
  2. Severely competitive orientations (e.g., excessive need to dominate others)
  3. Need not met for personal consideration, caring, or regard
B. Group Member Confusion on Role Functions
  1. Inability to agree on who can perform needed leadership functions
  2. Poor relationship between member's personality and role requirements
  3. Lack of consideration of one another's feelings
  4. Inappropriate, or ineffective, attempts to perform leadership functions
C. Difficulties Caused by Personal Characteristics
  1. Lack of attractiveness of group members for each other
  2. Lack of cohesiveness of status, or prestige of group
  3. Dysfunctional group norms (e.g., tardiness, absenteeism, all talk at once, discourtesy, etc.)
  4. Disagreement concerning individual's status, or power (perhaps power struggle is evident)
  5. General apathy (e.g., poor motivation on part of members to be helpful to each other)
  6. Size of group—either too small or too large
D. Inability to Handle or Resolve Conflict
  1. Inability to separate (a) honest disagreement on problem, or value of a possible solution, from (b) interpersonal dislike
  2. Inability to handle cognitive dissonance (e.g., inability to be comfortable with honest, reasonable disagreement on problem or task issues)
  3. Inability to produce attitude congruence through communication

Process Analysis

In addition to observing behaviors demonstrated in a group, data may be gathered regarding the impressions, feelings, and orientation of the participants in the group process. Self-reports by participants and observations of a group by an outsider can provide insights to group quality.

Self-Reporting

One way to assess the effectiveness of a group is to ask the members directly how they think they are doing. Although subjective, such data provides an interpersonal index of feelings and opinions. Rating sides can help in pinpointing areas of strength as well as areas of weakness; benchmarking can also be utilized.

The Interpersonal Perception Scale (IPS) can be used to compare one's self-perception with the perceptions of others, and can serve as a check on the degree to which an individual's needs are being met by the group.[4]

Interpersonal Perception Scale (IPS)

The questions listed below refer to the group interaction experience in which you have just participated. The other members of the group will be interested in knowing how you perceive them, and you will be interested in knowing how they perceive you. Please answer the questions as carefully and honestly as possible using the following response format.

Very Little	*Little*	*Average*	*Much*	*Very Much*
1	*2*	*3*	*4*	*5*

1. To what extent does this person *indicate willingness to let others interact with them*?
Circle your response: 1 2 3 4 5

2. To what extent does this person *show a need to interact with others*?
Circle your response: 1 2 3 4 5

3. To what extent does this person *express a need to control others*?
Circle your response: 1 2 3 4 5

4. To what extent does this person *indicate willingness to be controlled by others*?
Circle your response: 1 2 3 4 5

5. To what extent does this person *show affection toward others*?
Circle your response: 1 2 3 4 5

6. To what extent does this person *indicate a desire to be shown affection by others*?
Circle your response: 1 2 3 4 5

The Task/Person Scales

These scales may be used for self-evaluation in terms of one's orientation toward task (problem-solving) and people (relating to other members of your group).[5] The Task/Person Questionnaire (see below) is filled out by each group member.

The Task/Person (T/P) Questionnaire[6]

The following items describe aspects of group member behavior. Respond to each item according to the way you would be most likely to act if you were in a problem-solving group. Circle whether you would be likely to behave in the described way always (A), frequently (F), occasionally (O), seldom (S), or never (N).

If I were a member of a problem-solving group:

A F O S N   **1.** I would be very likely to act as the spokesman of the group.
A F O S N   **2.** I would encourage overtime work.
A F O S N   **3.** I would allow members complete freedom in their work.
A F O S N   **4.** I would encourage the use of uniform procedures.
A F O S N   **5.** I would permit the others to use their own judgment in solving problems.
A F O S N   **6.** I would stress being ahead of competing groups.
A F O S N   **7.** I would speak as a representative of the group.
A F O S N   **8.** I would encourage members toward greater effort.
A F O S N   **9.** I would try out my ideas in the group.
A F O S N   **10.** I would let the others do their work the way they think best.
A F O S N   **11.** I would be working hard for personal recognition.
A F O S N   **12.** I would be able to tolerate postponement and uncertainty.
A F O S N   **13.** I would speak for the group when visitors were present.
A F O S N   **14.** I would keep the work moving at a rapid pace.
A F O S N   **15.** I would help identify a task and let others go to it.
A F O S N   **16.** I would settle conflicts when they occur in the group.
A F O S N   **17.** I would be likely to get swamped by details.
A F O S N   **18.** I would represent the group at outside meetings.
A F O S N   **19.** I would be reluctant to allow the others freedom of action.
A F O S N   **20.** I would decide what should be done and how it should be done.
A F O S N   **21.** I would push for better results.
A F O S N   **22.** I would let other members have some authority.
A F O S N   **23.** Things would usually turn out as I predicted.
A F O S N   **24.** I would allow the others a high degree of initiative.
A F O S N   **25.** I would try to assign group members to particular tasks.
A F O S N   **26.** I would be willing to make changes.
A F O S N   **27.** I would ask the others to work harder.
A F O S N   **28.** I would trust the group members to exercise good judgment.
A F O S N   **29.** I would try to schedule work to be done.
A F O S N   **30.** I would refuse to explain my actions when questioned.
A F O S N   **31.** I would persuade others that my ideas are to their advantage.
A F O S N   **32.** I would permit the group to set its own pace.
A F O S N   **33.** I would urge the group to beat its previous record.
A F O S N   **34.** I would act without consulting the group.
A F O S N   **35.** I would ask that group members follow standard rules and regulations.

It is then scored as follows:

A. Circle the item number for items 1, 4, 7, 13, 16, 17, 18, 19, 20, 23, 29, 30, 31, 34, and 35.
B. Put an "X" in front of only those circled item numbers for items to which you responded "S" (seldom) or "N" (never).

C. Put an "X" in front of items whose numbers are not circled, only when you responded to such items with "A" (always) or "F" (frequently).
D. Circle any "X" that you have put in front of any of the following item numbers: 3, 5, 10, 12, 15, 17, 19, 22, 24, 26, 28, 30, 32, and 34.
E. Count the circled "Xs." This is your Person Orientation (P) score.
F. Count the uncircled "Xs." This is your Task Orientation (T) Score.

An individual's T and P scores are then plotted on the T/P Grid and are interpreted in terms of the descriptive elements given in the appropriate cell; see Figure 10.1.

Name _____   Group _____

Locating oneself on the grid:

To locate yourself on the grid below, find your score on the Person dimension (**P**) on the horizontal axis of the graph. Next, start up the column above your P score to the cell that corresponds to your Task score (**T**). Place an "X" in the cell that represents your two scores.

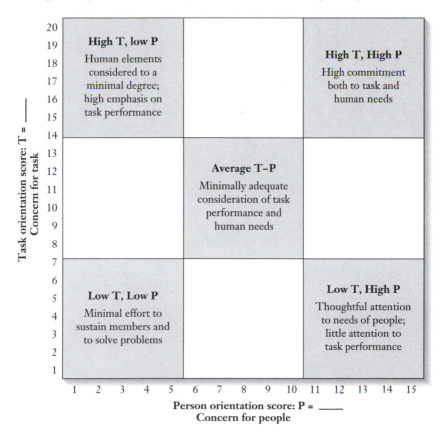

FIGURE 10.1 The Task/Person Grid

Systematic Observation

While a number of systems are available for observing a group systematically, we believe that one of the most functional is the Bales System of Interaction Process Analysis (IPA), developed by Robert Bales in the 1940s.[7]

The purpose of the IPA system is to identify and record the nature (not the content) of each separate act in ongoing group interaction. The act is the verbal or nonverbal behavior noted by the observer. Twelve acts constitute the system, as shown in Figure 10.2. They are arranged in two broad areas, a *task* and a socioemotional area, which may be equated with *maintenance* functions. The task area consists of questions and answers, and the socioemotional areas are respectively "positive" and "negative."

The observer does not record the content of a given verbal message but, rather, the behavior it represents. In scoring he notes the interaction "from whom to whom" and renders an interpretation of the act in terms of the 12 categories. A simple sentence is a single unit while complex sentences may contain several units. The observer also scores, on the same sheet, the nonverbal behavior of all the members at one-minute intervals. After much training he is able to find high correlations, ranging from 0.75 to 0.95.[8]

Fragments of sentences, words, and phrases are scored as communication acts (unit) when you can understand the meaning as a unit of thought in context. For example, "What?" may mean "What did you say?", or "Me?" may mean "Were you referring to me?" Such scraps of conversation as "Huh" or "Mm" may have fairly clear meaning in context. Also included are nonverbal acts, when a message is clearly implied. For example, a nod of the head may clearly signify agreement, and shaking the head may, in context, mean disagreement or even an unfriendly reaction.

As well as being able to identify the communication behaviors, the observants must determine which of the following 12 categories best describe interactions in the group. The 12 categories are briefly described as follows.

1. *Seems friendly.* Any act showing hospitality, neighborliness, sympathy, or similarity of feeling; indications of being attracted; demonstrations of affection; urging of unity or harmony; expressing desire for cooperation or solidarity; showing a protective or nurturing attitude; praising, rewarding, approving, or encouraging others; sustaining or reassuring a person having difficulty; complimenting or congratulating; exchanging, trading, or lending objects (e.g., cigarettes or matches); confiding in another; expressing gratitude or appreciation; surrendering or giving in to another (e.g., when interrupted); friendly submission so that another can go ahead; confessions of ignorance; acts of apology; grinning with pleasure; smiling directly at another. This category should be used whenever an act primarily appears to convey good feeling toward another person.[9]

2. *Dramatizes.* Any act that emphasizes hidden meaning or emotional implications or is especially self-revealing about a person. Most frequently these are jokes or stories *with a double meaning.* They may take the form of an anecdote

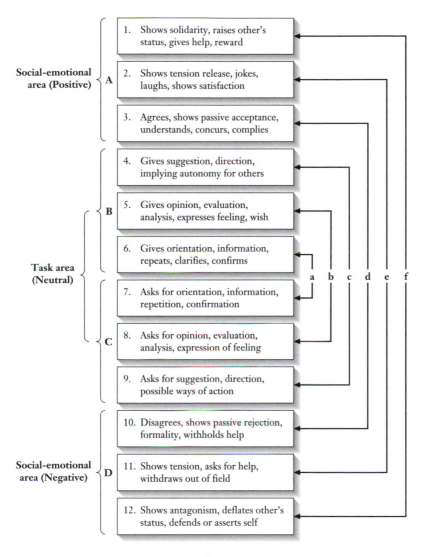

Key

a. Problems of orientation   **A.** Positive reactions

b. Problems of evaluation   **B.** Attempted answers

c. Problems of control   **C.** Questions

d. Problems of decision   **D.** Negative reactions

e. Problems of tension management

f. Problems of integration

FIGURE 10.2   Bales's System of Categories, Used in Observation, and Their Major Relations. Note that "acts" 1 and 12 are complementary, as are 2 and 11, 3 and 10, and so on, to 6 and 7. On an actual form there is more space for filling in by the observer. (From R.F. Bales, *Interaction Process Analysis* [Reading, Mass: Addison-Wesley, 1950], p. 59.)

about a particular person in which emotional feelings are expressed, or they may be symbolic actions, such as shrugs or bodily and facial expressions portraying great amazement, surprise, fear, or anger. More than one meaning is nearly always implicit in dramatizations as here defined; for example, a posturing, a facial expression, a remark, or all three together may imply: (1) "He certainly thinks he is something!" and (2) "I don't agree." The personal tone of this dramatic bit, coupled with the overtones of partially hidden emotional feelings, are typical of acts scored in this category.[10] According to Bales, "The joke is a very common form of dramatization in group interaction. The joker expects, though perhaps not always too clearly, to produce a shock of recognition of the hidden meaning, to provoke a laugh, a sudden release or display of tension."[11] Bales goes on to suggest that the concept the joker offers is loaded but that whoever laughs admits "the hidden truth."[12] The essential quality of this category is that of some special, personal, partially hidden meaning subtly exposed in a way that is emotionally releasing even though risky; thus, one ordinary hallmark of such acts is that they seem to have two meanings, one dangerous to expose and the other somewhat amusing on the surface.[13] Behavior such as this may seem to be dangerous or better avoided; however, Bales makes this evaluative comment: "In terms of psychological services performed, and general importance in the group as well as individual life, these activities are not task-oriented, but they are nevertheless serious psychological business."[14]

3. *Agrees.* Any act that shows accord, concurrence, or assent about facts, inferences, or hypotheses: "I think you are right," "That's true," "Yes, that's it." Nonverbal agreement may involve nodding the head, showing special interest, or giving significant visible attention to what is being said. Another variation may be overtly expressing comprehension or understanding: "Oh, now I get it."

4. *Gives suggestions.* Any act that takes the lead in the task direction. This category includes routine control of communication and directing the attention of the group to task problems when they have been agreed on by the group. Thus, mentioning calling a meeting to order, referring to agenda, and opening a new phase of activity—all of these are scored as "giving suggestions," if they are routine, agreed on moves and if they are brought forth in a way that implies the acceptability of dissent if anyone so desires.[15] Bales gives this definition: "In general, direct attempts to guide or counsel, or prepare the other for some activity, to prevail upon him, to persuade him, exhort him, urge, enjoin, or inspire him to some action, by dependence upon authority or ascendance rather than logical inference are called *giving suggestions.*"[16] Such suggestions usually propose ways of modifying the problem situation, the group, certain members, or the norms.

5. *Gives opinions.* Any act that involves a moral obligation, offers a major belief or value, or indicates adherence to a policy or guiding principle. Such acts should be serious but not personal, sincere but objective. If such an act is not serious or is insincere, you should score it in category 2, *dramatizes.* Category

5, *gives opinions,* includes expressions of understanding or insight besides those of value judgements: "I believe I see your point" or "I think we should recognize our obligation to . . ." or "I feel we are on the right track." *Gives opinions* should be distinguished from category 6, *gives information,* primarily on the basis of its use of inference or value judgment.[17]

6. *Gives information.* Any act reporting factual (not necessarily true) or potentially verifiable (testable) observations or experiences. Bales gives this instruction: "Any statement too vague in principle to be tested is not classified as giving information, but, usually, as giving opinion."[18] Common cases of giving information are reports on problem situations confronting the group: "The legislature has not yet acted on that bill" or "We have three days left" or "I contacted the City Council and they can meet with us on Tuesday."[19]

7. *Asks for information.* Any act that requests a factual report. Bales' definition includes requests for "descriptive, objective type answers, an answer based upon experience, observation, or empirical research."[20] The questions making these requests are not always direct but sometimes indirect: "I have forgotten whom we appointed." You should include in this category only requests for simple factual answers; if an inference, an evaluation, or the expression of a feeling is requested, such should be tabulated as category 8, *asks for opinions.*[21]

8. *Asks for opinions.* Any act that seeks an inferential interpretation, a statement involving belief or values, a value judgment, or a report of one's understanding or insight. It may include a request for a diagnosis of a situation or reaction to an idea. A warning should be given here regarding questions such as "Do you know what I mean?" and "Do you see?" These are examples of attempts to elicit agreement and should be identified as persuasive effort, properly tabulated in category 4, *gives suggestions.*[22] Another problem you may encounter occurs when an elected chairperson or leader serves the group in ways that the group commissioned them to, and they are struggling to fathom and comply with the group's wishes. In such a case the leader might ask for an opinion in this manner: "Would you like to have a committee work on that?" But a question such as "What should we do about increasing our membership?" implies that the leader is asking for suggestions regarding ways of solving a group problem. This kind of question should be identified as belonging in category 9, *asks for suggestions.*[23]

9. *Asks for suggestions.* Any act that requests guidance in the problem-solving process, is neutral in emotional tone, and attempts to turn the initiative over to another. Such requests sometimes indicate a feeling of confusion or uncertainty.[24] To fit this category properly the request should be "open-ended," without the implication of any specific answer: "What do you think we should do about that?" If, on the other hand, the question is asked in such a way that a specific answer is implied, it should be coded in category 4, *gives suggestions.* An example of a veiled suggestion is: "I wonder if there are any other ways of getting information from the Legislature?" This seems to imply there are other ways and suggests they be considered.[25]

10. *Disagrees.* Any *initial* act in a sequence that rejects another's statement of information, opinion, or suggestion. It is a reaction to another's action as defined by Bales: "The negative feeling conveyed is attached to the content of what the other has said, not to him as a person. And the negative feeling must not be very strong, or the act will seem unfriendly."[26] (It would, in such a case, be scored in category 12, *seems unfriendly.*) Statements that follow the initial rejection of another's position, such as arguments, rebuttals, and questions, are not scored as disagreement; rather, they are scored in other categories. Examples of acts scored in this category are "I don't think so" and "I don't think that's right."[27]

11. *Shows tension.* Any act that exhibits conflict between submission and nonconformity yet does not clearly show negative feeling toward another person.[28] Bales gives this general definition: "Signs of anxious emotionality [that] indicate a conflict between acting and withholding action. Minor outbreaks of reactive anxiety may first be mentioned, such as appearing startled, disconcerted, alarmed, dismayed, perturbed, or concerned."[29] Other behaviors Bales suggests are hesitation, speechlessness, trembling, flushing, gulping, and licking of the lips.[30] Of special import in this category is laughter. On the surface laughter may seem to indicate a reduction of tension, and it may in part serve that purpose. In fact, however, it appears to be more dependable as a sign of tension rather than a sign of its reduction.[31] We are not here speaking of friendly smiles with a relaxed atmosphere of interpersonal warmth; rather, we are identifying embarrassed or *tense* laughter. Bales gives this explanation: "Laughter seems to be a sudden escape into motor discharge of conflicted emotional states that can no longer be contained."[32] An additional behavior to be included in this category is any embarrassed reaction to disapproval, as the appearance of being chagrined, chastised, or mortified.[33]

12. *Seems unfriendly.* Any act that is personally negative; when negative, it is not content oriented, which would be classified as category 10, *disagrees,* but is oriented toward another person. It includes very slight signs of negative feeling, arbitrary attempts to subjugate another, uninvited attempts to "settle" an argument, to judge another's behavior, to override, interrupt, deflate, deprecate, disparage, or ridicule.[34] Also included are attempts to "show off," embarrass a generally accepted authority, or inordinately make a nuisance of oneself.[35] In general, Bales suggests that this category be used to identify all overt acts that seem to the observer to be in any way both negative and personal.[36]

In addition to the category descriptions and suggestions for deciding how to use the categories for interaction analysis, Bales offers four general rules to employ when an observer has difficulty in deciding where an act should be tabulated:

1. Give priority to category 2, *dramatizes,* or to category 11, *shows tension,* when there is a question between either one and any other category.

2. Give priority to category 1, *seems friendly,* or to category 12, s*eems unfriendly,* when any element of interpersonal feeling is shown.
3. Give priority to category 4, *gives suggestions,* or to category 9, a*sks for suggestions,* over category 5, *gives opinion.*
4. After an initial act of either disagreement or agreement the scoring reverts to the appropriate impersonal categories, as the basis for the disagreement is explained.[37]

The observations may be of further value in a tabulation of the relative frequencies of the types of interaction in a given group. In observations of 24 different groups, ranging in size from two to seven members, working on a standard task, Bales noted the following relative percentages:[38]

1.	Shows solidarity	3.4
2.	Shows tension release	6.0
3.	Shows agreement	16.5
4.	Gives suggestions	8.0
5.	Gives opinions	30.1
6.	Gives information	7.9
7.	Asks for information	3.5
8.	Asks for opinion	2.4
9.	Asks for suggestion	1.1
10.	Shows disagreement	7.8
11.	Shows tension	2.7
12.	Shows antagonism	0.7

Note that in these norms the positive emotional expressions (1, 2, and 3) greatly outweigh the negative (10, 11, and 12) and that opinions, information, and suggestions are given far more often than they are requested (56 percent as against 7 percent). Bales was careful to note that different groups will yield different profiles.

As you have been reading the category descriptions and the suggestions for scoring, you may have felt that the use of the IPA will be complex and confusing. It is a common feeling our students report *before* they attempt to gain experience with it; it is also common for them to report increased confidence in their scoring ability as they follow our suggestions for practice. We equip them with scoring sheets illustrated by Figure 10.3. Familiarity with the line on the sheet where each category is located is of great help and is obtained with a little practice.

Four levels of analysis are possible. The first level of analysis involves the calculation of the percentage of total group interaction for each participant; see Table 10.1.

With data from this first level of analysis you can detect the spread of participation through your group and compare your own degree of participation with that of the others. The gross amount of participation from an individual

For each interactional act (a simple sentence or equivalent part of a complete sentence) put one mark in each category. For example, after some period of time your tabulation for "seems friendly" might look like this:

1. Seems friendly   ////   ////   ///

Code number for person observed _____

| 1. Seems friendly |
| 2. Dramatizes |
| 3. Agrees |
| |
| 4. Gives suggestions |
| 5. Gives opinions |
| 6. Gives information |
| |
| 7. Asks for information |
| 8. Asks for opinions |
| 9. Asks for suggestions |
| |
| 10. Disagrees |
| 11. Shows tension |

FIGURE 10.3   Tabulation Sheet for IPA Data

member is generally a good indicator of attempts to gain status, or achieve influence over others, especially in groups in which no appointed leader is present.

The second level of analysis requires the computation of the percentage of the total group interaction in each of the 12 categories; this will tell you how much your group is participating in what way. With these data you can list the estimated norms presented by Bales and compare the manner of participation from your group members with these suggested norms, as illustrated in Table 10.2.

In the table the column of estimated norms gives ranges, the high and low cutoff points. Although these points are not supported by as much evidence and experimentation as we would like to have, they may be taken as general guidelines to what may be considered high or low in each category. Whenever these bounda-

TABLE 10.1 Participants' Share of Total Observed Group Interaction

Name	Percent
Joe	10.3
Mike	7.2
Bill	42.8
Mary	28.3
Jill	11.4
Total:	100.0

ries are exceeded, you should give careful thought to what may be happening in your group. For example, look at the data presented in the percentage column. Here seems to be a nice, friendly group—overly so, according to data for category 12. The data for category 10 shows they are not disagreeing with each other in a normal way, and the degree of tension shown by the data for category 11 tends to support our inference; they appear afraid to disagree normally. This inference, of course, is not a *firm* conclusion but only a lead for this group to explore further by discussing their feelings and attitudes and monitoring their ensuing behavior.

An additional point for them to consider is that they appear to be giving an inordinate number of opinions and an unusually low amount of information. Are

TABLE 10.2 Percentage of Total Observed Group Participation in Each IPA Category, Compared with Estimated Norms

Category	Percent	Estimated Norms
1. Seems friendly	3.5	2.6–4.8
2. Dramatizes	7.0	5.7–7.4
3. Agrees	18.5	8.0–13.6
4. Gives suggestions	3.8	3.0–7.0
5. Gives opinions	24.5	15.0–22.7
6. Gives information	8.3	20.7–31.2
7. Asks for information	10.3	4.0–7.2
8. Asks for opinions	12.5	2.0–3.9
9. Asks for suggestions	2.3	0.6–1.4
10. Disagrees	1.0	3.1–5.3
11. Shows tension	7.8	3.4–6.0
12. Seems unfriendly	0.5	2.4–4.4
Total:	100.0	

they in need of informing themselves about their problem areas? They may have intuitively sensed that they are ignorant about their problem topic; here appears to be some solid confirmation. They should at least give this their careful consideration. From their work in analyzing data from many groups, Bales and Hare suggest that whenever the *combined* scores in categories 7, 8, and 9 yield low percentages, the group should give special attention to seeking more specific information about its problem area.[39] The normal estimated ratio is 5 to 1, or 6 to 1; in the illustrative example given in the table the ratio is less than 2 to 1, which is a fairly convincing sign of a lack of needed information for successful group problem solving. In such fashion your group can analyze the percentage of total group participation in each category and compare it with the estimated norms given in Table 10.3.

As we have indicated, data collection by the Bales IPA can provide information on your group on both task-oriented (problem-solving) behavior and on interpersonal (group maintenance) behavior. Data in categories 4, 5, 6, 7, 8, and 9 (giving and asking for suggestions, opinions, and information) are problem-solving, or task-oriented, behaviors. Data in the remaining categories, 1, 2, 3, 10, 11, and 13 (seeming friendly or unfriendly; agreeing, or disagreeing; dramatizing and showing tension), are primarily interpersonal in nature and relate to the maintenance of effective human relations among group members. Comparisons of these two classes of data may be made with data obtained (from the same group) via the Task/Person Scales.

The third level of analysis you will wish to perform is to calculate the percentage of total group participation of *each* of your group members in each of

TABLE 10.3 Percentage of Total Observed Group Participation in Each IPA Category for Each Group Member

Category	Percentage of Group Participation				
	Joe	*Mike*	*Bill*	*Mary*	*Jill*
1. Seems friendly	—	0.9	1.2	0.2	1.2
2. Dramatizes	3.4	1.3	—	—	2.3
3. Agrees	—	.4	11.4	5.5	1.2
4. Gives suggestions	—	—	2.6	1.2	—
5. Gives opinions	3.4	—	13.0	8.1	—
6. Gives information	—	—	6.2	2.1	—
7. Asks for information	—	—	7.1	3.2	—
8. Asks for opinions	—	1.2	0.1	8.0	3.2
9. Asks for suggestions	—	—	1.2	—	1.1
10. Disagrees	1.0	—	—	—	—
11. Shows tension	2.0	3.4	—	—	2.4
12. Seems unfriendly	0.5	—	—	—	—
Total:	10.3	7.2	42.8	28.3	11.4

the 12 categories; see Table 10.3. Comparisons of these data can give you a good idea of who is making which type of contribution and to what degree; it can also identify members who may need encouragement to participate in certain ways as well as those who might wish to do the encouraging, especially if they are somewhat inconsiderate in their total time available to the group. For example, the group data in Table 10.3 theoretically describes that Joe needs encouragement to participate in almost all of the task-oriented categories (4, 6, 7, 8 and 9); Bill and Mary probably are spending a bit of the group's time talking with each other; they could well afford to encourage Joe (besides Mike and Jill) to participate more in task-oriented ways.

The fourth level of analysis is a personal one. Calculate the percentage of an *individual's* total participation for each category. Looking back at Table 10.3 let us assume that you are Joe. In terms of total group interaction you contributed 10.3 percent, with 3.4 percent in category 2, *dramatizes*. Dividing 3.4 by 10.3, you derive 32.6 percent, that portion of your (Joe's) own individual participation scored in this category. In such a fashion you can produce a set of data like that presented in Table 10.4.

Using the information presented in Table 10.4, you can compare your own participation with the estimated norms, the medium-range column, provided by Bales. You may recall that in Table 10.3 these normative data were used for comparison with group data; the same norms may be used for an evaluation of individual participation.[40]

According to the data in Table 10.4, Joe is extraordinarily high in interaction that *dramatizes,* category 2; of his own total participation, 32.6 percent was identified as fitting this category. This amount is very high compared with a normative medium-range of 5.4 to 7.4 percent.

TABLE 10.4 Individual IPA Data Compared with Estimated Norms

Category of Interaction	Percent of Joe's Total	Medium Range
1. Seems friendly	—	2.6–4.8
2. Dramatizes	32.6	5.4–7.4
3. Agrees	—	8.0–13.6
4. Gives suggestions	—	3.0–7.0
5. Gives opinions	32.6	15.0–22.7
6. Gives information	—	20.7–31.2
7. Asks for information	—	4.0–7.2
8. Asks for opinions	—	2.0–3.9
9. Asks for suggestions	—	0.6–1.4
10. Disagrees	9.7	3.1–5.3
11. Shows tension	19.4	3.4–6.0
12. Seems unfriendly	4.9	2.4–4.4

This interpretation can give Joe a fairly good impression of the way he is seen by others for about one third of the time that he is participating. As he pursues similar interpretations of other data in Table 10.4 he may note category 5, *gives opinions:* 32.6 percent (very high), interpreted as task oriented and concerned with the work of the group. So for at least one third of the time he is participating, Joe is seen as contributing to the achievement of the goals of the group. As Joe thinks about these data and their interpretations, he may decide to be less of a clown and more of a problem-solving participant. He may also remember that, when a tense situation arises in the group, he is seen as a person who might be able to reduce the tension by providing a good round of laughter. You should view such interpretations as suggestions rather than firm labels; these suggestions should be evaluated further by observing the reactions of other members as you continue to interact in your group; in addition, you should observe your own behavior in the light of these suggestions. In this way the approach Bales has developed and we have illustrated can be useful in evaluating your behavior and deciding in what ways, if any, you might wish to change.

Case Study

A group of students at the University were taking a course entitled "Problem-solving Group Interaction." One of the major assignments was to observe a group in action and determine the quality of the group performance based on process measures. The group elected to observe the McCollum Hall Social Committee, a student group representing a residence hall at the University of Kansas. The Social Committee is responsible for all social events planned in the dormitory that require the utilization of hall facilities and the usage of allocated hall funds.

The group consisted of approximately 30 members, with each individual representing a specific section and floor of the residence hall. The average attendance for a group meeting was approximately 25 members.

Among the instruments used to observe the Social Committee, the observing group elected to use the Bales Interpersonal Perception Scale (IPS). They observed the group planning a Halloween party and examined such factors as the details of the party, including publicity, contests, decorations, admission procedures, policies regarding liquor, clean-up arrangements, and financial matters.

Discussion

Due to the large size of the group, the observing team selected the four most vocal group members and lumped the remaining individuals into a residual category. The amount of participation time is shown in Table 10.5. The percentage of the total observed participation in each of the Bales's IPA categories is shown in Table 10.6 and compared to estimated norms in Table 10.7.

**TABLE 10.5 Participants'
Share of Total Observed
Group Interaction**

Name	Percent
Joanne	20.5
Nancy	17.6
Bruce	15.8
Lori	14.8
Others	31.3
Total:	100.0

According to the group analysis, the Social Committee was shown to be high on task information and below average on maintenance-related categories. It appears that the group did not openly express disagreement, tension, or unfriendliness.

As Bales has observed, increasing group size produces greater dominance by a few members. Although group membership and centrality are inevitable accompaniments of a dormitory situation in which all floors desire representation, several measures could have been adopted to improve group performance and member satisfaction; floor representatives should be encouraged to contribute opinions and suggestions to a greater extent.

TABLE 10.6 Percentage of Total Observed Group Participation in Each IPA Category for Each Group Member

Category	Percentage of Group Participation				
	Joanne	Nancy	Bruce	Lori	Others
1. Seems friendly	0.5	0.3	2.9	1.4	1.2
2. Dramatizes	1.0	0.3	0.6	1.4	0.6
3. Agrees	0.3	1.0	2.3	1.6	4.0
4. Gives suggestions	0.4	1.5	1.8	2.2	1.4
5. Gives opinions	0.9	1.3	1.9	3.3	3.0
6. Gives information	10.7	7.4	2.3	2.1	15.1
7. Asks for information	3.9	4.3	2.6	1.9	5.0
8. Asks for opinions	1.2	0.3	1.2	0.6	0.2
9. Asks for suggestions	0.8	0.1	0.1	0.3	0.1
10. Disagrees	0.4	0.0	0.1	0.0	0.6
11. Shows tension	0.3	0.3	0.1	0.0	0.3
12. Seems unfriendly	0.1	0.8	0.0	0.0	0.0
Total:	20.5	17.6	15.9	14.8	31.5

TABLE 10.7   Individual IPA Group Data Compared with Estimated Norms (Rounded to Nearest Percentage)

	Percent of Each Person's Total					
Category	Joanne	Nancy	Bruce	Lori	Others	Norms
1. Seems friendly	2.5	2.0	18.5	9.6	3.7	2.6–4.8
2. Dramatizes	4.8	1.5	3.9	9.6	2.0	5.7–7.4
3. Agrees	1.3	5.5	14.6	10.8	12.7	8.0–13.6
4. Gives suggestions	2.2	8.5	10.7	15.0	4.6	3.0–7.0
5. Gives opinions	4.3	7.5	12.4	22.2	9.6	15.0–22.7
6. Gives information	52.4	42.2	14.6	14.4	48.0	20.7–31.2
7. Asks for information	19.0	24.1	16.3	12.6	15.8	4.0–7.2
8. Asks for opinions	5.6	2.0	7.3	4.2	0.6	2.0–3.9
9. Asks for suggestions	3.7	0.4	0.6	1.8	0.3	0.6–1.4
10. Disagrees	2.2	0.0	0.6	0.0	2.0	3.1–5.3
11. Shows tension	1.3	1.3	0.6	0.0	0.8	3.4–6.0
12. Seems unfriendly	0.4	4.5	0.0	0.0	0.0	2.4–4.4
Total:	100.0	100.0	100.0	100.0	100.0	

Based on the data here included, what inferences could you make about the following:

1. The possibility of hidden feelings or dissatisfaction. Is leadership an issue in this regard?
2. Why is there such a high percentage of asking for information? What does this tell us about the group?
3. What additional information would you seek if you were in the position of observing the group?

Chapter Summary

It is important that your observations of other groups contribute to the evaluation of your own behavior. In fact, the primary point of this chapter has been to provide a way of enhancing your learning and improving your own performance, even though at times it may have seemed to you that we were presenting guidelines or classroom procedures to be used by your instructor.

As you observe others, you may find yourself saying, "I do that, too—and I wish I didn't!" You must remember that it is always easier to see such things and even to say such things than it is to actually accomplish these personal changes. Changes in one's behavior ordinarily require these conditions (at least): (1) specific knowledge of the new (to you) behavior you would like to adopt, (2) a strong desire to carry out the new behavior, and (3) the assistance of another person who will show patience (not critical impatience) and give you feedback on their perception of the degree to which you have demonstrated the new behavior. If these conditions are present, and these new behaviors are actually within your range of capabilities, the experimental attempts to change can be successful. It is important to remember that practice does not make perfect if you are practicing an inefficient way of behaving. Practice (without change) simply makes for permanence: permanently inefficient behavior, if such is the behavior practiced. Our students have used their project groups somewhat as a laboratory in which they can, in an exploratory fashion, attempt new behaviors in a search for individual self-improvement. By "project groups" we mean the in-class student groups who worked together to observe and critique out-of-class real-life groups. Sometimes members of these student groups have shared an experience like the following: "You know, when I saw a member of the city council behaving the way I caught myself doing in our own group, I made up my mind I just shouldn't be that way anymore!" It seems clear to us that the observation of others, the interpretation of the effects of various behaviors, and the comparison of these observations with one's own performance are important steps in attempting to improve one's own behavior.

In this chapter we have emphasized the point that individuals can gain insight into and understanding of their own behavior by observing the task-oriented techniques and interpersonal relations exhibited by members of other groups. We have described procedures of observing, analyzing, and interpreting such behavior—procedures that our own students have generally found useful to them in gaining personal insight and understanding.

APPLICATIONS

10.1 Evaluate the reports presented in this chapter. Are the inferences reasonable, based on the data presented?

10.2 Select an outside group that would be agreeable to your investigation and analysis. Decide as a team on the instruments that would be useful for such an examination.

10.3 Following the outline provided in this chapter, formulate an approach and methodology for observing the outside group and preparing a detailed report.

REFERENCES

1. From R.C. Camp, *Benchmarking* (Milwaukee: Quality Press, 1989), p. 10.
2. M. Bolon and A. Weber, *Benchmarking: A Manager's Guide* (Arlington, VA: Coopers and Lybrand, L.L.P., 1995), pp. 3–5.
3. For a detailed explanation and a model of normative benchmarking, see B.R. Patton and K. Giffin, *Decision-Making Group Interaction* (New York: Harper and Row, 1978), pp. 213–228.
4. See R.S. Johnson, *TQM: The Mechanics of Quality Processors* (Milwaukee: ASQC Quality Press, 1993), pp. 203–205.
5. T.J. Sergiovanni, R. Metzcus, and L. Burden, "Toward a Particularistic Approach to Leadership Style: Some findings," *American Educational Research Journal,* 6 (1960), pp. 62–79.
6. J.W. Pfeiffer and J.E. Jones, *Structured Experiences for Human Relations Training* (Iowa City, Iowa: University Associates Press, 1969), pp.

7–10. The T/P scale is reproduced here with permission of the authors and publisher.

7. R.F. Bales, *Personality and Interpersonal Behavior* (New York, Holt, Rinehart & Winston, 1970), p. 92, also p. 62.

8. R.F. Bales and A.P. Hare, "Diagnostic Use of the Interaction Profile," *Journal of Psychology,* 67 (1965), pp. 239–258.

9. Bales, *Personality and Interpersonal Behavior,* pp. 100–103.

10. Ibid., pp. 105–108.

11. Ibid., p. 108.

12. Ibid.

13. Ibid., p. 477.

14. Ibid., p. 108.

15. Ibid., pp. 109–112.

16. Ibid., p. 111.

17. Ibid., p. 112–116.

18. Ibid., p. 118.

19. Ibid., p. 116–119.

20. Ibid., p. 119.

21. Ibid., pp. 119–120.

22. Ibid., p. 121.

23. Cf. ibid., p. 121.

24. Ibid., p. 121.

25. Ibid., pp. 121–122.

26. Ibid., p. 123.

27. Ibid., pp. 123–124.

28. Ibid., p. 124.

29. Ibid.

30. Ibid.

31. Ibid., p. 125.

32. Ibid.

33. Ibid., pp. 124–127.

34. Ibid., pp. 127–129.

35. Ibid., pp. 129–132.

36. Ibid., p. 127.

37. Ibid., pp. 134–135.

38. R.F. Bales and A.P. Hare, "Diagnostic Use of the Interaction Profile."

39. Ibid.

40. Bales, *Personality and Interpersonal Behavior,* p. 15.

11 Presenting the Findings of the Quality Group

Scenario

A major aerospace company conducted an experiment with participative employee groups assigned the task of reducing errors and increasing employee satisfaction. For four years, groups were assembled and assigned specific problems and compared to other groups that did not deal with the problem. The differences were pronounced. One group comprised of all women requested and received music in their work area by tapes and earphones; their output increased significantly. This music was provided unilaterally to another group, and no changes in work output resulted. One group requested that their workbenches be turned around to avoid facing a bare wall. This change was effected for three groups, and only the one requesting it was found to be more satisfied; the other groups were indifferent. These results demonstrate how the way in which a change is made can have more influence on acceptance than the nature of the change itself. Over the four year period, in the groups encouraged to participate in the study, production increases averaged between 20 and 30 percent and error reduction averaged between 30 and 50 percent.[1]

Effective decision making requires data and analysis. The group must clearly understand the data if it is to be used effectively. Visualization and specificity are usually required. In this chapter we shall suggest tools that can assist in the gathering and in the presentation of the data.

Data Collection and Analysis Tools

Data must be relevant, representative, and reliable—the three Rs. *Relevant* data are what is important to your group and to decision makers. *Representative* data means that any population cited is truly a subset of the whole. Statistical sampling

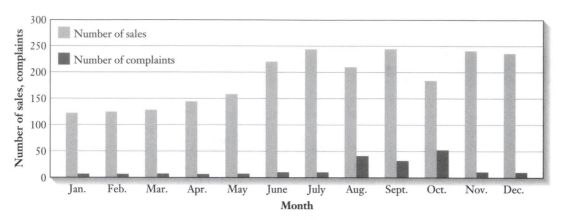

FIGURE 11.1   Control Chart—Sales versus Complaints

techniques need to be followed. *Reliable* data means that you will get the same results if the study is replicated. Analysis tools make data easier to understand and help show the significance. We shall examine five such tools.

Control Charts

A control chart is a graphic comparison of measured characteristics, either quantitative or qualitative, with desired or projected norms. For example, how many times does a phone ring before it is answered in an office, or how many hours are lost to a unit due to absenteeism? Such charts can compare units, trace a phenomenon over time, or establish targets and goals based on historical data.

Control charts are frequently used in manufacturing and service businesses. In Figure 11.1, the number of complaints can be compared to the amount of sales, and variable strategies can be tested to see if complaints can be reduced. Service training of employees and identification of reasons for the complaints can be charted and addressed. In manufacturing, the defect rate or overall time to complete a project can be charted.

Cause-and-Effect Diagrams (or Fishbone Charts)

If there is a problem, a first step in analysis is determining what causes the problem. The group may brainstorm and list all the potential causes that can be related to the problem. The diagram is an attempt to show the relationship between the problem (effect) and the potential causes of the problem. It provides a visual system to organize thoughts and determine relative consequences of different actions.

Characteristically, a horizontal line across the middle of the paper labels the problem (e.g., customer complaints). The "fish ribs" are vertical lines that show the

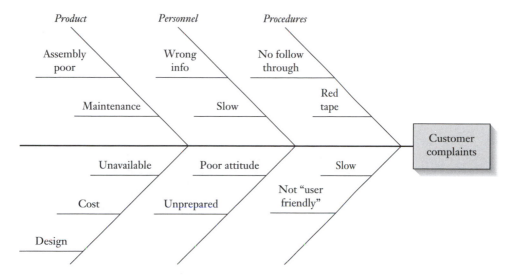

FIGURE 11.2   Cause-and-Effect Diagram

potential causes of the problem. In Figure 11.2, we have shown an analysis of the problems of customer complaints. The cause-and-effect diagram helps to focus discussions and clarify what actions would be helpful in developing an action plan to solve the problem. For example, the Phoenix Medical Center used cause-and-effect diagrams to analyze the causes for post-operative infection rates that exceeded the national average of 2 percent. They then were able to develop solutions that lowered the rate to 0.4 percent, less than one-fourth of the previous level.[2]

The Cause-and-Effect Diagram both assists the group in analyzing problem areas and in determining how well the process functions.

Pareto Charts

A nineteenth century economist, Vilfredo Pareto, in studying the uneven distribution of wealth, observed that 20 percent of the population owned 80 percent of the wealth. In looking for the most frequently occurring process problem, the Pareto Chart shows that the most important effects are likely the result of very few causes.

A group used Pareto Charts to better understand causes of customer complaints and how frequently they occur in a motel chain. Figure 11.3 shows the analysis that revealed that most of the problems were occurring at the front desk. Further analysis broke the causes into the functions performed and the areas of dissatisfaction. Customers complained of long waits standing in line, unfriendly staff, lost messages, and mistakes in billing. The chart helps the group select the significant causes and focus their attention.

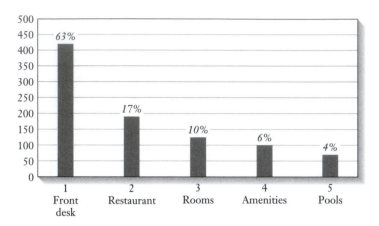

FIGURE 11.3 Pareto Chart

Flow Charts

One of the best ways to determine how the process works is through a flow chart. Members of the group are challenged to identify all the things that must happen to create the product, service, or experience being studied. By drawing a picture representing the steps in a process, members of the group will better understand the total process and how the individual steps interrelate. There is no single set of symbols, but they should be as simple as possible and all members should know what they mean.

In Figure 11.4 a flow chart was begun to study the process for students adding a course of study at a university. Steps calling for signatures of administrators were able to be eliminated as insignificant to the efficiency or accuracy of the data to be entered, thus saving time and student effort.

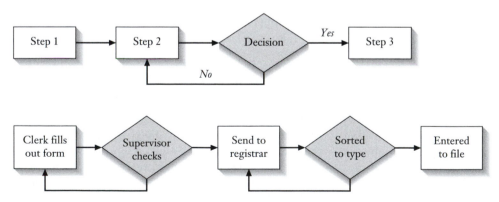

FIGURE 11.4 Flow Charts

PERT

The acronym "PERT" stands for Program Evaluation and Review Technique. It was developed for the space program as different contractors had to plan and build extremely complex components that had to work together. By developing a chart that laid out the steps in detail, project managers could see how each step depended on the successful completion of the previous one. The major contribution of the PERT chart is that relationships are shown, and everything in the process can be identified.[3]

PERT is a useful tool during the final implementation phase of the group process. This procedure clarifies who will do what and by when. These five data collection and analysis tools have been developed to assist groups in

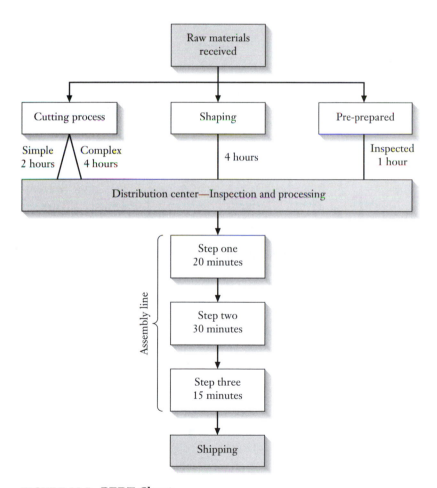

FIGURE 11.5 PERT Chart

gaining a clearer view of how communication functions within the group. The understanding and improvement of performance can be enhanced through their use.

Mobilizing External Resources

In some cases your group will face problems that cannot be solved through the efforts of your group members; they will then need the help of persons outside your group. If the degree of help thought to be needed is significant, your group should redefine the problem as a *community* responsibility; that is, a social problem needing to be brought to the attention of the larger unit of society of which your group is only a part. This operation is not easy and is somewhat complicated. It will require procedures and skills of advocacy in addition to skills of group interaction. In part, however, the procedures of problem identification and analysis, as well as ways of evaluating proposed solutions, as described in previous sections, will be of value to you.

One effective approach is to reorganize yourselves into a new, larger group involving the entire community, or unit of society, having a concern or interest regarding this problem. If this can be done, well and good, and all that you have learned about working together as a group may be called upon in this new social environment. In many situations, however, the larger social unit may not share the concern felt by the members of your own smaller group. They have the resources and, in fact, they have the problem (although they do not recognize it), but you have the concern. In such a case you must think both for yourselves and for them and, when possible, explain your thinking to them, hoping they will adopt your proposed plan of action.

The first step is to follow standard procedures of group problem solving. Meet with other concerned persons, identify clearly this mutual concern, analyze impelling and constraining forces, identify the possible approaches, evaluate the suggested alternatives, and develop a detailed plan of action. In doing these things, however, you must also inform yourselves regarding the thinking of the "others" in the community or larger social unit. You must familiarize yourself with their thinking, their feelings, their other primary concerns, and their biases or "blind spots."

Starting with your concern, you must analyze and solve their problems *as if you were they.* This, of course, is never easy, but you must do it as best you can. While this procedure is in progress, you will discover areas of their thinking you cannot accept. What should you do?

First, make sure you have obtained an accurate understanding of their thinking: invite them to your meetings, ask for their opinions, read their published statements, and interview their spokespersons. If you are satisfied that you clearly understand their views but you still disagree, you must bolster your personal courage, because you will probably need it. Do not adopt their thinking if you honestly disagree with it; do not "find where the people want to go and get out in front" just so they will like you. If you are not sincerely in agreement, quite likely you will be found out, and you will then be neither liked nor effective.

If you cannot satisfy both yourself and others, seek to *understand* their view. *Eventually, however, you must satisfy the demands of your own logic and conscience, and then you must, as honestly and clearly as you can, offer them the essence of your thinking.* You must, in fact, become an advocate of your beliefs. As an advocate you will attempt to get others to adopt your analysis of the problem and your proposed plan of action.

Integrating Your Thinking With That of the Audience

As you prepare to influence the beliefs and actions of others, no matter how careful and valid your thinking has been about your topic, you must consider how your listeners will receive your thoughts. Very likely they have done some thinking of their own. They may have come to certain conclusions (perhaps on information that is different from yours); some of them have prejudices, vested interests, or prior commitments. You must familiarize yourself with their thinking for them, at least in part. The objective is to *integrate* your thinking with theirs, to think like they do, and then to add your information and reasoning to theirs—not an easy task. How do you proceed?

Begin by discussing the problem with as many people as you can; ask for their opinions; read their published sources of information. Do not adopt any data or conclusions with which you honestly disagree; do not, as above, "find where your listeners want to go and run out in front" just to be accepted or approved. If you are not straightforward and sincere in dealing with your audience you will most likely be found out and lose the respect of your listeners. Make sure you understand their thinking, accept what is credible to you, integrate it with your thinking, and present the composite to them, hoping that they will do the same for you. In the long run, however, *you must satisfy the demands of your own logic and conscience*. Then you must, as honestly and clearly as you can, offer them the essence of your thinking.

The suggestions for your proposed attempt to influence others are beginning to take the following shape: (1) tell your listeners what you believe, (2) indicate the reasons why your belief is credible, (3) make sure that they realize that you clearly understand what they believe and that you have carefully evaluated its basis, (4) show them why your belief is credible, and (5) tell them *why* you want them to change their beliefs. Do not be afraid to reveal that your motives are mixed— some satisfaction for you and some advantages for them. Be as clear and honest as you can. It will work best for you in the long run.

Changing Your Listeners' Attitudes

Attitude may be defined as a predisposition to behave in a particular way under a specified set of conditions. Some people who have a definite belief in God feel strongly about the value of prayer in our public schools. Yet others, who also believe in God, are opposed to prayer in public schools because they believe that church and state should in all instances be kept separate. Atheists, on the other hand, may be opposed to prayer in public schools as a general principle. As can readily be seen, our beliefs, from which our attitudes arise, tend to govern what perspective we bring to problems and what we think the proper course of action or policy should be in dealing with that problem. Thus knowledge of listeners' attitudes is a vital concern to any advocate.

In a general way, you can assess people's attitudes by observing their behavior. However, you must be careful; studies have shown that such behavior may be deceptive.[4]

Attitudes are *not always consistent* with observable behavior.[5] The verbal expression of an attitude is called an opinion. It is also somewhat risky to infer an attitude (predisposition to act) from an expressed opinion because many circumstances can cause a person to express an opinion inconsistent with a real attitude. Your best bet is to determine if any of the following circumstances are present: (1) pressure from groups or organizations of which the person is a member, or (2) influence of status persons who hear the opinion. If one or both of these factors appear to be present, you need to discount an expression of opinion. Even so, behavior and expressed opinions do tend to reflect attitudes of your potential listeners.[6]

The amount of information individuals have about a subject may influence their reaction to your effort to change their viewpoint. When people are well informed they tend to have more intensive, less changeable attitudes, either for or against that about which they are well informed.[7] Such information about your listeners can be helpful as you seek to present your thinking to them.

Some of you may have read some studies of attitude change that reflected easy, successful experiences in influencing people. Indeed, you may have had such an experience yourself. In one way or another you may have formed the notion that there are tricks and formulas for manipulating people easily. In some instances this seems to be the case, but for the most part, once a person has formed an attitude, it is not easily changed; attitudes tend to persist over long periods of time. You will need to be aware of certain factors that cause their retention. The most important one appears to be a tendency of people to seek information consistent with their currently held attitudes; this practice has been called *selective exposure*. People tend to form friendships, join organizations, and subscribe to newspapers and magazines that reinforce their own previously held attitudes.[8] When people cannot avoid information inconsistent with their attitudes, they tend to pay more attention to available information with which they can agree.[9] Some of your listeners may try to avoid hearing information that is inconsistent with their present attitudes. Often they will distort their perceptions of the nature or substance of such information.[10] In some cases, if such undesired information cannot be ignored, or distorted, they will simply derogate or attempt to discredit the source (you), perceiving you as dishonest.[11]

All of these tendencies for an existing attitude to persist (once acquired) have direct bearing on your task as an advocate. They must be considered as you attempt to gain the support of your listeners.

Listeners appear to have an area or latitude of acceptance around a currently held attitude, a range of positions that are near their own, different to some degree, but still tolerable to them.[12] They also appear to have a similar "latitude" of rejection, a range of positions more distant from theirs that they find more or less objectionable. In essence, your listeners may be quite tolerant of your position if they perceive it as relatively close to their own.

If your listeners see a position as different from their own, you must be careful not to present your message in its most extreme form. In such a case, proceed with care. To the extent that you can show that your position is similar to that of your listeners, do so. Show them elements of similarity, placing less stress on those areas of disagreement. In no case, however, should you be dishonest or leave out a significant part of your reasoning supporting your position. Be completely clear, honest, and forthright, and stress areas of agreement between yourself and your listeners.

Helping Listeners Decide Questions of Policy

There are many situations in life where you can perceive that you and other people have a mutual problem—but they don't see it. Perhaps you and your classmates are working on a project; all of you wish to see it completed in good fashion, but you believe that by following procedures you have adopted, the project will not be finished by the agreed-on deadline. You see the problem, but other members of your group do not. Or perhaps you ride to work in a car pool. All riders know that you have a problem of ordinarily using a highway that is undergoing construction. The others are content to negotiate this tortuous route, but you are convinced that a smoother but longer road would be a wiser choice. In cases such as this, you have done some thinking along problem solving lines. You hope your associates would realize the value of your thinking. In fact, you would like to have them change their behavior—cooperate with you—to help you and them solve a problem that is, as you see it, of mutual interest.

In essence, you are seeking to think for other people, to identify problems and achieve solutions for others who are affected by the problems but who are uninformed about important things in their environment. Your own thinking must be done with care, and then it must be presented to them with accuracy. What should be the guidelines for such careful thinking and accurate presentation? They should include procedures for analyzing a problem and choosing the most reasonable solution as they were utilized in the group. In Chapter 5 we introduced the concept of "stock issues" for evaluating courses of action. These issues, in question form, can also guide your attempt to change attitudes: (1) Is there a need for a change? (2) Will the proposed solution meet the need identified? (3) Will the proposed solution introduce inherent disadvantages?

Stock Issue 1: Is There a Need For a Change?

How did your group arrive at the decision that something should be done? How did you reach the conclusion that a particular proposal should be adopted? Very likely you started with a feeling of concern about a certain part of your environment. Some of the things around you—situations, conditions, or ways in which people behaved—bothered you. You sensed that, in some way, things were not the way they could be and perhaps ought to be. The following three steps will help you answer these questions:

1. *Carefully compare the existing condition that seems to bother you with the condition you desire.* This process of comparison is the first step in analyzing a problem and should be the first step in getting yourself ready to influence the action of others. By definition, a problem is an undesirable situation.

   Describe very specifically the condition or situation that you want to see brought about. If you cannot do this, you are not prepared to try to explain what you would like to see brought about; if you aim at nothing in particular, you are likely to hit it, and nothing more.

   Analysis of a problem essentially consists of determining the *difference* between what exists and what you wish would exist. However, the determination of this precise difference is a fairly complex process. The essential issues are these: Is there a realistic *need* for people to change what they are doing? Does their current behavior constitute a clear and present deterrent or danger to a desirable common cause? Is this desired goal realistic? Is it within the realm of reasonable achievement? Is it a practical goal, not too idealistic or ethereal? Can you state this desired condition in specific terms? All of these questions must be answered in your thinking when you have adequately identified the problem your proposed change of actions of others is to meet.

2. *Analyze the nature of the problem.* You must carefully consider the field of forces that are inherent in it. You must gain a perspective of it in terms of its environmental conditions. Specifically, this means that you should identify two kinds of forces that are at work in the situation: impelling forces and constraining forces that were described in Chapters 3 and 5.

   Both the impelling and constraining forces must be carefully considered as you approach the next logical step in your thinking: What are the various possible alternative ways that the problem might be resolved? As you consider various approaches, you need to be sure that you don't miss any; you must carefully evaluate all possible approaches before you are ready to advocate change of other people's behavior. You cannot afford to take a position of advocacy favoring one particular line of action only to have one of your listeners point out to you and your audience a better way, one that you have utterly ignored in your thinking.

3. *Carefully identify all possible significant approaches to solving the problem you have analyzed.* Adequate consideration of impelling and restraining forces (as we have just described this procedure) can be very valuable in preparing you for

this third step. For example, you may become aware that a major restraining force to providing opportunities for teenage recreation in your community is an assumption that all boys and girls work after school and on weekends (a common assumption in many traditional farming communities). However, let us say that your town has been growing, becoming more urbanized, and that there are now over 400 teenagers whose parents work on jobs where youngsters cannot be expected to help. Changing the existing, erroneous assumption may be a reasonably viable approach to the problem. Similarly, identification of impelling forces may suggest possible ways of approaching the problem. For example, to find that petty crime and vandalism by young people has rapidly increased in your community may suggest the need to provide facilities for more constructive use of teenagers' time—perhaps by development of science fairs, athletic programs, swimming pools, and part-time employment programs.

All possible solutions to the identified problem should be considered; none should be missed or ignored. Only by giving fair consideration to all viable approaches can you be sure that your proposed solution will be worthy of your time and effort as a responsible advocate.

Stock Issue 2: Will the Proposed Solution Meet the Need Identified?

Once you have determined that a change is called for, you are ready to advance a proposal that you feel provides the best solution to the problem. *Carefully evaluate the probable workability of each of the optional approaches you have identified.* Remember that your objective is to influence the action of others. In order to do this, you must advocate a plan of action that will stand the criticism of your listeners. Careful analysis of practical experience has made students of advocacy aware of a basic criterion that can be used to test any proposed plan of action: Will this proposal produce the desired changes in the current situation?

To determine the degree to which any proposal or approach to a policy problem meets this criteria, you must go back to the results of your problem analysis. Compare the impelling and constraining forces in your force-field analysis with the actual changes indicated by various proposed action plans. Does one or another proposal actually change one or more of the existing impelling or con-straining forces? It should never be too late to change the crowd decision about the plan of action you will advocate if a new approach is, in your own estimation, better able to achieve the change you desire. Note that each possible approach or proposal should be evaluated in terms of its probable effect on each of the impelling and constraining forces earlier identified. Thus, the quality of work you have done earlier in identifying these factors inherent in the problem situation will directly affect the quality of the proposal you eventually choose to advocate. The basic issue involved is: Will your chosen plan really work?

Stock Issue 3: Will the Proposed Solution Introduce Inherent Disadvantages?

As you consider the third stock issue, you will need to consider this criterion: *Avoid serious disadvantages in a proposed plan of action.* You may agree that many times we could think of a proposal that really would produce a desired change but would also cost too much, perhaps in terms of money, effort, or even severe loss of human liberty. For example, small children *can* be made to be quiet in church—by taping their mouths and tying their hands and legs; yet the cost of such a plan would be too severe and it does not really achieve the desired goal—a worshipful demeanor. Disadvantages inherent in a proposal usually consist of risks that your listeners cannot afford. Costs are probably judged to be too severe if they are greater than the benefits likely to be achieved. They are also judged to be too severe if they are greater than the cost of other proposals that can also achieve the desired results. Once again, before you decide that you will advocate a particular proposal, you should evaluate all possible plans of acting against this criterion; for each alternate plan, what will likely be the cost—in money, time, effort, or loss of human values?

In the practical affairs of the world, any one of the considerations detailed in this chapter may be the limit to which you can analyze a problem; that is, you may be able to do valid thinking beyond the second step in consideration of the first stock issue: Analysis of the *nature of the problem*—identification of the impelling and restraining forces involved. Presentation to others of your thinking can make a significant contribution. Perhaps you have not been able to thoroughly identify all possible alternative ways of solving this problem. Any presentation should reflect your thinking, starting with the first step of Stock Issue 1: Comparison of existing conditions with the conditions you believe ought to exist or are desirable; your presentation should then cover, in order, each of the stock issues, so far as you can go on the basis of your careful, informed thinking. Many credible presentations have been given by speakers who clearly analyzed a problem and concluded their presentation by an appeal to their listeners to help them search for a solution. However, it is likely that if your thinking has been well done, covering all the stock issues, you will then want to cover the final step in advocacy: *Description of a detailed plan of action that you have determined to be the best solution.* Remember, however, that a presentation that covers all stock issues is rather rare and reflects the thinking of a very thoughtful and well-informed investigator.

The Persuasion Paradigm

At this point you may feel that we have presented an extensive treatment of the problems you face as an advocate of policies without giving you adequate instructions on how to proceed. For this reason we offer four specific suggestions. They cover, in essence, the principles discussed in this chapter.

1. *Show shared concern.* Show that you share the concerns of your listeners, that you and they have basic cares in common, that there is common ground.

2. *Demonstrate need for change.* This should be *their* need as well as yours. Point to the condition that is dangerous, intolerable, or undesirable. Compare what *is* with what *ought* to be or is desirable.

3. *Compare alternatives.* Identify alternative approaches or actions. Show why you have chosen one over the others. Give reasons backed by facts.

4. *Paint a picture of your plan in action.* Describe how your listener will look, act, and feel living under your new program. Paint a word picture; "romance the product," as experienced salespeople say. As you conclude, your listeners should know how it will feel to enjoy the situation or condition that will be the *result* of your plan being adopted.

Case Study

The American Speech and Hearing Association became concerned a few years ago with the plight of people in our society with communication handicaps. People who are deaf or hearing impaired did not always have appropriate visual displays of information that are equivalent alternatives to information transmitted via public address systems in large public buildings such as hospitals, schools, and airports. Sometimes fire and other emergencies were only signaled by sound rather than with any visual message. In addition, a number of meetings and conferences did not have appropriate interpreters for the deaf. While many people with other types of disabilities are able to be identified by virtue of canes, crutches, or wheelchairs, people with communication disorders are a hidden subgroup in our society.

To identify the problem and to formulate a way of changing public policy and perceptions, the Association formed a specific task force to plan a campaign.

Despite the Rehabilitation Act of 1973, which compels colleges and universities receiving federal funds to make their educational programs accessible to students with disabilities, very slow progress had been made, particularly for people with hearing or speaking difficulties.

Response

The task force developed a Bill of Rights for the severely communicative disabled. Included in the Bill of Rights were things such as a comprehensive evaluation by several professionals, if necessary; the right to quality and equal education; the right to an interpreter; and the right to a normal lifestyle with counseling support as needed.

In endorsing these rights the Association sent speakers around the country who addressed the problems locally and were able to call upon the national organization for data support. Speeches were designed to appeal to the sensitivities of the audience on behalf of the communication handicapped, and for the listeners to contact senators and congressional representatives in support of public laws that assisted the civil rights of the disabled. One speaker used the following conclusion:

In conclusion, I hope I have sensitized you to some of the special rights of the communicatively impaired, but more important, I hope that I have alerted you to the need for a civil rights viewpoint in dealing with the problems of disabling conditions. I believe it important that we do not focus too narrowly on the issues of speech, hearing, and deafness but that we form coalitions with other handicapped groups to keep the rights movement alive. Many of us concerned about handicapped rights have felt that in the past five or so years we have made significant strides in creating a new beginning for the disabled. However, recent actions in Washington have convinced me that we still have a long, hard battle before us. I believe that it is totally inexcusable and unacceptable to deny civil and legal rights to the handicapped on the grounds that the federal budget is currently too fat. In essence, this is to say that a disabled person cannot be a first-class citizen in our country, with all the rights and privileges of a nondisabled person, because it is just too expensive to insure justice and equality under the law. I urge you to contact your senators and congressmen to resist budget cuts in Public Law 94-142 and the Rehabilitation Act of 1973. We cannot allow ourselves to assume the inferior and neglected minority status we are just beginning to shed. We recently gained a vision of what the world might become for the disabled. Now that we have such a vision we must not allow it to be clouded by darkness.[13]

Chapter Summary

As people make their way through life, most of them find ways of cooperating and negotiating with other people. From time to time, however, we find ourselves in situations where we need to have others see the situation as we do, and act accordingly. As we seek to help others reach decisions that agree with our thinking, occasionally we find it appropriate to give speeches of advocacy.

In seeking to let others "know what we know," we must explain to them what we believe and why we believe it. The basis for seeking to influence the beliefs and behavior of others is grounded in our perception of reality. To be sure of our ground we must carefully evaluate our own beliefs. We must examine our motives and our perceptions.

As we seek to influence the beliefs of others, we must first gain their attention, then establish our credibility. Nothing will be more important than that our listeners see us as credible speakers. If we have carefully identified our beliefs, examined the bases of our beliefs, and studied conflicting beliefs, we then may want to express concern for a problem to an audience we think can profit from our thinking.

As we seek to influence the *actions* of others by having them act as if they believe as we do, we must review our reasons for believing as we do; if our reasons are sound, they will show that we have done as follows:

1. Compared the existing condition with the condition we desire
2. Analyzed the nature of impelling and constraining forces inherent in the problem situation
3. Identified all possible valid ways of solving the problem

4. Evaluated the workability and potential cost of each approach
5. Developed a detailed plan of action that we believe should be adopted and implemented

If we have accomplished well these five steps we are now ready to present our thinking to others. As we do, we will need to familiarize ourselves with our listeners' thinking, "start where they are," and integrate our thinking with theirs.

APPLICATIONS

11.1 Based on one of your previous projects in which a solution was proposed to a societal problem, develop a plan in your group to disseminate your recommendations.

11.2 Analyze a public campaign utilizing the tools of data collection and analysis and the persuasion paradigm.

11.3 Discuss a local or national political campaign in terms of the major points in this chapter. Consider using an agenda item from a political campaign or a social change agenda prevalent in your community or culture (e.g., handgun controls or drug awareness programs).

REFERENCES

1. H.K. Brelin, K.S. Davenport, L.P. Jennings, and F. Murphy, *Focused Quality-Managing for Results* (Delray Beach, FL: St. Lucie Press, 1994).

2. Ibid.

3. D.R. Siebold, "Making Meetings More Successful," in *Small Group Communication: A Reader,* 6th ed., ed. by R.S. Cathcart and L.A. Samovar (Dubuque, Iowa: W. C. Brown Publishers, 1992), pp. 185–188.

4. For classical study of the relation of attitudes to behavior, see R.T. LaPiere, "Attitudes vs. Actions," *Social Forces,* 13 (1934), pp. 230–237.

5. C. Kutnev, Wilkins, and P. Yarrow, "Verbal Attitudes and Overt Behavior Involving Racial Prejudice," *Journal of Abnormal Social Psychology,* 47 (1952), pp. 649–652.

6. See for example, M.L. DeFleur and F.R. Westie, "Verbal Attitudes and Overt Acts: An Experiment on the Salience of Attitudes," *American Sociological Review,* 23 (1958), pp. 667–673.

7. See for example, G. Nettler, "The Relationships Between Attitudes and Information Concerning the Japanese in America," *American Sociological Review,* 11 (1964), pp. 177–191.

8. J. Mills, E. Aronson, and H. Robinson, "Selectivity in Exposure to Information," *Journal of Abnormal Social Psychology,* 59 (1959), pp. 250–253.

9. See L.K. Canon, "Self-Confidence and Selective Exposure to Information," in *Conflict, Decision and Dissonance,* ed. by L. Festinger (Stanford, California: Stanford University Press, 1964), pp. 83–95.

10. J.L. Freedman and D.O. Sears, "Selective Exposure," *Advances in Experimental Social Psychology,* ed. by L. Beerkowitz, vol. 2, 1965, pp. 57–97. New York: Academic Press.

11. D.K. Berlo and H.E. Gulley, "Some Determinants of the Effects of Oral Communication in Producing Attitude Change and Learning," *Speech Monographs,* 25 (1957), pp. 10–20.

12. C.W. Sherif, M. Sherif, and R.E. Nebergall, *Attitude and Attitude Change* (Philadelphia: Saunders, 1965).

13. B.R. Patton, K. Giffin, and W.A. Linkugel, *Responsible Public Speaking* (Glenview, Ill.: Scott, Foresman and Company, 1983), p. 227.

12 Quality Groups in the Twenty-First Century

*"While the 20th century has been the century of productivity, the
21st century will be the century of quality."*[1]

Scenario

Computer and electronic producer Texas Instruments has been attempting to reposition itself to compete more effectively in its highly competitive and rapidly changing market. Their plant in Kuala Lampur instituted quality improvement teams made up of managers, engineers, and experts as needed from various departments. The plant moved toward a "flexible organization" in which self-managed teams of workers set up their own equipment, kept track of attendance, and monitored outcomes without the need for supervisors. The plant manager Mohd Azmi Abdullah noted the benefits: "Technicians, in the past, some of them, as they stepped into the plant, parked their brains outside the fence . . . Now, by getting into the self-managed team concept, we are creating an environment where there is a certain amount of freedom to choose what they want to do . . . We are very excited because there is a lot of potential we can tap if we provide the necessary training, coaching, and support."[2]

These changes paid off as the company's sales exceeded $10 billion, Texas Instruments became one of the world's 200 largest companies, and the company won the prestigious Malcolm Baldridge National Quality Award.[3]

Dimensions of the Future

People have not always been accurate in predictions about the future. For example, a Western Union memo in 1876 suggested, "This telephone has too many short-comings to be taken seriously as a means of communication. The device is inherently of no value to us." H.M. Warner of Warner Brothers Pictures said in 1927, "Who the hell wants to hear actors talk?" Similiarly, in 1962 Decca Recording Company said in rejecting the Beatles, "We don't like their sound, and guitar music is on the way out." In 1975, Ken Olson, the founder of Digital Equipment Corporation, is reported to have stated: "There is no reason anyone would want a computer in their home."[4]

As we know, interest in change and concern for the future are tied together. Eons ago, when nothing was changing perceptually (except the seasons in recurrent cycles), humans had little reason to speculate about the future. Tomorrow would be like today, and today is like yesterday; next year will be like this year.

Our prime task in the future, unlike that in the past, will not be to deal with the similar, or even with increases in the similar, but to adjust to a world where conditions are more different than similar. There are at least three fundamental ways in which today is converting tomorrow into a world that will not resemble yesterday. These three themes—rate and magnitude of change, interrelatedness, and continuing escalation of human aspirations—can be viewed as dimensions of the future.[5]

Rate and Magnitude of Change

Social and technological changes have accelerated to the point at which the old habits of "waiting to see what happens" will no longer work. We must develop new strategies for living with change, for anticipating problems, and for designing creative alternatives. The faster we go, the greater lead time we need for recognizing trends, preparing solutions, and revising our course of action. An analogy of travel is valid. If we drive an automobile down the road at 25 miles an hour, we can leisurely watch for signs and landmarks; we can turn off at the last minute. If, however, we are driving at 55 miles an hour, we have to be more alert to exits ahead. In other words, we need early warning systems as we anticipate the amount of change in our future. Our future is likely to include too many people, too many decisions, and too much information. We will have a constant sense of overload. One expert has suggested that recorded knowledge doubled between the year 1 A.D. and 1750, and another doubling occurred between 1750 and 1900, a third time between 1900 and 1950, a fourth time between 1950 and 1960, and a fifth time between 1960 and 1963. Since then knowledge has been said to be doubling approximately every six months. In this world of quantitative overload, it is easy to lose perspective and become disoriented.

Electronic media have added to the information overload. Periods of time away from a desk result in a deluge of e-mail messages, and new Web sites offer pages of information. Unfortunately, not all the information distributed is accurate or useful.

The meanings of change are many and subjective. With the harried and harassed, additional change may represent more pressure; it may be threatening. For the bored, change may create excitement, may be appealing. In terms of the magnitude of change, "more" has no absolute value, and is not necessarily good or inevitably bad. The real question is "more of what?" To most of us, more income is good, but more bills are bad, and the difference between the two may determine happiness or unhappiness. There's nothing inherently threatening or frightening in the increase in the number of things in our environment. Expanded awareness has always been a major thrust in the evolution of humankind. In studies of child development, for example, we call home environments *rich* when they have ample sources of stimulation; *poor* when there are few. Psychological experiments in sensory deprivation have demonstrated that the human nervous system may become seriously disoriented when removed from normal sense excitements, a situation analogous to the withholding nourishment from the physical body. Human experiences will continue to be enriched by greater interaction with more people and places. Radio, television, computers, and satellites have put us in touch with the remote, the strange, and the previously inaccessible. Through electronic communication our senses are connected directly with the rest of our globe and with outer space. These connections help us take the halting but vital steps toward feeling a unity with the rest of our globe and with the cosmos.

However, with the opportunities also come threats. For the first time in human history, we have the power to make decisions that have no reverse gear. The paths we take may never be retraced. Biologically, we can remake the human species, but behind our capacities for genetic engineering lurk the threats of the monster suggested in the story of Dr. Frankenstein. Who is wise enough to decide what should be done and how will it be decided? The same questions are present in nuclear physics and technology, through which it is possible to devastate our entire planet. And in a more immediate sense, how do we confront the issue of terrorism? We know that fanatics have the power to blow up cities and contaminate public water supplies. These are not pleasant thoughts, but we must improve our odds at anticipating the problems and plan our responses. The worst crises are those that are unforeseen.

Interrelatedness

No longer is it possible to be separate or isolated from other people. The world and its people form one gigantic system. What goes on in any one place, in some way, affects every place. The ecological model is universal. We are all members of and served by complex systems. Some of these are systems of nature, some are massive human organizations, some are huge technological systems. Self-sufficiency in our society has diminished and dependency has increased. One of the consequences in government has been a tendency toward more and more regulation to the point that many suggest is over-regulation. Threats of pollution and nuclear explosions are global in potential impact. There is no place to hide.

Most of the problems we face today are people-made problems. Most of the solutions we must find tomorrow will be people-made solutions. Our achievements in science and technology have contributed both to the problems and to the potential solutions. Pollution is a worldwide threat; population pressures and food shortages have global implications. As we have suggested, communication and transportation technologies have brought all parts of the world into direct contact with each other. However, much of our thinking from past models is parochial and provincial; most of our habits and our institutions are based on models from earlier ages. We instinctively compete with each other and define winning as ending up with more than our neighbors. It is important that we note that the world has changed. In the future, winning will be measured by how successfully we can make the world work for everybody. The real enemies will *not* be other people but starvation, disease, illiteracy, and terrorism. The world will be run as a whole, or not at all. Cooperation will be a necessity, not a luxury. We are in a race between our old instincts and the new demands of our global culture.

Any human act sends ripples across the entire human pond. All of us are affected by the problems that affect any nation. No national wall is high enough to shield us from the difficulties that affect our neighbors. For a moment we may talk of self-sufficiency in energy resources, for example, but no nation can be truly self-sufficient in a world that is crowded, finite, and closely connected. We are all passengers on Spaceship Earth. Either we learn to live and share with each other, or we will wreck the vehicle before we travel much farther into the orbit of the future. To use a more homely metaphor, we are one large family on a summer's vacation in a camper. Either we learn to get along in limited space and with limited supplies, or we ruin the trip. The only alternative to compromise is chaos. Our figurative family can always call it off and turn back, but our world doesn't have that choice. We can only go forward to a short and disastrous trip, or to a long journey in harmony in time and space.

Continuing Escalation of Human Aspirations

Human beings all over the world look for and long for more satisfying lives. Some of the longings are material, such as for food, medical care, and a higher standard of living. But many of the longings are spiritual and ethical: rights of personal dignity, political autonomy, and religious worship. The crucial change, however, has been the shift from a mere longing to expecting. In the latter part of the twentieth century, hopes and wishes were replaced by demands and insistencies. The reason was an expanded sense that humankind can do better if it so wishes, and we are not simply helpless victims tossed on waves of chance. A second contributing factor was the effect of the mass media. Through television's window of the world, underdeveloped countries and deprived masses could see and envy varying degrees of influence in the lifestyles of the "rich and famous."

As with the other dimensions, the expectations explosion has both positive and negative features. Both human philosophy and human experience are centered on a few major counterpoints. For example, good and bad; right and wrong; war and peace; truth and untruth; beauty and ugliness. As governments and societies have evolved, one key counterpoint has always been the individual and the group, or sometimes the individual versus the group. This is a recurring issue in national political matters with the rising expectations of the population.

What rights should an individual have that transcend the rights of the group? What rights should the group have to control the behavior of the individual? Diverse cultures and political regimes have given different answers to these questions over time, and these different answers have ignited wars and revolutions. For nations and for individuals, development has three phases. The first phase of any game is *how to play.* A young child raises this question as they watch brothers and sisters bat balls or shoot baskets. "Can I play? Show me how." A young nation has the same problem as ours did 200 years ago, and we learned fast. The second phase of any game is *how to win.* After a while, just playing is not enough. The youngster learns to score points, do well, beat other people. This is the spirit of competition. It is a strong motivator and helps to sharpen skills. Once again, the same is true for nations and for organizations or institutions within nations. In our nation, what we mean by capitalism is innovation, enterprise, economic competition in the private sector, etc. Our captains of industry have won in the marketplace because they have the same motivations and the same sharpened skills as our best athletes.

But it is also true that some of our captains of industry and some of our athletes have been known to cut corners here and there, to wink occasionally at the rules, and to put winning ahead of ethics. Thus we come to the third phase of any game—*how to keep the game fair.* The real question today and in the future is how to preserve the game and keep it fair for all players. Some social games have been rigged or fixed in the past, with unfair rules for women, blacks, and other minorities. Many of us are unwilling to accept these rules any longer, and we will no longer accept the uncontrolled freewheeling and free dealing by unethical leaders in any of our professions.

A Projected Future of Groups

So where do we go from here? What are our alternatives? We believe that there are only three possible directions. First, we can wait and watch and see what happens. Second, we can escalate our efforts at control and regulation. Third, we can start trying to reinvent human nature.

The first alternative is no answer at all; it is a tragic spectator sport; we have been a crisis society for too long—waiting until the disaster comes, then trying to figure out a remedy. We must switch to an anticipatory strategy. The risk is too great for us relying on the old wait-and-see approach; we must aim at prevention. The second alternative of control and regulation can never be our long-range answer. Controls and regulations may indeed be indispensable as stop-gap measures in a scary world—but new and greater ingenious threats will emerge, and we could only spiral into a type of police state. Thus, we believe that the third alternative is the only viable one—the one that seems the most unrealistic on first examination. Is it possible to change "human nature"?

It is simply a recognition that the same brain and nervous system (same mental habits included) that got us to the twenty-first century must be modified before long, or we will self-destruct.

To understand that point, we must face up to the truth that we often miss. Remember the old axiom "what a fish is least aware of is water." The key truth is that we live in a human-made world we have invented; look at other animals, then look at us. Most of what we do, use, and pay attention to is of our own creation. In a very literal sense, the human world is an unnatural world, an artificial world. This is not a criticism but a fact. But the human organism itself, including the brain and the nervous system, has changed little over the ages. We know we can never put a moratorium on technological invention. So, if we are to hope for a viable change, we must start exploring ways to reinvent human nature. Surely we can find ways to modify sources of greed, selfishness, and hostility. This alternative is not an option; it is an imperative. Is this a call to homogenize or tranquilize the human race? No, rather it is a call to utilize psychology, with all the marvelous ingenuity and energy that we have devoted to technology.

Over 100 years ago, in connection with the world's Colombian exposition in 1893, the American Press Association and 74 experts predicted the nature of life in America a century later. Two central forecasts emerged: 1) technology could and would solve society's problems, and 2) human nature would change dramatically for the better. While these predictions may seem naïve, they do help clarify our perspectives. Technology provides us with tools, wondrous tools, but only tools. Human nature will always dictate how we use technology, and human nature will not change without our help.

The last transition in the fundamental paradigm of our society was the shift from the agrarian to the industrial economy. Many of the theories and practices, procedures and organizational structures of modern management, education, and government were formulated during that period of transition and the Industrial Age that evolved. The practices were modernized by twentieth century improvements and by a new layer of information technology designed to improve their efficiency. But at heart there remained the vestiges of earlier times. As we are engaged in a shift in paradigms to the Information Age, two key lessons can be learned from the last transition. The first lesson is that some underlying technology both enables and pushes the transition. For the Industrial Age, the steam engine, internal combustion engine, and jet engine were important, sequentially pushing technology development. For the transition to the Information Age, the emergence of computing, the fusing of telecommunications with computers, and the emergence of ubiquitous networking are pushing the transition to the new information-based economy. New generations of powerful applications will be a future driver. The second lesson is that productivity gains require both incorporating the new technology and developing new enabling organizational structures and methods for accomplishing work.

Today, bureaucracy and its culture are incompatible with the new Information Age organization. Time is now a critical competitive factor. Every possible variation and circumstance cannot be foretold. The model for providing command, control, and communication needs to be recast to serve Information Age realities. Rules need to be replaced by informed judgement and action, and bureaucracy by self-informing, self-correcting systems.

The choice is clear: an organization may accept either the risks of pursuing the transformation of its ways of doing business, in the Information Age model, or the certainty of stagnation and decline as the remnants of the Industrial Age fall further and further from favor. Achieving quality needs to be the driving force behind every group experience.

During a period of fundamental change, it is often more dangerous to stand still than to risk change. The Industrial Revolution did not alter the basic patterns of group life. Now, digital capabilities are creating new ways of expressing, interpreting, and knowing; clearly new does not always mean better.

Interprofessional Communication—Means to Quality

As we look to the future, our goal is not to predict with certainty what will happen in the group environment. Rather our goal is to help you, the reader, to imagine and shape the future. We want you to develop your talents and abilities to be leaders of innovation and responsible citizens of the world.

Of the variables and attributes contributing to quality groups, one is likely to become even more important in our future—*interprofessional communication*. Electrical engineers must be able to work effectively with lawyers and architects; business managers must work with chemical engineers and psychologists. Specialized professionals talk to each other, but often have difficulty relating their knowledge to the needs of a diverse society.[6]

Professionals who can communicate and work in collaboration with professionals from other fields will have a greater probability of developing the innovations needed to solve some of the world's most complex problems. In health care, it is not only the health professionals, but the engineers, lawyers, business executives, and government officials who are working together to determine new ways to deliver and finance health care. Nutritionists, chemists, biologists, lawyers, chemical engineers, and administrators must develop rules for the importation, processing, and packaging of food.

The needs for professionals in almost every major field to be able to communicate and collaborate is significant, whether dealing with problems of environment, housing, world security, space exploration, or telecommunications. To get things done in an increasingly complex world requires such abilities.

Interprofessional communication may well be the basis for a new educational paradigm for the twenty-first century. Such a model has been developed at the Illinois Institute of Technology. They have redefined their undergraduate curriculum in interprofessional terms and launched new research initiatives in this area. All students are now required to conduct a minimum of two interprofessional projects during the course of their undergraduate studies. Each project team is led by a graduate student and includes 10 to 15 students from all academic levels (sophomore through graduates) from across different professional programs such as engineering, law, humanities, social sciences, business, architecture, art design, and the physical sciences.

One of their recent examples of such interprofessional work in 1998 was called "Project Bosnia." The underlying premise of the project was that Internet technology can help to rebuild Bosnian law libraries, the court system, and legislative processes. In one semester the team accomplished the following:

- Convinced Sun Microsystems, U.S. Robotics, Cisco Systems, and Motorola to donate the needed equipment
- Designed and developed the networks
- Developed the software to enable Bosnian journalists to post and retrieve information from anywhere in the world
- Trained Bosnian journalists and wrote training manuals
- Built the Bosnian legal information database and established it on a Web site
- Took everything they had done and went to Bosnia and Serbia over spring break and installed and tested all the equipment and software.[7]

A faculty committee member stated in implementing the program: "Students should be learning to express what they know in terms that are understandable to intelligent, interested nonexperts. They must learn to talk to members of the other professions in understandable language."[8]

The elements of listening, understanding, and acting together is the crux of interprofessional experience. As in any quality group situation, the students complete the project having understood the project's objectives and outcomes from perspectives other than their own, while in the process having learned to inform others about issues unfamiliar to them.

Recognizing Quality—Award-Winning Projects

In addition to the Malcolm Baldridge Awards that are given annually to the organizations that exemplify accomplishments utilizing Total Quality Management principles, a Quality Cup is awarded annually by RIT/USA Today in six categories: education, government, manufacturing, small business, health care, and service industry.[9] Competitors are judged on the use of teamwork and the principles of total quality management to cut costs, solve problems, and increase efficiency. An examination of the 1998 winners will demonstrate how such practices can yield positive results.

Education[10]

The winning entry in the Education category was the "Parking Team" for the University of California, Irvine. The problem addressed by the group was the cumbersome, time-consuming process of obtaining a parking pass. The team critically examined the existing practices and determined that: (1) less information was needed from students; much was read that could be obtained from other sources; (2) parking passes could be made portable and hung from the rear-view mirror; abuse by multiple uses proved minimal; (3) computers can handle visitors who call ahead, with passes prepared in advance and available from a visitor kiosk.

As a result, the team substantially reduced the administrative costs, as well as the amount of time needed and the number of steps in the process of purchasing university parking permits.

Government[11]

The Tennessee Valley Authority (TVA) at its Allen Fossil Plant needed to adapt to new environmental rules requiring coal plants to emit less high-sulfur dioxide, which contributes to acid rain. The team's analysis of the problem determined that the cause of the problem was slag buildup. Slag is similar to the leftover ash in a fireplace; too much slag keeps the coal from burning properly. Experimentation proved that adding limestone or mixing the coal with other low-sulfur coal can prevent slag buildup.

The team involved TVA coal buyers, suppliers, and vendors in a program to ensure a consistent quality of emissions controls and to quickly identify potential problems. The sulfur dioxide emissions dropped from 80,000 tons annually to 26,000 tons, well exceeding the government guidelines.

Manufacturing[12]

Air travelers are delayed if an indicator lamp signals a problem. The Allied Signal Aerospace ATA-31 Team in Tempe, Arizona, had members drawn from American Airlines, Federal Express, Airbus Industries, General Electric, and Allied Signal. The team spent days in hangars determining what happens when a fault light goes on. In a typical fix, an air valve that adjusts the airflow from the engines to other systems such as cabin air temperatures is the most likely cause of the signal, and can be quickly replaced. However, the team found that most of the $37,000 valves actually did not need to be replaced.

The team determined better methods of determining faulty valves, and were able to cut flight delays resulting from such problems in half, as well as saving significant dollars.

Small Business[13]

Diamond Packaging Services operates multiple assembly lines without supervisory support, increasing the company's profitability, flexibility, and quality. Twenty temporary workers take directions from 11 full-time colleagues deciding who will fold cartons and who will fill the boxes. To motivate the team, a daily scorecard is used on each assembly line, each shift. It measures performance in five areas: profit (maximum 45 points), quality (35), cleanliness (20), training (15), and safety (5). For every 100 points scored a $5 tally is made for the team, and when $1,000 is reached, the money is divided.

Since the team scorecards were started in 1996, the following results have ensued:

1. Everyone has a training and development plan with about three times the amount of job skills developed.
2. New ideas or improved operations are up 52 percent.
3. The average score per shift has increased from 86 to 94, with awards increasing commensurately.
4. Customer complaints fell 25 percent.
5. Profits increased 350 percent.

Health Care[14]

The Cardiac surgery team in Rochester General Hospital, New York, has reorganized the way it operates. It has standardized everything from how anesthesia is administered to how towels and tools are stacked. Each task is synchronized so that everyone knows what to do and when to do it, even with different surgeons in charge. They cut steps that wasted time so that cardiac surgery is shorter and more efficient for patients.

Since the program went into effect, the following results were benchmarked for patients:

1. Time in the operating room—2 to 3 hours instead of 3 to 5, the national average
2. Days in hospital—4 instead of 7
3. Value of blood needed—$347 compared to $481 before the program
4. Readmission rates—decreases from 18 percent to 9 percent
5. Mortality rates—0.68 percent compared to 2.2 percent the previous year

The team was able to improve patient health, lower costs, and serve as a model for other hospital units.

Service Industry[15]

People may stop making their mortgage payments due to job loss, illness, divorce, or other misfortunes. General Electric Mortgage Insurance in Raleigh, North Carolina, must deal with 8,000 delinquent loans a year. Representatives of the company must determine if foreclosure is called for, or if the situation can be improved with possible financial recovery for the buyer.

An eight person team created a computer program that asks company representatives to input data such as future income, willingness to pay, depreciation on property, assets, and other debts or loans. The program has proved to be nearly perfect in predicting which borrowers eventually will agree to pay for default losses and at what percentage.

The first year of this new approach resulted in 1,600 foreclosures being avoided, up 43 percent over the previous year. General Electric saved over $8 million by making decisions quicker and more accurately, and satisfaction from customers the mortgage lenders insured rose from 61 percent to 76 percent.

These examples illustrate how groups of the future, utilizing quality principles, can genuinely make a difference.

Building Quality Decision-Making Groups

Unfortunately, too few people have been members of a truly cohesive, committed, and involved group. In such a group, trust is taken for granted, roles are understood, and authority is delegated according to ability. Such a group has the potential for providing creativity, support, motivation, skilled inquiry, and effective problem solving.

New information technologies, consumerism, and increasing resource restraints are prompting change in our ways of interacting and conducting business. CD-ROMS, the Internet, video conferencing, and other modes of communicating make it possible to open contact with people at all times and in all places. Previous restraints on interaction are no longer problems.

In the previous chapters, we have identified a number of principles that address the quality issues in the group. These principles, drawn from research and our own experience, represent a package that can lead to enhanced performance. Four of these principles consistently emerge as critical variables that determine the ultimate success of the group.

Quality Leadership

Harvard researchers John Katter and James Heskett have shown that the single most important factor distinguishing successful groups from those that fail is competent leadership.[16] Without visible, committed, and skilled leaders, most groups fall far short of expectations.

Quality Data Gathering

In some groups, data gathering efforts often disappoint because the data are either too voluminous to digest, too aggregated to inform meaningfully, or too outdated to be useful. The process must help the group ask the right questions and find the data that are relevant and critical to the needed decision.

In most groups, "hard" data is not enough. People know more than what the data suggests. The group must create discussion based on the data that truly reflects on the information and its meaning. Henry Mintzberg suggests using hard data to stimulate thinking, and then tapping into the wisdom of the group participants.[17] This process involves people's intuitions and often leads to deeper understanding and creative solutions.

Quality-Group Communication Skills

From experience we know that bringing a group of people together does not mean that they will automatically work well together. Often the collective intelligence of the group is less than that of some of the individual participants. Rather than take risks to openly explore issues, people will blame others for poor decisions and withhold information to avoid criticism. Some will act to protect their control and influence in situations they find threatening.

Groups and the individuals in them must have feedback on productive behaviors and an atmosphere where participants can think aloud without fear of criticism or judgment. We have suggested the need for open dialogue—the capacity of group members to suspend judgments and enter into true thinking together. Such quality interaction requires a sense of shared values and purposes among the numbers.

Trust and Relationships

In his study of effective people, Steven Covey has observed that "the fundamental reason that most quality initiatives do not work is because of the lack of trust in the culture—in the relationships between people.[18] Without mutual trust there can be no true relationship, and without relationships groups cannot develop loyalty and collective commitment.

"Organizations which rely on trust as the principle means of control are more effective, more creative, more fun, and cheaper to operate," asserts one authority.[19] Relationships provide the connections for exchanging information between different parts of the systems, and the basis for establishing the collaboration necessary for taking action. Well-established relationships provide the electric current for the group to learn, develop, and respond to problems. Trust is the key. To develop the necessary trust, groups must provide greater flow of information, broader participation in decision-making, and more evenly distributed power structures.

Case Study

One university campus that has taken continuous improvement seriously is the University of California at San Diego. There every year an outside research firm arrives to let the students, faculty, and other users of services grade the quality of campus business service (not academic departments). They rate them from terrible to superb with a score of 5 being best. When averaged, the responses generally range from 2 to 4. This approach is similar to what many corporations do in what is called a "balanced score card" program. All administrative department heads and business operation directors on the campus gather to review the findings and set goals for the following year.

Examples of improvement include the payroll department, which reduced its errors by 80 percent over a three-year period after the survey showed dissatisfaction. Improvement increased the score of the department from 3.4 in 1995 to 3.8 in 1998. In another office, the amount of time needed to process travel reimbursement checks was cut from up to two months to as little as three days. The score from this category rose from an average of 3.0 in 1996 to 3.6 in 1998.

Some business operations were doing so well that no changes were required. The office storehouse had such a positive review that there was no need to attempt improvement. Such areas as the bookstore have found ways to provide on-line information to parents about the costs and type of personal computers the university-bound student will need, and greatly increased their sales as a result.

As a result of this effort the campus received the RIT/USA Today Quality Cup Award for education in 1999.[20]

Chapter Summary

The success of any group attempting to reach the best possible decision depends on many factors. Extensive research efforts in the social sciences have given us abundant clues to the variables that are likely to have positive or negative impact on a group's performance. Yet the complexity of human interaction still leaves a great deal to be discovered. In many ways, promoting quality group interaction remains as much an art as a science.

One of the consistent themes emerging from the research that we have cited has been the recurrent finding regarding the interlocking nature of task and maintenance behaviors. We believe that this dual emphasis is requisite for the long-term success of a decision-making group. Both a sense of accomplishment in the decision made and a feeling of positive regard for self and coworkers are important if a group is to continue to function. Product and process are thus interdependent.

APPLICATIONS

12.1 With the advent of the twenty-first century, many people took the opportunity to express their predictions for the future. Discuss these predictions in terms of the dimensions presented in this chapter.

12.2 From the different fields of study and capabilities of the members of your group, discuss the future potential and problems associated with interprofessional communication.

12.3 Compare and contrast the award-winning projects cited in this chapter. What are the common threads that determine high-quality decision making?

REFERENCES

1. J.M. Juran, "What Japan Taught Us about Quality," *The Washington Post,* August 15, 1993, pp. H.1–H.6.

2. A.B. Cheney, H.P. Sims, Jr., and C.C. Manz, "Teams and TQM," *Business Horizons,* September 1994, p. 16.

3. "The Global 500," *Fortune,* July 1994, p. 168.

4. L. Collens, "Innovation and Leadership: The Search for the Renaissance Professional." Symposium presentation to the Rose-Hulman Institute of Technology, August 27, 1998.

5. W.A. Conboy, "The Future at Risk—The Mismatch Phenomenon." Paper presented to the Eighth General Assembly, World Future Society, July, 1996.

6. Collens , op. cit.

7. Loc. cit.

8. Loc. cit.

9. *USA Today,* Friday, May 1, 1998, pp. 4B–5B.

10. C. Woodyard, "University Takes Pain Out of Parking Passes," *USA Today,* May 1, 1998, p. 4B.

11. E. Eldridge "Enterprising Team Solves TVA Coal Problem," *USA Today,* May 1, 1998, p.4B.

12. D. Levy, "Manufacturing Winners Teamed to Trouble-shoot Valve Problem," *USA Today,* May 1, 1998, p. 4B.

13. K.K. Choquette, "Team Approach Wins Points With Workers," *USA Today,* May 1, 1998, p. 5B.

14. K.K. Choquette, "Streamlined Surgery is Win-Win Situation," *USA Today,* May 1, 1998, p. 5B.

15. D. Jones, "GE Turns Decision-Making 'Art into Science,'" *USA Today,* May 1, 1998, p. 5B.

16. J. Katter and J. Heskett, *Corporate Culture and Performance* (New York: Free Press, 1992).

17. H. Mintzberg, *The Rise and Fall of Strategic Planning* (New York: Free Press, 1994).

18. S. Covey, *The Seven Habits of Highly Effective People* (New York: Fireside Book, 1989), p. 211.

19. C. Handy, *The Organization of the Future* (New York: The Drucker Foundation, 1997), p. 164.

20. C. Woodyard, "Productivity Improvement Measures Up," *USA Today,* May 7, 1999, p. 7B.

INDEX